D0567434

THE FALL OF **CONRAD BLACK**

WRONG WAY

Also by Jacquie McNish

The Big Score:
Robert Friedland and the Voisey's Bay Hustle

THE FALL OF **CONRAD BLACK**

WRONG WAY

JACQUIE McNISH &
SINCLAIR STEWART

THE OVERLOOK PRESS
Woodstock & New York

This edition first published in the United States in 2004 by
The Overlook Press, Peter Mayer Publishers, Inc.
Woodstock & New York

WOODSTOCK:
One Overlook Drive
Woodstock, NY 12498
www.overlookpress.com
[for individual orders, bulk and special sales, contact our Woodstock office]

NEW YORK:
141 Wooster Street
New York, NY 10012

∞ The paper used in this book meets the requirements for paper
permanence as described in the ANSI Z39.48-1992 standard.

Cataloging-in-Publication Data is available from the Library of Congress

Printed in Canada
ISBN 1-58567-636-5
1 3 5 7 9 8 6 4 2

Contents

Authors' Note

HOLLINGER INTERNATIONAL'S ANNOUNCEMENT of Conrad Black's departure as CEO in November 2003 triggered a series of events that provided a rare glimpse into the inner workings of a troubled company and the private communications of its embattled executive ranks. Lawsuits, court testimony, and reports from an internal investigation team laid bare the contents of confidential emails, faxes, letters, and, in some cases, the minutes of board meetings. These documents, which span thousands of pages, provided the skeleton of our research, fleshed out by interviews with more than seventy-five people involved in this corporate drama, many of whom were key insiders. The combination of legal evidence and interviews has enabled us to piece together an extensive chronology of the behind-the-scenes activities of Hollinger International's managers, directors, and advisers. Every major character in this book was either interviewed or presented with a request to speak to the authors and provide comment. Several granted these interviews with the understanding that their comments would not be directly quoted, but rather would be used to help recreate conversations or scenes vital to the book. The authors recognize that it is impossible for any one person to recall exactly what was said in a meeting that may have taken place some time ago, but we have endeavoured to capture as accurately as possible the essence of these exchanges by relying on testimony or interviews with at least one person who participated in the dialogue. In the case of meetings involving a group of people, we most often relied on the recollections of more than one participant to aid our reconstruction.

Two books were enormously helpful in our research. Peter C. Newman's 1982 classic, *The Establishment Man: A Portrait of Power,* is an enduring account of Black's early ascent. And Conrad Black's 1993 autobiography, *A Life in Progress,* was a key reference that allowed us to include his perspective on the many controversies that have shaped his career.

Cast of Characters

The Executives

Conrad Black, chairman and CEO, Hollinger International and Hollinger Inc.
Daniel Colson, CEO of Telegraph Group Ltd.
J.A. "Jack" Boultbee, executive vice-president, Hollinger International
David Radler, deputy chairman, president, Hollinger International
Peter Atkinson, executive vice-president, Hollinger International
Peter White, chief operating officer, Hollinger Inc.
Paul Healy, vice-president corporate development, Hollinger International
Mark Kipnis, corporate counsel, Hollinger International

The Special Committee

Gordon Paris, CEO of Hollinger International, 2003–present
Graham Savage, chairman, Callisto Capital LP
Raymond Seitz, former U.S. ambassador to the United Kingdom
Richard Breeden, adviser to the special committee, former chairman of the
    Securities and Exchange Commission

The Directors

HOLLINGER INTERNATIONAL

Dwayne Andreas, 1996–2002, former chairman, Archer Daniels Midland Co.
Barbara Amiel Black, 1996–present
Richard Burt, 1994–present, chairman, Diligence, LLC
Raymond Chambers, 1996–2002, chairman, Amelior Foundation
Dr. Henry Kissinger, 1996–present, chairman, Kissinger Associates, Inc.
Marie-Josée Kravis, 1996–2003, senior fellow, Hudson Institute, Inc.
Shmuel Meitar, 1996–present, vice-chairman, Aurec Ltd.
Richard Perle, 1994–present, resident fellow, American Enterprise Institute
Robert Strauss, 1996–2002. Akin Gump Strauss Hauer & Feld
Alfred Taubman, 1996–2002, chairman, The Taubman Company
James Thompson, 1994–present, chairman, Winston & Strawn

Lord Weidenfeld, 1996–2002, chairman, Weidenfeld & Nicholson
Leslie Wexner, 1996–2002, chairman and CEO, The Limited Inc.

Hollinger Inc.

Ralph Barford, 1983–2002, president Valleydene Corporation Ltd.
Douglas Bassett, 2003–2003, chairman, Windward Investments
Dixon Chant, 1978–2002, former deputy chairman, Ravelston Corp. Ltd.
Charles Cowan, 1981–2003, vice-president and secretary, Hollinger Inc.
Fredrik Eaton, 1979–1991; 1994–2003, chairman, White Raven Capital Corp.
Donald Fullerton, 1992–2003, former chairman, Canadian Imperial Bank
    of Commerce
Allan Gotlieb, 1989–2003, senior adviser, Stikeman Elliott
Henry Ketcham, 1996–2003, chairman and CEO, West Fraser Timber Co. Ltd.
Richard Rohmer, January to September 2004, co-founder Rohmer & Fenn
Maureen Sabia, 1996–2003, president, Maureen Sabia International
Gordon Walker, 2004–present, principal, Walker Consulting, Inc.

Senior International Advisers*

Margaret Thatcher, former prime minister of Great Britain
Valéry Giscard d'Estaing, former president of France
Lord Carrington, former secretary general of NATO
Henry Kissinger, former U.S. secretary of state
Zbigniew Brzezinski, former assistant to the president for U.S. National
    Security Affairs

The Lawyers

Hollinger International

Martin Flumenbaum, partner, Paul, Weiss, Rifkind, Wharton & Garrison
Toby Myerson, partner, Paul Weiss

Special Committee

Jonathan Rosenberg, partner, O'Melveny & Myers
Andrew Geist, partner, O'Melveny & Myers
Norman Harrison, Richard C. Breeden & Co.

---

*As of 2000. The special advisory board was disbanded in 2001.

AUDIT COMMITTEE
James McDonough, partner, Gardner Carton & Douglas

BLACK AND HOLLINGER INC.
Jesse Finkelstein, Richards Layton & Finger
John Warden, partner, Sullivan & Cromwell
Benjamin F. Stapleton, partner, Sullivan & Cromwell
David Boies, managing partner, Boies, Schiller, & Flexner
Edward Greenspan, senior partner, Greenspan Henein & White
Brendan Sullivan, partner, Williams & Connolly
Darren Sukonick, Torys

The Bankers

Bruce Wasserstein, Lazard Frères & Co.
Louis Zachary, Lazard Frères & Co.
Rick Fogg, managing director, Wachovia Securities
David Haase, managing director, Wachovia Securites

The Auditors

Marilyn Stitt, partner, KPMG LLP

The Suitors

Sir Frederick and Sir David Barclay, Press Holdings International Ltd.
Nelson Peltz, Chairman and CEO, Triarc Companies, Inc.
Thomas Hicks, Chairman and CEO, Hicks, Muse, Tate & Furst Inc.
Richard Desmond, Chairman, Northern & Shell Networks

The Shareholders

TWEEDY BROWNE CO.
Christopher Browne, managing director
Laura Jereski, analyst
Robert Curry, Kirby McInerney & Squire

CARDINAL CAPITAL MANAGEMENT
Eugene Fox, managing director
Robert Kirkpatrick, managing director

SOUTHEASTERN ASSET MANAGEMENT INC.
Mason Hawkins, chairman
Staley Cates, president

OMEGA ADVISERS, INC.
Leon Cooperman, chairman

The Shareholder Advisers

Herbert Denton, president, Providence Capital, Inc.
Jay Hill, head of research, Providence Capital, Inc.

The Newspapers

Jeremy Deedes, CEO and publisher, the *Telegraph*
John Cruickshank, publisher, the *Chicago Sun-Times*

The Black Empire

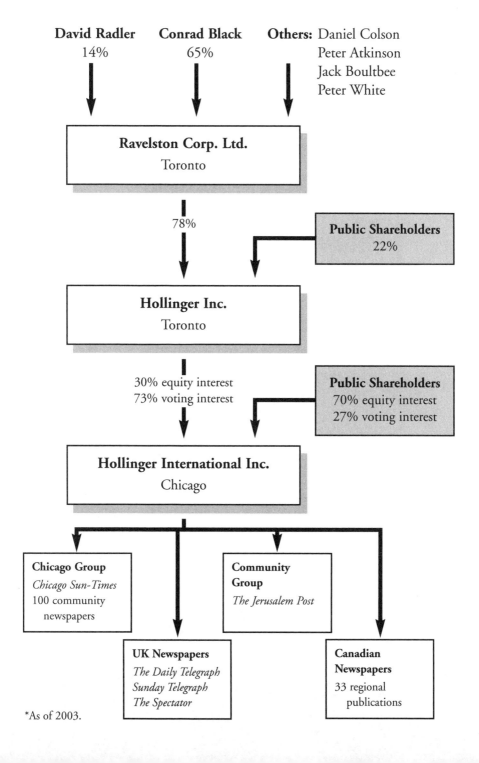

David Radler
14%

Conrad Black
65%

Others: Daniel Colson
Peter Atkinson
Jack Boultbee
Peter White

Ravelston Corp. Ltd.
Toronto

78%

Public Shareholders
22%

Hollinger Inc.
Toronto

30% equity interest
73% voting interest

Public Shareholders
70% equity interest
27% voting interest

Hollinger International Inc.
Chicago

Chicago Group
Chicago Sun-Times
100 community
newspapers

Community Group
The Jerusalem Post

UK Newspapers
The Daily Telegraph
Sunday Telegraph
The Spectator

Canadian Newspapers
33 regional
publications

*As of 2003.

Prologue

November 13, 2003

WHEN THE ELEVATOR DOORS OPENED, four men, their faces grim, emerged on the eighteenth floor of a building on New York's Fifth Avenue. In a few seconds, they would step into the elegant, wood-trimmed offices of Hollinger International Inc. and deliver an ultimatum to the company's notoriously combative chairman and chief executive officer, Conrad Black. They were braced for a showdown.

Black had built one of the world's most formidable newspaper empires, amassing hundreds of publications in Canada, the United States, and the United Kingdom. His aggressive corporate manoeuvres and ostentatious lifestyle frequently ignited controversy, but Black had a history of deflecting criticism by bludgeoning his adversaries, including a prime minister, with lawsuits. He had always remained defiant. When provoked, the domineering press lord typically responded with a fierce counterattack, and no one knew this better than the four men who were arriving to meet him.

Gordon Paris, James Thompson, Richard Breeden, and James McDonough walked into Hollinger International's boardroom at 1 P.M. Black had not expected so many visitors. Thompson, the former Illinois governor who served on Hollinger International's board and chaired its audit committee, had phoned Black the previous day and requested a meeting with him and Paris. He had not mentioned that he would be bringing McDonough, the audit committee's lawyer, and Breeden, the former head of the U.S. Securities and Exchange Commission. The four visitors were on a mission: they were going to topple a bloated regime at Hollinger International, an emerging symbol of executive greed in an era defined by corporate scandal. The men knew their task would likely unleash a series of unpleasant events. The reputations of dozens of powerful business and political figures could be tarnished, if not destroyed, and hundreds of millions of dollars in investor money was at risk.

After the men had seated themselves around a large mahogany conference table, Paris launched into a carefully rehearsed speech. The New York investment banker was in charge of a special committee of Hollinger International directors that had been appointed to investigate millions of dollars in payments that had been siphoned out of the company by Black and three other executives. Only a week earlier, they had written Black with their preliminary conclusions: he and his lieutenants had pocketed, without authorization, more than $30 million.

Now came the difficult part. Paris explained that the special committee had decided to take action. He told Black that he would have to repay the money. Furthermore, Paris said, the special committee would be recommending to Hollinger International's board that several of his long-time allies be forced to leave the company. Then, hesitating slightly, he delivered the final demand. Black would have to resign as CEO and Paris would replace him.

Black, his face drained of colour, had remained uncharacteristically quiet through most of Paris's speech. This last indignity, however, was too much to bear. In calling for Black's removal, Paris was essentially firing the man who had approached him to join Hollinger International's board just nine months earlier. The kick in the face was that Paris, an investment banker with no corporate experience, was going to replace him.

"You are spectacularly unqualified," Black sputtered. "The idea that the chairman of the special committee should replace me as chairman of the board is too humiliating."

Paris did not waver. If Black refused to sign the agreement, he explained, the committee would take legal action to remove him. Black immediately turned to Breeden, the former securities regulator who had been advising the special committee, to protest his innocence.

"I acknowledge that there may have been some paperwork issues," he said, explaining the lack of approvals for the executive payments, but "I had nothing to do with all of this." Removing him as CEO, Black insisted, was "excessively severe and unwarranted."

For the next few hours the group debated the committee's demands. The discussion was tense, but aside from Black's initial outburst, it was curiously devoid of the fireworks they had been expecting. Instead, Black repeatedly excused himself from the room, explaining that he had people waiting for him. The four men were bewildered. They had just served Black with a corporate death warrant and yet he continued to juggle appointments as if nothing had happened. Late in the afternoon, just before the meeting concluded, Black's behaviour grew even more bizarre: he invited his visitors to dine with him that night at Le Cirque, the famed French restaurant frequented by Manhattan's elite.

The men agreed, but as they walked away, McDonough shook his head in disbelief. "This is exceedingly odd," he muttered to his companions. Usually, it was the condemned man who was offered a last supper.

Tonight, the doomed CEO would treat his executioners.

CHAPTER ONE

Uprising

WOULD CONRAD BEHAVE? Paul Healy glanced at his watch. It was after 11 on the morning of May 23, 2002, and the meeting was starting late. As usual, Conrad Black was behind schedule and only now making his way through the crowded room to the podium. The annual meeting of Hollinger International was finally about to begin and Healy was agitated. As Hollinger International's vice-president in charge of investor relations, he was the person shareholders called when they had issues to discuss. Lately there had been plenty of issues.

Healy had fended questions for months from some of the company's biggest shareholders about multi-million-dollar payments and fees paid to Black and some of his top lieutenants. Investors demanded explanations. They wanted more information, analyses, anything that would justify why so much shareholder money was being diverted into the pockets of executives. Healy had been passing the complaints on to Black, who generally greeted them with royal indifference. Lately, however, Lord Black of Crossharbour had been chafing at the pestering. A few days earlier, irked by a query from one shareholder, Black had fired a caustic email to Healy, ridiculing the concerns as an "epidemic of shareholder idiocy." The boss, Healy feared, was spoiling for a fight.

Healy surveyed the meeting room and observed Barbara Amiel in the front row. Black had married the slender brunette in 1992, shortly after divorcing his first wife, Joanna, who left him and their high-society London life for a former Catholic priest in Toronto. Amiel, a one-time receptionist with the Canadian Broadcasting Corporation, had launched her media career in 1966 by appearing in a TV satire as a bikini-clad seductress tempting hockey wildman Eddie Shack. She attracted further attention in the 1970s and 1980s as one of Canada's most outspoken conservative political columnists and editor of the right-wing *Toronto Sun*. Long before Reagan economics and the Thatcher revolution paved the way for such liberal-bashing media celebrities as Rush Limbaugh, Amiel established herself as a unique right-wing phenomenon. Sexy and smart, she was an intoxicating brew of William F. Buckley, Jr. and Ava Gardner. By the late 1980s, Amiel had left Canada and three marriages and found a new outlet for her conservative views as a columnist for *The Times of London*. Her marriage to Black, four years her junior, opened a new career as a corporate director with Hollinger International and a variety of other Black interests. In 1998 she moved her column from *The Times* to Black's *Telegraph*. Known as much for her revealing designer clothes as her arch-conservative columns, Amiel was nicknamed "Glamour Puss" in the British tabloids. The pussycat, Healy had learned the hard way, also had sharp claws. When annoyed, she was a woman to be avoided.

Sitting behind Amiel in the meeting room on the first floor of New York's Metropolitan Club were about seventy-five shareholders and guests. Ever since New York financier J.P. Morgan had built the club in 1894 on the corner of Sixtieth Street and Fifth Avenue, the white stone shrine with its polished marble interior, burgundy carpets, and chandeliers had been called the "Millionaires' Club." It proved an ideal theatre for Black, who took advantage of the showcase to plump and flatter business allies and dazzle shareholders at annual meetings. But few would notice the grandeur this morning.

What transfixed most people was a table on the dais at the front of the room where Black was sitting. The table to his right was empty. Resting on it was a small white sign that read RESERVED FOR DIRECTORS. None of Hollinger International's eight outside directors had shown up. Underlining the void was the table to Black's left. Occupying it were four sombre men in dark suits whom he introduced as Hollinger International president David Radler, vice-chairman Daniel Colson, executive vice-president Jack Boultbee, and corporate counsel Mark Kipnis. No one mentioned the missing directors.

It was time for Black's annual speech to shareholders. Black usually delivered speeches that left listeners impressed with his boundless enthusiasm for the company's international holdings, which included such trophies as *The Daily Telegraph,* the *Chicago Sun-Times,* and *The Jerusalem Post.* Over six feet tall, with a barrel torso, rumbling baritone, and a vocabulary that flew across centuries, Black was an imposing, almost boastful presence at the podium. This morning, however, the master orator didn't seem so sure of himself.

For most of his twenty-minute speech, he led shareholders through a confusing thicket of Hollinger International's financial inner workings. He talked inscrutably about discounts on debt notes: "15 percent, 17 percent on 90 percent of the quantum, partially offset by the super-normal rolled-up yield." Then he moved to financial formulas for measuring gains on recent asset sales: "average total multiple of EBITDA," or "unadjusted EBITDA multiple," and, not to be forgotten, "a recession-reduced EBITDA." As for taxes on asset sales, he intoned, "… we did not pay tax on re-captured depreciation."

Glancing at some of the furrowed brows in the audience, Healy knew he wasn't the only one in the room mystified by Black's presentation. His speech was as clear as mud. He's obfuscating, Healy thought. When Black ended his speech, Healy saw a slim, pale woman with a short bob of thick brown hair raise her hand for a microphone. It was Laura Jereski. Known to many in the room as a hard-hitting financial journalist whose exposés had brought her notoriety, Jereski for the past three years had been quietly working as an analyst with one of Hollinger International's largest shareholders, Tweedy Browne & Co.

Healy had tried with little success in the past year to answer Jereski's increasingly insistent questions about personal payments to Black and some of his executives. All he could do was refer her to Hollinger International's public financial filings. Details about the payments in these filings were so meagre that they would have barely filled a classified ad in one of Hollinger International's newspapers. Frustrated with the stonewalling, Jereski and her boss Chris Browne wanted other shareholders to hear their concerns at the annual meeting. Jereski's first query was about multi-million-dollar payments made to Black and some of his executives by companies that had acquired newspapers from Hollinger International.

"Why do you feel it is appropriate," Jereski asked Black, "for those payments to go to you and not to our company?" Black answered with ease. The personal fees had been requested by the purchasers, he assured Jereski. For example, when Hollinger International sold more than three hundred newspapers, including the *National Post*, to Winnipeg-based CanWest Global Communications Corp. a year earlier, Black and his team had received $53 million. Black insisted in his speech that CanWest owner Israel Asper "demanded" that the Hollinger International team sign non-compete agreements. Furthermore, Black added, it was Hollinger International's board of directors that had reviewed and approved the CanWest payments. "That was not a matter negotiated directly by us."

The next shareholder to grab the microphone was Lee Cooperman, a short, portly Wall Street investing legend in his sixties. Cooperman had made a fortune trading securities for his former employer Goldman Sachs and now operated his own hedge fund. Given what Black had just said, Cooperman wanted to know why Hollinger International's independent directors were not there to back him up. Why were Alfred Taubman, chairman of Sotheby's Holdings Inc., Leslie Wexner, chairman of U.S. retail chain The Limited, Inc., Marie-Josée Kravis, economist and wife of Wall Street takeover titan Henry Kravis, Shmuel Meitar, an Israeli communications mogul, James Thompson, former governor of Illinois, and one-time Washington heavyweights Henry Kissinger, Richard Perle, and Richard Burt missing in action?

Black was sympathetic to Cooperman. "I think it is not a flattering reflection on them as a group, they're not here," he said, then explained that a few directors had other obligations or were travelling. As for the other absent directors, Black said: "I'm not going to go through kind of a schoolboy thing and say, you know, the cat ate Mr. Wexner's homework or something.... It's a freakish thing, though, I mean there are usually some [directors here]."

The interrogation continued. Why was Hollinger International paying tens of millions of dollars in annual management fees to Black's private holding company? Why wasn't there more information about how the fees were calculated? Although each question was asked calmly and respectfully, Black grew increasingly indignant.

"We haven't been sitting here feathering our nest," he told one shareholder.

"We certainly aren't using the fact that we're owners to stuff our pockets," he told another.

"You're not dealing with greed here and you're not dealing with sneakiness."

As the questions grew more pointed, Black inadvertently echoed the memorable denial by Claude Rains's character in *Casablanca* when he ordered the closure of a gambling room. "I would be shocked, I would be shocked," Black blurted, "if I thought [you] ... were trying to suggest there was anything unethical about what we're doing."

Black was not the only person in the room who had grown impatient with the questioning. Edward Shufro had not planned to attend the meeting. He ran a small investment firm started by his father more than sixty years earlier and had recently sold most of his Hollinger International shares after watching them lie dormant for three years "like a dog that wasn't barking." On a whim, minutes before the meeting began, Shufro had decided to take the two-block walk from his office to the Metropolitan Club. As he sat there listening to shareholders, he grew frustrated with the polite and deferential tone of their questions. Shufro thought, These guys are afraid to tell him what they think.

Waving impatiently for a microphone, Shufro stood up and addressed Black. "Fortunately we represent only a fairly modest amount of your shares," Shufro began. "We have had more in the past. I've been listening to what my distinguished—and I do mean distinguished—colleagues have been saying to you. They're trying to be polite about it, but what they're telling you is that they consider you a thief...."

Turning red, Black growled at Shufro, "Then you shouldn't be here."

"Well, I'm here," said Shufro.

"Sell your shares and get out," Black shot back. "If you think I'm a thief, go. I'm not going anywhere."

Unfazed by Black's outburst, Shufro replied, "Well. Yeah, well, I thought it would be interesting for you to hear my viewpoint on it."

"If we lived in a country or were now in a country where the civil torte of defamation still existed, I'd—my response would be a juridical one," Black thundered. Turning back to the audience he asked: "Do we have any more intelligent or civilized comments than that?"

———

One hour later, Black walked into Hollinger International's New York boardroom, located a few blocks south of the Metropolitan Club. The room was the largest in Hollinger International's small New York office, located on the eighteenth floor of a Fifth Avenue tower. The sumptuous office had been designed by famed British decorator David Mlinaric, the force behind the restoration of London's Royal Opera House, Spencer House, and British embassies in Paris, Brussels, and Washington. Mlinaric specialized in evoking the elegance of old-world money and he spared no expense in the $3-million makeover of the half-dozen rooms in Hollinger International's New York base. He also spent millions of dollars decorating Black's London mansion and Park Avenue condominium.

The boardroom was the centrepiece of Mlinaric's work at Hollinger International. Anchoring the room was a massive, custom-built mahogany table surrounded by twenty-four dark wooden chairs padded in cobalt-blue fabric. The table was so enormous that the movers had had to lash it beneath an elevator to carry it up to the offices. Inlaid into the table's surface were several miniature teleconference microphones, so discreet than an unsuspecting cleaner once covered them in wax; after a muffled teleconference, new raised speakers had to be installed.

The boardroom's walls were covered in wheat-coloured silk. To the north were windows with a view of Central Park and on the south wall hung some of the artifacts from Hollinger International's growing collection of Franklin Delano Roosevelt memorabilia: photos, letters, and a painting of a battleship that once ferried the president through the Panama Canal. In a nook near the boardroom's door was a small black-and-white photo of a chubby-faced man with slicked-back dark hair. The signature beneath the photo read *Al Capone*. Black liked to quip that the Chicago gangster was a Hollinger International shareholder.

The room was buzzing when Black arrived. Seated at the table were Radler, Colson, Kipnis, Healy, Jack Boultbee, and Peter Atkinson, Black's long-time lawyer from Toronto who had just been appointed a director to Hollinger International. Two other men joined them: former governor Thompson and Pentagon adviser Richard Perle, one of the architects of George W. Bush's Iraq policy. Thompson and Perle, Hollinger International's independent directors, had not bothered to make an appearance at the annual meeting a few blocks away, but they did manage to attend the business lunch.[1] Butlers in short white tunics served a selection of grilled fish, chicken, and salad on the company's navy blue–rimmed Bernardaud Limoges plates.

As the men dug into the meal, Healy wondered how Thompson and Perle would digest the news about the stormy shareholders session. After everyone had eaten, Black called to order the meeting that had been scheduled to follow the shareholder gathering. Listening in via teleconference was his wife Amiel, who had been so angry about the shareholder uprising that a company executive had to drive her back to her Park Avenue apartment to calm her down. Richard Burt, Shmuel

Meitar, and Alfred Taubman also listened in. Absent were Kissinger and Kravis.

Black opened the session with a summary of the morning shareholder gathering. "The meeting went fine today," Black said, glancing at Thompson and Perle. "Some of the shareholders were concerned that you didn't show for the meeting. It would be a good idea if you showed up next year."

Healy was disgusted. Conrad wasn't telling his independent directors about the angry shareholders. And none of his senior executives who had attended the rancorous annual meeting spoke up to contradict him. After the meeting, Healy pulled Radler and the company's lawyer Kipnis into his office. He knew the two would be flying back to Chicago that afternoon with Thompson. The former governor was making a name for himself as a corporate governance expert and he chaired Hollinger International's audit committee.

"You've got to tell Governor Thompson what happened today," Healy implored the two men. Kipnis agreed with Healy, and after a few minutes Radler seemed to capitulate.

Healy had hoped the media would draw attention to shareholder complaints, but, inexplicably, the few reporters who had attended the annual meeting played down the dramatic encounter. A few hours after the annual meeting, Reuters ran a short story on its news wire that focused exclusively on Black's hints to reporters that he might sell assets or take the company private. Bloomberg News was closer to the mark, quoting shareholder concerns about the need to improve the transparency of Hollinger International's business dealings. But the story was so brief that the few who published it buried the story in their business sections.

The next day, Healy phoned Kipnis to find out how Thompson had responded. When Kipnis said the former governor had not been told, Healy again asked Hollinger International's lawyer to meet with Thompson. Nothing happened, but Healy kept pushing. This time he phoned Radler at his Chicago office in the *Sun-Times* building and urged him again to tell Thompson about the angry shareholders. Radler didn't say much.

A few days later, Healy made his way home after work to his condo on New York's Upper West Side. He picked up his phone and punched the number pad to check his voice mail. He had three messages. They were all from Black, who was calling from his home in London, where it was close to midnight. As he listened to the messages, Healy could hear the anger building in Black's voice. He said that Healy had "stepped out of line" by pushing Radler to disclose shareholder complaints to Thompson. Then Healy heard a *beep* on his phone. He had another call. Switching to his other line, Healy found Black, still fuming. His boss had worked himself into a fury.

"This is my company," he roared. "I will decide what the board knows and when they know it."

CHAPTER TWO

Holy Mackerel

CONRAD BLACK RULED his boardrooms with a steely grip for more than two decades, but he reigned over a coalition of the willing. His directors were virtually hand-picked from a supportive circle of close friends and aging political and business legends who embraced his ardent right-wing views and were energized by his attention. He magnanimously entertained them at star-studded gatherings and engaged them in heady discussions about world events. He was charming and courteous to his friends and colleagues and heaped flattery and perks on his directors and advisers. To gain membership to this boardroom club of like-minded people was to join an exclusive salon where socializing and political debate dominated the agenda. It was a world where Black's authority was seldom challenged and his influence was always on display.

On one memorable occasion, the morning of September 6, 1989, Black went to great lengths to impress his colleagues. He led a group of men in a convoy of limousines from London's Four Seasons Hotel to a dark Georgian home with a solid black door bearing a lion's head knocker and the brass numeral "10." Ushered quickly inside, they were met in the marble entrance hall by a middle-aged woman with a carefully landscaped headdress of auburn hair. Black stepped forward and exchanged pleasantries with Margaret Thatcher and then turned to introduce Britain's prime minister to his Hollinger Inc. directors.

"I'm terribly sorry," Thatcher explained to her visitors, "but the room we were going to meet in upstairs is unavailable. Would it be all right if we met in the Cabinet Room?" Hearing no protests, the prime minister invited the businessmen into the chamber where British cabinet members have gathered since 1856. The course of history had been charted from the room's boat-sized oval table, but this morning a different kind of politics was at work. As head of a thriving newspaper empire whose publications included the Tory stalwart the *Daily Telegraph,* Black enjoyed special access to the Conservative Party's leadership—so special that Thatcher was letting Black strut his influence by granting directors of his distant Canadian company a private audience.

Under the watchful gaze of a portrait of Britain's first prime minister, Robert Walpole, Thatcher sat at her customary chair in the middle of the cabinet table facing Downing Street. Apart from Black, the only Hollinger Inc. director familiar to her was Lord Peter Carrington, her former foreign secretary, who resigned in 1982 after he was caught off guard by Argentina's invasion of Britain's Falkland Islands. The retired blueblood would become one of many political celebrities to ornament Black's boardroom.[1]

The most prominent Canadian in the Cabinet Room was Black's childhood friend and reliably loyal Hollinger Inc. director Fredrik Eaton. Great-grandson of legendary Toronto retailer Timothy Eaton, the boyish-looking heir had recently yielded his post as president of Eaton's department store chain, a fading company that would sink into bankruptcy proceedings by 1997. When Black asked for Eaton's backing during a controversial takeover in the 1970s, the retail heir assured Black, "I don't really understand all this, but you've got my vote."[2]

Joining Eaton at the cabinet table were Black's most trusted advisers. There was his older brother Montegu Black, who had sold his corporate holdings to Conrad during an acrimonious divorce. Alongside him was David Radler, Hollinger's famously intense and penny-pinching president, who had been Black's shadow ever since their first newspaper venture in the 1960s. Daniel Colson, the son of a Montreal policeman, was an elegant, globe-trotting lawyer for Toronto law firm Stikeman Elliott. Colson would soon be devoting himself to Hollinger full time as a London-based executive. Dixon Chant, Hollinger's diminutive and stooped seventy-seven-year-old deputy chairman, a Toronto accountant, had long passed retirement, but he had been such a crucial ally to Black during an early corporate conquest that he lingered as a paid Hollinger executive and director until shortly before his death in 2002 at the age of ninety. Towering over Chant was Hal Jackman, irreverent heir to a Toronto financial conglomerate. Annual shareholder meetings at public companies he controlled were such rushed affairs that Jackman occasionally timed the sessions with a stopwatch. His record was an eighty-second annual meeting.

Black had advised the Hollinger Inc. directors that Thatcher would have only a few minutes to spare. But when the *Telegraph*'s owner asked the prime minister to comment on current events, she launched into a discussion that lasted nearly an hour and a half. The men listened appreciatively as she shared her thoughts about the troubles in Northern Ireland, Estonia, and the Falklands. When Eaton asked her if she would again defend the Falklands if the Argentine army returned to the British territory, Thatcher turned and snapped, "Mr. Eaton, if a thief came into your house, would you go after him?" The room erupted with laughter. As they filed out, Eaton joked with fellow directors about the encounter. He had just been "handbagged" by the Iron Lady. He couldn't believe his good fortune at sharing such an intimate moment with one of the world's most powerful leaders. Eaton thought, *Holy mackerel, are we lucky.*

There would be more "holy mackerel" moments that day. From 10 Downing Street, the directors were ferried to Fleet Street, where, at the time, the *Telegraph* had its headquarters. During what Jackman would later describe in his diary as a "boring lunch" and "perfunctory board meeting," Conrad proposed an "exceedingly generous" tripling of directors' attendance fees at Hollinger Inc. from $500 to $1,500 for each board meeting and a raising of their annual fee to $12,000. Fond of needling Black about his ostentatious social life, Jackman responded to the increases by saying, "Your lifestyle is an inspiration to Canadians, you mustn't let us down by not paying us $1,500 a meeting." Although Jackman's sarcasm would eventually sour their friendship, Black appreciated the humour that day. "Yes, we must keep up appearances," he said.

To that end, Black entertained his directors at London's exclusive Brooks's Club later that evening. Joining them were a few dozen of the city's elite, including buccaneering financier Sir James Goldsmith, merchant banker Rupert Hambro, SG Warburg chairman Sir David Scholey, and right-wing satirist Auberon Waugh. Shortly before midnight, the weary Hollinger directors climbed back into their limousines. This time they were headed for London's Docklands, a long drive to a remote location where a cavernous new plant on the Isle of Dogs was printing the next day's edition of the *Telegraph*. Black had arranged for his directors to arrive at the facility at that late hour so they could witness the final stages of the print run. When they arrived, Black took them to a dial that counted papers as the presses spat them out. As the directors stood there, the dial clicked past the one million mark. The moment was not lost on them. More than a million readers would be flipping the pages of their company's premier newspaper tomorrow. It was an intoxicating ending to a day filled with high-octane hobnobbing. "It certainly showed us," recalled Eaton, "how important the *Telegraph* was, and therefore, how important the proprietor, Conrad, was, that he could do this kind of thing."

———

Conrad Black is not the first CEO to woo directors with star-studded excursions. He did, however, transform directors' meetings into unique salons decorated with ambassadors, former heads of states, and lords. Who else would be allowed to interrupt a prime minister's workday with a caravan of businessmen-tourists?

Conrad Black's mentor in boardroom manoeuvres was John Angus "Bud" McDougald, a crass, tough-talking former bond salesman who showed off his millions by hanging chandeliers in his garage and serving food on gold-plated china. In the 1970s, McDougald was chairman and a major shareholder of Argus Corp. Ltd., a publicly listed Toronto conglomerate named after the Greek mythological giant with one hundred eyes. Argus's far-flung subsidiaries included the farm-implement maker Massey-Ferguson Ltd., grocery store chain Dominion Stores Ltd., and a variety of prominent Canadian mining, forest product, broadcast, and financial companies.

Critical to McDougald's corporate clout and personal wealth were allies he recruited to Argus's board of directors, including Conrad's father George Montegu Black. When McDougald and some of his associates sold personal assets to Argus at inflated rates—according to Black's autobiography and an earlier biography by Peter C. Newman— the board did not stand in his way.[3] These directors, Black would later write, were brilliantly finessed by McDougald with "Stalinesque thoroughness and cynicism" through the use of "perquisites and preferments and unlimited use of the corporate plane."[4]

Black would know. By the mid-1960s, when Black's father retreated from corporate life to live like a recluse, McDougald curried the senior Black's favour by holding Argus executive committee meetings in the Black family home. On Conrad's twenty-first birthday, McDougald made him one of the youngest members of the Toronto Club, a starchy gathering spot for the country's business chiefs. In 1968, as McDougald was cultivating George Black's support for a corporate reorganization, the Argus chairman presented Conrad with a valuable portrait of Napoleon, whom the young Black had admired since an early age. When Black later reviewed his corporate ascent with biographer Newman he explained: "One of the reasons my brother and I succeeded while the others didn't is that they never really understood his technique. They never recognized the McDougald system as I did. It was all based on manoeuvring personalities.... You put one man's son into the Toronto Club and let another one ride in an antique car—just the way he gave me that painting of Napoleon."[5]

McDougald's boardroom cunning was one of many qualities that Black took from the Argus chairman. After he replaced McDougald at Argus, Black began to assume a lifestyle that was similar to that of his predecessor. "He wanted to be like Bud McDougald," said former director Jackman. "[McDougald] was his idol. He had an aura that impressed Black." Like his mentor, Black shuttled on company airplanes between luxurious homes in Toronto, London, and Palm Beach. Both men were chauffeured around London in vintage Rolls-Royces, gained memberships to exclusive clubs, and insinuated their way into the upper echelons of British society. They mixed business and pleasure, entertaining British royalty in their homes, and escorting queens, princes, and princesses to a variety of ceremonies.

———

Black began recruiting celebrities to his boards after he gained entry in 1981 to one of the Bilderberg conferences, cloistered gatherings of royal, business, and political elite who meet annually under heavy security at various five-star international resorts. Prince Bernhard of the Netherlands launched the meetings in 1954 to nurture military and economic co-operation among non-Communist countries during the Cold War. Although Prince Bernhard was disgraced in 1976 when the Dutch government revealed he was involved in a bribery scandal, the annual get-together he initiated has grown to include more than one hundred high-ranking officials.

At home with the group's predominantly conservative business and political elite, Black wrote in his autobiography that "Bilderberg has been the closest I have known to ... camaraderie."[6] The speed with which Black, then in his late thirties, ingratiated himself to the inner circle of Bilderberg was breathtaking. Faithful members such as Lord Carrington, Henry Kissinger, Giovanni Agnelli, chairman of Italian automaker Fiat, and Dwayne Andreas of Archer Daniels Midland agreed to serve long terms as directors on some of his corporate boards or as paid advisers. David Rockefeller, one of Bilderberg's earliest patrons, lent his Maine cottage to Black during his 1992 honeymoon with Amiel. Others made speeches or guest appearances at the Hollinger group's annual dinners.

In the blinding light of so many luminaries, directors at Hollinger Inc., and later at its U.S. subsidiary, Hollinger International, sometimes appeared to lose sight of the professional obligations they shouldered. Under North American corporate and securities law, directors of companies with publicly traded shares are bound by a duty to ensure that business decisions are made in the best interests of all shareholders. At companies such as Hollinger International, which are controlled by a majority shareholder, the duty falls to independent or outside directors who do not work at or have any business ties to the company.

Joining the big names on the boards of Hollinger companies was a mixed bag of not-so-famous directors who tended to be grateful for their membership in Black's exclusive boardrooms. Some, such as former Hollinger Inc. director Ralph Barford, viewed his twenty-year tenure as "the best theatre tickets in town."[7] Others were thankful to be invited into Hollinger boardrooms because their controversial business history, advanced age, or lack of experience made them less-than-desirable boardroom candidates at other companies.

Retired Catholic Archbishop Gerald Emmett Carter, who presided over Black's 1986 conversion from Anglicanism to Catholicism, was invited onto the board of Hollinger Inc.'s publicly traded affiliate Argus Corp. Ltd. in 1996 at the age of eighty-five. Despite Carter's lack of business experience, Black gushed in Argus's annual report that the man was "one of Canada's most distinguished citizens" with an "extensive background in general management" thanks to his work with Catholic schools. Joining the former archbishop on Argus's board was Anna Porter, whose Toronto firm published Black's 1993 autobiography, *A Life in Progress*. That same year, Porter resigned as a director of a troubled, publicly traded Toronto jewellery store chain, protesting, "I'm a book publisher. What am I doing in this mess?"[8]

Black was partial to high-profile business and political leaders who suffered reversals. Real estate developer Paul Reichmann was invited to sit on Argus's board in 1993, one year after his family's Olympia & York Developments Ltd. collapsed into bankruptcy. Movie chain and theatre operator Garth Drabinsky joined the board of Black's Toronto holding company Hollinger Inc. in 1996, five years after he was squeezed out of the cash-strapped Cineplex Odeon Corp. movie theatre chain. Hailed in a Hollinger Inc.'s 1995 annual report as "one of the most accomplished impresarios in the world," Mr. Drabinsky served on the governance committee of Hollinger Inc.'s board until 1999, when a U.S. federal grand jury in New York indicted him on charges of conspiracy and fraud relating to his theatre company Livent Inc. Although a Hollinger Inc. subsidiary saw most of its 10-percent stake in Livent virtually wiped out by the company's subsequent bankruptcy, Black donated money to Mr. Drabinsky's defence fund and hired him as a creative marketing consultant.[9]

Black was similarly loyal to Alfred Taubman, chairman of Sotheby's Holdings Inc., when in 2001 he was convicted of fraud for his role in a price-fixing scandal at the auction house. The seventy-eight-year-old Taubman was a director of Black's U.S. subsidiary Hollinger International, and Black told shareholders at the company's 2002 annual meeting in May that he refused to accept the resignation of the "outstandingly valuable director" because his conviction was under appeal. "We do not desert our friends," Black told shareholders. After Taubman was sent to jail two months later, Black travelled to a Rochester, Minnesota, prison to visit him. Price fixing tainted another Hollinger International director, Dwayne Andreas, former chairman of grain-processing titan Archer Daniels Midland Co., which in 1998 saw three of its executives convicted after one of the largest antitrust investigations in the United States. One of the convicted was Andreas's son, who served a three-year term in a Minnesota prison a few hundred miles north of where Taubman was doing time. Andreas senior continued as chairman of Archer Daniel until 1999 and as one of Hollinger International's U.S. directors until 2002.

A directorship on one of Black's boards could be personally lucrative. Some early directors were minority investors in the private holding company Ravelston Corp., through which Black controlled a maze of companies and partnerships. These directors scored in the mid-1980s when Black, according to his autobiography, purchased their Ravelston shares at a price that tripled their original net investment.[10] Others made extra money by collecting fees and salaries as directors, advisers, consultants, or executives on active and not-so-active companies in Black's domain. For example, Argus Corp. in 1982 shouldered a large board of eighteen directors, most of them Black cronies, even though the storied former conglomerate had by then largely been reduced to a repository for shares of affiliated companies. Incredibly, Argus directors such as Eaton, Jackman, and Radler, each of whom had a full-time job elsewhere, doubled as vice-presidents at the company. Of the C$7.6-million Argus generated in income in 1982, nearly C$2 million was spent on officers' and directors' pay and general office expenses, according to its annual report. When Black reflected in his autobiography on his loyal fraternity of directors, he said "… not a brusque word had been exchanged among any of us throughout our association. They all remain friends."[11]

———

Black's cultivation of the elite moved into high gear in 1991, when his Toronto-based parent company Hollinger Inc. formed an international advisory committee. Advisers at these mini-Bilderbergs included so many elderly statesmen in their seventies and eighties that it resembled a retirement club. Complementing the geriatric politicians was a handful of prominent U.S. journalists, including syndicated columnist George Will and William F. Buckley, Jr., who would later praise Black in their columns or endorse his books. By the late 1990s, Black's U.S. subsidiary Hollinger International was paying more than $1 million annually in expenses and fees to fete his friends on the advisory board. One weekend a year, members and their spouses were flown first-class—many on the Concorde—given a car and a driver, ensconced in a room in a five-star hotel, and entertained at gala dinner parties set in such neoclassical shrines as London's Spencer House, Washington's

Folger Shakespeare Library, and Chicago's Cultural Center. The gatherings were such a draw that Fiat's Agnelli continued to attend sessions even wnile undergoing debilitating treatments for prostate cancer, which in 2003 took his life. For their trouble, Hollinger's advisory directors were each paid $25,000. Regulars such as Republican Defense Department heavyweight Richard Perle, Buckley, Kissinger, Andreas, and Carrington each would have pocketed more than $200,000 if they attended every session over an eleven-year span.

At the advisory board's once-a-year meeting, more than a few oversized egos wrestled for control of discussions about global politics and economics. Black, according to participants, served as "maitre d'discussion," kicking off each session with personal comments and then moving to a prearranged "tour de raison" of world events during which advisers were allotted set times to speak. Invariably the agenda broke down, one adviser said, because some guests such as Margaret Thatcher "usually grabbed most of the discussion."

The highlight of these annual gatherings was the Hollinger dinner. The traditional gathering originated in the 1920s as a raucous party for prospectors and promoters at a time when Hollinger reigned as one of Canada's biggest mining companies. Under McDougald, however, the evening was a staid affair populated by cigar-chomping Canadian business executives in the exclusive Toronto Club's back rooms. Black used the dinners to showcase his growing influence. The events became such a hot ticket that William Thorsell, then an editor at his old nemesis, *The Globe and Mail,* was star-struck when he was invited in 1992. "Conspicuous by his capabilities was Conrad Black himself. Beatific in his role as host to a business and social elite that generally pales beside his intelligence," gushed Thorsell in a column.

Flattery was as common as black ties at Hollinger dinners. In 1988, Black was so effusive about Prime Minister Thatcher's accomplishments that she began her speech by saying, "You've left me nothing to say." At the next year's dinner he introduced Ronald Reagan, who had retired only months earlier, as a president who had "altered for the better the course of American and of world history."[12] At the 1992 dinner, he championed a frail seventy-nine-year-old Richard Nixon, omitting his observation ten years earlier to his biographer that Nixon was "sleazy," "neurotic," and "paranoid."[13]

When shareholders queried the costs of the social club, Hollinger officials defended the expense on the grounds that its advisers were enlightening the newspaper company's executives and senior editors about international affairs. Privately, however, Black had another agenda. "He told me it was social climbing," former director Hal Jackman said, quoting Black's response in the early '90s, when he asked him why he was bothering with "all the fancy people." Although Black has denied it, some associates believe that one of the reasons he courted so many pedigreed advisers, particularly in Britain, was that he had his eye on a British peerage.

Black was introduced into England's House of Lords in October 2001 as Lord Black of Crossharbour, a name borrowed from the underground station near the *Telegraph's* Canary Wharf offices.

That same year, Hollinger disbanded its advisory council.

CHAPTER THREE

Black Factor

CONRAD BLACK'S FIRST BUSINESS venture flopped when the masters of Canada's elite private boys' school, Upper Canada College, caught him selling stolen exam questions to fellow students in June 1959.

It was an audacious scheme. With the help of three accomplices and a purloined key, fourteen-year-old Black broke into the Toronto school's offices and removed a number of upcoming final exam questions and a copy of the academic records of every student, so that, as he put it, "I could easily identify those who would be prepared to pay the most dearly for them."[1] Fellow students paid money for the test questions, but the school's teachers noticed almost immediately that some of its underachievers were suddenly scoring near-perfect marks. Black and the three co-conspirators were expelled.

Thirty-three years later, Black would strike back at his prosecutors, whom he termed "sadists." He was unapologetic about the theft and characterized the incident in his autobiography as a rebel hero's triumph over an oppressive regime.[2] "I am neither proud nor ashamed of what happened. It was an awful system whose odiousness was compounded by banality and pretension, but I was becoming somewhat fiendish and in the end inconvenienced hundreds of unoffending people, students, and faculty."[3] It would not be the last time in his career that the self-styled renegade blamed others for his troubles and minimized the consequences of his misdeeds as an "inconvenience."

———

Black's academic record didn't improve much after his expulsion. After trying a number of private schools and nearly flunking his first year at an Ontario university, he was so unmotivated that by 1963 he declared himself "an academic failure."[4] Unresponsive to structured education, Black chose his own path of learning by reading from his father's collection of books on European, military, and shipping history, subjects upon which he would develop an almost photographic recall. Although his generation was fond of hippie catchphrases, Black removed himself from the mainstream by cultivating an ornate manner of speech heavily embroidered with multisyllabic words. Instead of "cool" and "groovy," he favoured "pusillanimous" and "oleaginous."

Black persevered in university and, although he failed law school in Ontario, graduated from Quebec City's French-language university, Laval, in 1970 with a law degree. He drifted and travelled for a while and eventually found an outlet for his talents when he joined forces with Peter White and David Radler, two fellow conservatives he met during his university years. White at the time was an aide to Quebec premier Daniel Johnson, leader of Quebec's conservative Union Nationale Party. Black met Radler at the Radler family's Montreal restaurant Au Lutin Qui Bouffe, which was a popular hangout for Union Nationale members and where customers could have their photographs taken with a live baby pig. White and Black had dabbled in community newspapers in the mid-1960s, but in 1969 Radler joined the pair, and they went after bigger game and acquired the *Sherbrooke Record*. At the *Record*, a small Quebec newspaper, Black, Radler, and White followed a management pattern that they would use for more than two decades. Black focused on a variety of administrative tasks and the regional paper's editorial policy, personally writing glowing profiles of U.S. presidents, analyses of international affairs, and other non-local stories. It was the beginning of his lifelong affection for flattering political greats and advancing his deep-seated political conservatism. Radler plumped profits by trimming editorial space to make room for more advertisements. He also assailed costs; within weeks of the takeover he fired nearly half of the paper's thirty-two employees. White helped out with administrative duties between lengthy stints as an adviser, candidate, and executive with a variety of conservative provincial and federal political parties.

The budding newspaper barons were so impressed with the volume of profits that could be squeezed from aging newspapers that they began buying other regional Canadian papers, naming their chain Sterling Newspapers. But by 1974 Black had tired of rural life and returned to his family and friends in the Canadian establishment by opening a tiny Sterling Newspapers office in downtown Toronto. There, Black adopted a daily routine that would become one of his trademarks. His workday began late morning from his home, where he made phone calls to Radler and White for business updates. Just before noon he made a "cameo" appearance at the office, after which he typically lunched at the Toronto Club "maintaining and building contacts."[5] After lunch he devoted himself to writing articles and the occasional book, sessions that usually kept him up until 3 or 4 A.M. His first book, an admiring 743-page biography of controversial Quebec premier Maurice Duplessis, was published in 1977 to mostly favourable reviews. However, one critical review by a noted Canadian history professor prompted Black to rage that the academic was "a slanted, supercilious little twit."

Black was presented with an opportunity to move from the fringes of the Canadian establishment to its inner core when Bud McDougald died of a heart attack on March 14, 1978. McDougald had left no successor to steer the sprawling Argus conglomerate. Black and his brother Monte had inherited a minority stake in Argus's parent company Ravelston from their father, but they were shunted aside by senior Argus directors who appointed themselves to run the company.

Infuriated that he had been denied a management job, Black looked for another way to gain influence at Argus.

Argus's two largest shareholders at the time were McDougald's widow, Maude "Jim" McDougald, and her sister Doris, the widow of another deceased Argus executive; the women held their shares through the parent company Ravelston. Two months after McDougald's funeral, Black sent emissaries to visit the widows to ask them to sign an agreement containing a shotgun clause that effectively gave Black the right to compel some Ravelston shareholders to sell their stock to him.[6] The widows signed the documents, paving the way for Black and his brother Monte to seize the reins at Ravelston and its subsidiary Argus. Days later the women would protest that, despite advice from their lawyers, they hadn't understood what they were signing. "Like absolute idiots and birdbrains, we signed and signed and signed without reading at all," McDougald's widow said.[7] Black sued a number of journalists and authors who suggested that he used sinister means to seize control of Argus. If anyone's motives should be questioned, Black acidly observed in his autobiography, it should be those of the widows. "The whole arrangement was requested by the rapacious ladies, vetted by them, explained laboriously to them in monosyllables and with examples adapted to the mind of a child of ten, and they understood and approved every letter of every word of the agreement."[8] The women would fight Black's move, but Black, backed by other friendly Ravelston shareholders and the first of many supportive loans from the Canadian Imperial Bank of Commerce, successfully acquired the sisters' stake and in the process locked up control of one of Canada's most prominent companies. At the age of thirty-three, Black was the new Bud McDougald. For years after the controversial power grab, Black kept a framed copy of the widows' handwritten capitulation in his office.

With Black at the helm, Argus underwent a dizzying series of corporate asset shuffles that the proprietor boasted were inspired by the blitzkrieg methods of German tank commanders in the Second World War.[9] Black explained that the radical surgery was necessary to "exit the neuralgic corporate tangle ambiguously bequeathed to us by Bud

McDougald."[10] But the fringe benefit of some of the transactions was the funnelling of multi-million-dollar payments up to Ravelston, the private holding company now controlled by Black and his allies. Using public shareholders' money to feather executive nests was something of a tradition at Argus. According to Black and his biographer Peter C. Newman, McDougald embellished his personal fortune by selling his stock in a variety of companies to Argus at inflated rates.[11]

It was through Ravelston that Black accumulated his wealth. For example, in June 1979 one of the publicly traded companies in Black's orbit handed a C$90-million cash-and-stock windfall up to Ravelston. In exchange the public company got shares in another Black affiliate.[12] Argus also rewarded Ravelston with massive multi-million-dollar dividends and loans, some of which were interest free.[13] Ravelston got another cash infusion in 1983, when Argus paid C$49 million to the private company in exchange for shares in its ailing grocery store chain, Dominion Stores.[14] It is difficult to gauge the degree to which Argus shareholders benefited from these complex swaps, because the group's annual reports offer such scant detail that, in some Ravelston transactions, even the total dollar amount involved was omitted. The benefit to Black, however, is clearer. When he reflected on one of his first major shuffles, he said his private holding company Ravelston was put "in useful funds."[15]

By the early 1980s Black had completed most of the major surgery at Argus and was looking for new growth opportunities. He set his sights on the United States' third-largest iron ore producer, Hanna Mining Company of Cleveland, Ohio. Six months and an ugly legal battle later, Argus affiliate Norcen Energy Resources Ltd. and Black settled allegations of misleading disclosure about its takeover intentions by signing a so-called consent decree with the Securities and Exchange Commission, which regulates U.S. markets. Such decrees compel defendants to refrain from future violations of U.S. securities rules. That promise to play by the rules would come back to haunt Black.

After the bruising encounter with U.S. regulators, Black, White, and Radler revisited their expansion strategy. Recalling the easy money made from early newspaper ventures, they opted to return to their roots. Under the new banner of Hollinger Inc., the old Argus conglomerate empire was reborn as a newspaper company. Black and Radler concentrated initially on acquiring a variety of regional newspapers, but in 1985 they were handed an opportunity to enter a bigger league. In the spring of that year, fellow Bilderberg disciple, *The Economist*'s editor Andrew Knight, called Black to tell him that London's *Daily Telegraph* was seeking equity investors. Black was intrigued. The neoconservative had always admired the *Telegraph*'s right-wing views and its cachet with Britain's upper class. The paper had been such a supporter of the Conservative Party since it was founded in 1855 that its nickname was the "Torygraph."

A few weeks after Knight's tip, Black met with the *Telegraph*'s owner, Lord Hartwell, in a hotel room at New York's Kennedy Airport. Black advised Hartwell that he would invest close to $20 million for a minority stake in the *Telegraph*—but he had a condition. If the paper issued new shares, or if its controlling shareholders sold stock, Black wanted the first right to buy the equity. Desperate for cash to fund expensive new printing plants, Hartwell agreed. Six months later, as a result of his prescient demand for first rights, Black was able to take effective control of the *Telegraph* when the cash-starved paper's only hope for survival was to sell shares to him. As London newspaper baron Robert Maxwell famously told New York analysts, "Mr. Black has landed history's largest fish with history's smallest hook."

Building on his *Telegraph* conquest, Black and his top lieutenants, David Radler and Daniel Colson, continued buying dozens of small, regional newspapers and other international trophies. Soon Black owned *The Jerusalem Post* and the *Chicago Sun-Times,* and a minority interest in John Fairfax Holdings Ltd. Inc. of Australia, publisher of the *The Sydney Morning Herald.* Black had accumulated more than four hundred regional Canadian and U.S. dailies and weeklies, many with titles that sounded like abandoned railway stops—*Genesee Country Express, Boone County Headlight,* and *Shawnee Cridersville Press.*

By the mid-1990s, Black's Hollinger empire was the third-largest newspaper conglomerate in the world. To insiders, however, there was another side to the success story. Repeating the strategy that made Argus such a profitable enterprise for its proprietors, assets and money at Hollinger companies were in constant flux. Newspapers and other assets were swapped so often within the web of private and public companies in Black's domain that some of the group's executives internally referred to the Hollinger organization as a trading house.

The biggest migration of Black-owned newspapers occurred in the mid-1990s after his Toronto holding company Hollinger Inc. created a new publicly listed company on the New York Stock Exchange that would become known as Hollinger International Inc. By 1996, Black had transferred most of his newspaper holdings to Hollinger International. Though the company was based in Chicago, its small team of U.S. executives was divided between the *Sun-Times*'s offices and a Fifth Avenue high-rise in New York. As a result of the makeover, Black controlled his newspaper through an unwieldy chain of companies. At the top of his empire was his private holding company Ravelston, which controlled the now-depleted Hollinger Inc. in Toronto, which in turn controlled Hollinger International. Although Black only owned an indirect equity stake of 30 percent in Hollinger International, he controlled more than 70 percent of its shareholder votes through his exclusive ownership of a class of super-voting shares, also known as multiple voting shares.

Ever restless, Black was on the move again in 1996, when the *Telegraph* sold its stake in John Fairfax, publisher of the *Sydney Morning Herald*. The sale was a prelude to a much bigger purge in 1999 and 2000, when Hollinger International sold the vast majority of its U.S. and Canadian newspapers, including the two-year-old *National Post* in Toronto, to a variety of buyers. To the untrained eye, Hollinger International was still a major newspaper operator with big brands such as the *Telegraph, Jerusalem Post,* and *Sun-Times,* but its collection of stable and profitable community newspapers had been spun off at a cost that was not immediately apparent to the company's shareholders.

———

Black's frequent companion during this corporate evolution was controversy. When his business shuffles triggered protests, he inflamed the disputes with insulting and outrageous remarks. Black had long ago mastered the misdirection trick. When he bailed out of Massey-Ferguson's refinancing talks in 1980, a number of critics accused him of leaving the troubled farm-equipment maker in the lurch. He shifted the debate away from the main economic issue with a scathing denunciation in a letter to one of his critics, a columnist at the *Toronto Sun*:

> *For the record (not that the* Sun *is a newspaper of record to anyone who does not suffer from severe lip-strain after half-a-minute of silent reading) the* Sun*'s theory that we should mortgage all the assets … to bail Massey out of a mess that none of us had any hand in creating, is too asinine to merit further reply.*[16]

Black came under attack again in 1986, when one of his companies attempted to remove millions of dollars of surplus funds from Dominion Stores' pension fund. His response was to attack his employees. "We had C$30 million in produce stolen by employees (every year)," Black said in defence of the pension grab, which ultimately got government approval to relieve the plan of a C$30-million surplus. "We are not running a welfare agency for corrupt union leaders and a slovenly workforce."[17] He was on the hot seat again in 1996, when directors of Toronto-based newspaper chain Southam Inc. rejected as inadequate a proposed sale of some of its newspapers to a company controlled by Black. Black bellowed that the directors were an "obdurate rump"—and they were replaced two months later when he gained control of Southam.[18]

Black altered the course of another controversy when he heaped abuse on the Roman Catholic bishop of Calgary after the cleric showed sympathy for striking workers at Hollinger International's Alberta newspaper the *Calgary Herald*. In an opinion piece published in the *Herald* in April 2000, Black called Bishop Frederick Henry "a jumped-up little twerp of a bishop" and "a prime candidate for an exorcism."

The name-calling spawned numerous international stories, almost none of which examined the details of a bitter five-month strike by more than 150 employees, who feared job security was eroding. It is hard to think of another business leader who generated so much ink and yet so little critical analysis. By the end of the 1990s, Black had cultivated an image in the mainstream media as a bombastic tycoon who was known more for his defiantly right-wing views and corrosive insults than for his self-indulgent business practices.

The limited analytical scrutiny is partly explained by the sheer complexity of Black's corporate empire, a world populated with layers of transient public and private companies that frequently swapped loans, dividends, shares, and payments among themselves. Those financial analysts brave enough to cover a Black-controlled company usually complained that it was too difficult to follow. On the few occasions when Canada's reticent pension and mutual fund managers criticized Black's tangled corporate moves, Black pointed them to the door. "There are some elements in the financial community that have adopted the view that we regard deals involving the exchange of assets as a substitute for orthodox corporate administration," Black told former *Globe and Mail* reporter Jack Willoughby in 1981 after an early Argus makeover.[19] Unhappy shareholders, Black said, could "vote with their feet" by selling shares in his company. By the early 1990s, a number of Canadian institutional investors had done exactly that, and publicly listed shares in his Hollinger Inc. began trading at a discount to their peers, a phenomenon that became known as the "Black Factor."

Journalists faced a number of obstacles when they turned their attention to Black's business operations. Few business reporters had the financial training to deconstruct his Byzantine asset shuffles. Complicating matters, Canada's clubby business community frowned on financial analysts, investors, or executives who publicly spoke out against establishment figures. As a result, inquiring journalists were left with unsubstantiated mutterings about alleged self-dealing, which Black deflected with glib defiance. "The only charge that anyone can level against us is one of insufficient generosity to ourselves," Black told *The Globe and Mail* in 1981.[20]

Black had another powerful weapon to keep the media at bay. When reporters or authors suggested at the start of his corporate career that his treatment of the Argus widows or asset shuffles were not above board, he sued. By the mid-1990s, according to one count, Black had filed fifteen lawsuits against a variety of newspapers on the grounds that he had been libelled.[21] Black devoted enormous company resources to challenging journalists and at times seemed to take glee in his legal attacks. He launched a libel action against *The Globe and Mail* in 1987 after it published a critical profile of him that he later described as "an impetuosity for which my opponents could be painfully punished."[22] The suit was settled with one of the longest retractions in the paper's history.

––––––

The only constant in this quicksilver corporate world was Black's private Toronto holding company, Ravelston. Ravelston was named by Black's mentor McDougald after the Edinburgh-area home of one of his relatives, a Canadian senator, Wilfrid Laurier McDougald, who was forced to resign amid a federal bribery scandal in 1931. It would not be the last time that the name would be linked to scandal. Ravelston held the key to Black's corporate and personal success. It was through Ravelston that he sewed up control of Argus. It was the company that controlled his Hollinger empire, and it was the funnel through which he was accused of siphoning tens of millions of dollars in fees and payments from his various public companies.

In 1990, Black and his core executives found another way to extract money. Ravelston began collecting management service fees from Black's Toronto-based Hollinger Inc. In exchange for the fees, Ravelston provided the executive and administrative services of Black, his lieutenants, and other professional staff to Hollinger Inc. Most executives of public companies are paid salaries, bonuses, and stock options through compensation plans that are negotiated and approved by company directors. At Hollinger's group of companies, however, directors had little say about the details of executive compensation because Ravelston merely presented an annual bill for its management services. The system meant that it was impossible for shareholders to calculate how much Black and his executives were being paid individually, because they were only billed an aggregate fee once a year. Like a feudal tithe, Ravelston's annual management fees were charged to a number of Black's public companies. Hollinger International started paying multi-million-dollar management fees to Ravelston in 1998. The lavish fees were so over the top that Hollinger International said its tax advisers told the company it could deduct only a portion of the annual payments as a business expense because they could not be defended as reasonable.[23] Even some of the Hollinger group's smallest, money-losing affiliates paid management fees to Ravelston.[24]

In exchange for these fees, Black, his core senior executives, and about twenty accounting professionals negotiated asset sales and acquisitions, and managed tax, accounting, and financial reporting work for many of the companies in the Hollinger group. With Ravelston operating under a blanket of secrecy far from the U.S. operations, Hollinger International shareholders were kept mostly in the dark about how Black's holding company operated. Investors had no information about how the annual management fees were calculated or what top executives at Hollinger International were paid individually every year. If you followed the cash, however, one thing was certain: a river of money was leaving the public companies and flowing up to Ravelston.

The lines separating Ravelston and Hollinger were indistinct. Ravelston's staff worked in Hollinger Inc.'s head office on 10 Toronto Street, where they moved a variety of payments and assets between Black's companies. Confusing matters further, the same senior executives who operated Hollinger International and Hollinger Inc. were shareholders of Ravelston. By the late 1990s, Black was Ravelston's major shareholder with a 65-percent stake. The next-largest owner was long-time partner David Radler, Hollinger International's president, who owned 14 percent. Other Ravelston shareholders included Hollinger Inc.'s lawyer Peter

Atkinson, executive vice-president Peter White, chief financial executive Jack Boultbee, and the *Telegraph*'s CEO Daniel Colson.

Ravelston was the nerve centre through which Black and his team made most of the major decisions affecting companies in Hollinger's orbit. Typically, Black, Radler, Colson, Atkinson, and Boultbee personally negotiated major terms of various newspaper acquisitions, auctions, and reorganizations. It was only after a tentative deal was struck that the executives brought in their managers, lawyers, auditors, and bankers to hammer out details. Compounding the confusion, the top executives were scattered among three different countries and they sometimes mingled their private ventures with the public Hollinger companies. This became a particularly thorny issue in the mid-1990s, when Black and Radler began operating private companies that, among other things, bought a variety of Hollinger group newspapers.

The executives wore many hats at a variety of locations. Black and Colson operated primarily out of the *Telegraph*'s London offices, but by the late 1990s Black's office appearances grew more infrequent as he devoted an increasing share of his time to a massive biography of Franklin Delano Roosevelt. Atkinson and Boultbee worked in Toronto at Hollinger Inc.'s offices, but their primary executive duties were to the U.S. unit, Hollinger International.

Radler had by far the most complicated business life. Working from an office in Vancouver, where he lived, or at the *Sun-Times*'s Chicago offices, which he visited about once a month, Radler juggled many business interests. He was Hollinger International's president and chief operating officer and publisher of the *Sun-Times*. He owned large stakes in private companies that operated newspapers and he was a shareholder of Salman Partners Inc., a Vancouver-based investment banking firm that earned fees advising some companies in which Hollinger International invested.[25] On the side, he managed Jessop's Jewelers, a jewellery store in San Diego, which was owned by Ravelston. On various occasions Radler would offer to sell watches or jewellery at a special rate to some of his managers or clients, and at other times he asked his corporate staff to join him in meetings with diamond wholesalers to consider possible purchases for the store. If Hollinger International had a system for allocating how much time Black and his executives devoted to the company, it was never disclosed to shareholders.

Under Radler's direction, the *Sun-Times* seemed to operate as a family business. One of Radler's employees was his daughter Melissa Radler, who worked as a New York correspondent for *The Jerusalem Post*. Hollinger International claimed it doubled her salary to $62,000 after her father requested the raise.[26] His other child, Melanie Radler, was hired as a lawyer for Chicago's Winston & Strawn, whose chairman, Thompson, was a director with the newspaper conglomerate. Radler also appointed his wife, Rona, as chairman of a charitable trust operated by the *Chicago Sun-Times,* a position that paid her $126,000 in director's fees from 1998 to 2003.[27] The tangled business operations and insular decision making at Ravelston made it difficult for mid-level managers to keep track of the ebbs and flows of the Hollinger group's business. Internal communications deteriorated even further after 1992, when Black hired Colson, then a London-based lawyer, to help him run the *Telegraph*. The appointment triggered a rivalry between Colson and Radler, who had been Black's main deputy for decades. Radler, the harsh cost-cutter, thought Colson was spending too much at the *Telegraph,* while Colson believed Radler's sharp axe would cripple a paper recovering from a bitter circulation battle with Rupert Murdoch's *The Times*. Like squabbling children, they vied for Conrad's attention and, unless necessary, avoided direct contact with one another. The tension became so pronounced that Radler discouraged *Sun-Times* managers and editors from visiting or collaborating with the *Telegraph,* a team-approach move that could have benefited the smaller Chicago paper. If *Sun-Times* officials were unhappy with their strained work environment, their options were limited. Almost half of the *Sun-Times* top ten managers were Canadians who had been transferred by Radler to Chicago with limited U.S. immigration employment rights. Quitting the *Sun-Times* would have forced them to move their families back to Canada, a catch-22 situation that prompted some of the transferred managers to refer to themselves as "indentured servants."

By the mid-1990s, Black and his senior team were living increasingly lavish lifestyles. Black's largest home was the sprawling eleven-acre estate he had inherited from his father in north Toronto. He spent millions of dollars adding a massive security fence around the estate and a three-storey library with a copper cupola modelled after the dome of Saint Peter's in Rome. After he married Amiel, he acquired additional residences in some of the world's priciest neighbourhoods. In 1992 he purchased a ten-bedroom house in London's fashionable Kensington neighbourhood. The mansion had been fashioned out of two townhouses once owned by bankrupt Australian tycoon Alan Bond. In 1994, a Hollinger Inc. subsidiary spent $3 million to buy a New York apartment, which Black acquired personally, four years later, for the same amount. The residence occupied the entire floor of a Park Avenue building that was co-operatively owned by its residents. Cramped for space in the co-op, Hollinger purchased a smaller apartment in 1998 for about $800,000 to house Black and Amiel's staff and visiting senior executives. In 1997 the couple spent $9.9 million for an estate on Palm Beach's South Ocean Boulevard.

Like mini-Medicis, Black and Amiel hired craftsmen and such prized architects as New York's Fairfax & Sammons, London's Anthony Collett, and British designer David Mlinaric to gut and redesign their new homes. The designers dispatched teams of carpenters, stone-cutters, and painters to painstakingly transform their homes into ornate salons from another era. A team of trompe l'oeil painters spent a year hand-painting striped blue drapery, grille work, and birds onto the walls of the couple's two-storey dining room in London. One artist who spent months painting wallpaper in their Palm Beach mansion told *Vanity Fair,* "I feel like I'm a court painter living in Versailles."[28] The homes were a discordant jumble of European and Asian antiques, busts of historical figures, battleship models, and century-old portraits by such masters as George Stubbs and Sir Joshua Reynolds.

Into these gilded cages, Black and Amiel welcomed heads of state, business titans, ambassadors, royalty, actors, and other glitterati. Their parties were documented in newspaper society pages and their homes were showcased anonymously in architectural magazines and on websites. In 2000, *Architectural Digest* published a nine-page feature on a London residence, whose owners were not identified, but which Black's wide circle of associates recognized as their Kensington home. In the article designer Mlinaric outlined his client's ambitions for the baroque residence. "We needed the right background for laughter and challenging conversation; we needed the contents to be 'high' decoratively, to animate such a large space."[29]

Every year the Blacks hosted a summer party in their London home and filled it with hundreds of celebrities, including the likes of Britain's Prince Andrew, prime minister Tony Blair, and supermodel Elle Macpherson. In New York, Black hosted gatherings at the city's finest restaurants. In 2000 he threw a sixtieth birthday party for Amiel and eighty of her friends at New York's La Grenouille. The guests, who included Peter Jennings, Barbara Walters, Charlie Rose, and designer Oscar de La Renta, consumed $62,000 of Beluga caviar, lobster ceviche, and sixty-nine bottles of wine.[30]

To commute to their far-flung homes, Black and Amiel used one of two corporate jets owned or leased by Hollinger International. Their favourite was a leased Gulfstream IV with off-white seats, burled wood, $3,500 of silverware, and a blue sofa that opened into a bed. Hollinger paid for repairs to the Black's vintage Rolls-Royce, the lease of a chauffer-driven Bentley in London, and a Mercedes S-Class in New York. Salaries for their cooks, butlers, footmen, and other domestic staff were partly paid for by the company.[31]

Black's top deputies were also big spenders. David Radler lived in a mansion on Vancouver's exclusive Marine Drive, which he decorated with paintings by eighteenth-century masters and one by a member of the Group of Seven. He also had a desert home in Big Bear, Palm Springs, and a company-paid condominium in Chicago. He travelled between these locations in a Challenger jet, which Hollinger International had purchased for $11.6 million.[32] Colson had a sprawling townhouse near London's Regents Park, a country home in Quebec, and a Florida getaway in Highland Beach, about twenty minutes south of Black's Palm Beach spread. Atkinson commuted between homes in an affluent Toronto suburb and California's Napa Valley. Boultbee had a large home in Toronto's west end, a ski chalet north of the city, and a collection of cars that included an Aston Martin, the $200,000-plus sports car featured in early James Bond films.

By the 1990s, Black and Radler were dabbling in a variety of charities. Black and Amiel had a wing named after the Black family when they pledged C$3.4 million to Toronto's Sick Children's Hospital. Radler had a wing named after him in the business school of his alma mater, Queen's University in Kingston, Ontario, after a $168,000 donation. A trauma recovery unit bears his name and that of his wife at a Jerusalem hospital, and he pledged $110,000 to an Israeli college.[33] Black also directed the company to donate a further $2 million to charities linked to various Hollinger International directors.[34]

As the expenses soared, so too did the amount of money flowing to Ravelston. Most of the multi-million-dollar payments were disclosed in Hollinger's regulatory filings. If directors had any issues with the swelling tide of money to Ravelston, those issues were never aired in public. Many of Hollinger's directors were Black's loyal friends, executives, and ideological soulmates. They had stood by him for years. They trusted him. They had been enriched by him. When Black asked his directors to approve something, they were not in the habit of saying no.

CHAPTER FOUR

A Canterbury Tale

IN THE LAST WEEK of July 2000, Black and Amiel had retreated to the small town of Bayreuth in Eastern Germany, where they were attending the annual opera festival devoted to the works of composer Richard Wagner. It was something of an annual pilgrimage for the couple, yet this year was different. Between performances of Wagner's Ring Cycle, Black was putting the finishing touches on one of the largest media deals in Canadian history: the sale of $2 billion worth of newspapers to Winnipeg broadcaster CanWest Global Communications Corp. At one point in the negotiations, he sent CanWest a fax that began: "It's intermission at the opera."[1] It was quintessential Black, a man who never let a little business get in the way of pleasure.

Black portrayed the sale as a momentous step in the evolution of Hollinger International, and even likened it to a rebirth: by auctioning off all of the company's major city papers, as well as a 50-percent stake in the fledgling *National Post*, he was essentially abandoning the empire he had painstakingly assembled in his native country. But it was a necessary withdrawal. As Black would later explain to shareholders, he was following through on a promise to ease Hollinger International's punishing debt load and transform it into a leaner, cash-rich, and more investor-friendly company. Parting with half of his beloved *Post* may have been one of the most painful decisions he had ever been forced to make, but as he would later say in the company's annual report, it was all part of the "tortuous struggle" to improve the company's performance.[2]

> *In the course of the year, the senior management concluded that a radical change, a corporate slicing of the Gordian Knot, was necessary. We concluded that nothing less would break us out of the vise the Company had been in for two years between an undervalued share price and creeping debt.*[3]

For years he had been muttering about taking serious action—even privatizing Hollinger International—if its stock price did not improve, and the deal with CanWest, he insisted to shareholders, was proof that he did not make idle promises. Appearing uncharacteristically introspective about his controversial management record, he observed:

> *My impression was that after several years of such inveighing, I was running some risk of seeming to be a King Lear, becoming progressively less credible in threatening unspecific reprisals for an unsatisfactory (but far from dire) condition.*[4]

———

Black had officially unveiled the CanWest deal to Hollinger International's board of directors on July 26, 2000, while he was still at the Bayreuth festival in Germany.[5] Joining him on the teleconference were Kissinger, Richard Perle, Dwayne Andreas of Archer Daniels Midland, Alfred Taubman of Sotheby's, Richard Burt, the former U.S. ambassador to Germany, Robert Strauss, the former U.S. ambassador to the Soviet Union, Israeli businessman Shmuel Meitar, and Lord Weidenfeld. Amiel and Daniel Colson, the CEO of the *Telegraph* and a long-time Black ally, rounded out the participants. Two of the three audit committee members, James Thompson and Marie-Josée Kravis, were absent, although company records suggested Thompson had been briefed on the sale earlier that week.[6]

Black began by making sure everyone had received an information package outlining some of the key points of the deal and then briskly led his directors through some of the details.[7] He explained that $39 million would be deducted from the overall purchase price because of a management services agreement CanWest was planning to strike with Ravelston, Black's private holding company. Ravelston had traditionally charged Hollinger International millions of dollars each year to help manage these Canadian papers, but after the sale, CanWest would pick up the tab. According to the terms of the transaction, the broadcaster would pay Ravelston $3.9 million a year over the next decade for its advisory services. In addition, Black continued, Ravelston and other parties would receive payments from CanWest in exchange for signing so-called "non-compete" agreements.[8] Companies that sell papers are often required to sign agreements saying they will not reenter a market and compete with their former titles. Because company insiders would be receiving some of this money via their ownership interest in Ravelston, Black promised the arrangements would be scrutinized by the audit committee before the deal officially closed.

According to the minutes of the board meeting, the directors never sought an outside opinion on the fairness of the deal, nor did they seek information on exactly how much money was flowing to Black and his executive allies.[9] There is no indication that any of the board members questioned whether these management fees rightfully belonged to Hollinger International or whether it was proper for executives to be negotiating payments to themselves. Normally, these sorts of "related-party" issues are overseen by independent directors who have no personal stake in a deal. Nevertheless, after just one hour of discussion, the board adopted a resolution approving the sale to CanWest.[10] Everyone realized how transformative this deal would prove to be for Hollinger International. What they didn't know then was just how big a payday it would prove to be for Black and his inner circle.

Black had never intended to sell the *Post*. The previous April, he stunned the Canadian media establishment by announcing that he would seek buyers for all of Hollinger International's smaller community newspaper and some of its larger metropolitan dailies. However, the company initially said it was loath to part with its largest urban titles, including the Montreal *Gazette,* the *Ottawa Citizen,* and of course the *Post,* one of only two national papers in Canada. His withdrawal from his native country was a watershed moment, yet it wasn't entirely inexplicable. Black had become increasingly disillusioned with the Canadian government for not allowing him to accept a British peerage. Prime Minister Jean Chrétien, the object of many scathing attacks in Black-owned newspapers, was blocking Black's entry to the House of Lords by invoking an archaic clause prohibiting Canadians from receiving foreign titles. The whole episode had convinced Black that he might have to relinquish his Canadian citizenship as a last resort, a prospect that would certainly ease his exit from the domestic newspaper fold.

But Black's willingness to sell couldn't be explained solely by a political spat. He had more pressing reasons: about $1.8 billion worth, actually, which is the amount of debt Hollinger International had racked up to finance its acquisition spree in recent years. The annual interest payments alone had swelled to $143 million in 2000—an uncomfortable amount for a company of its size—and the financial burden of making these payments was exacerbated by the fact that Hollinger International had sold off many of its profitable U.S. papers the year before. If anything, Hollinger International's decision to dump its Canadian holdings, a chunk of publications representing almost half of its annual revenues, was further proof that Black's strategy of building a newspaper empire through myriad acquisitions and asset-shuffling simply wasn't working. The company was in desperate need of cash, and it had little choice but to begin selling.[11]

A solution appeared in the form of Israel "Izzy" Asper, the colourful, chain-smoking Winnipeg billionaire who had single-handedly built

CanWest into one of Canada's most formidable broadcasters. In 1979, Black had sold Asper a small financial company called Crown Trust, a deal the two men had consummated with a handshake. Now, two decades and a couple of empires later, the outspoken entrepreneurs were at it again. In early 2000, he and Asper had tentatively discussed a joint venture between their nascent Internet properties. Both men had watched mystified from the sidelines as twenty-something technology geeks amassed paper fortunes, and information age pundits began decrying the obsolescence of conventional media companies in the face of a new reality: "convergence."

Blending Internet content was one way to converge, but it did not hold nearly the same appeal as the idea of combining a coast-to-coast broadcaster with a dominant chain of newspapers. Once Black's papers were put on the auction block in April, the two men resumed their talks in earnest. They met several times, including face-to-face encounters at Hollinger International's New York offices, but the negotiations were always hamstrung by a crucial snag: CanWest was attempting to forge a national media company, and it wanted newspaper titles in all of Canada's major cities. It especially coveted a beachhead in Toronto, the headquarters for the *National Post*.

Black was conflicted. He had launched the *Post* with great fanfare in 1998 as an antidote to what he described as the "impenetrable soft-left group-think" of Canadian media.[12] Many viewed the *Post*'s conception as a means to wage war against Prime Minister Chrétien and the ruling Liberal Party. The paper's right-of-centre bent, and its almost obsessive fascination with Liberal scandals, taxes, and the perceived "brain drain" of Canadian talent to the United States, found an immediate following in the western provinces, which had long believed that "national" news was nothing more than a euphemism for what was happening in Toronto or Ottawa. Even those who inhabited the opposite side of the political spectrum were struck by the paper's bold design, its playful mix of paparazzi-style insouciance, serious financial reporting, and brash attitude.

The *Post* did more than breathe new life into the Canadian newspaper market—it sparked one of the most heated and costly newspaper wars in

North America. All four Toronto-based dailies—the *Post,* its bitter rival *The Globe and Mail,* the left-leaning *Toronto Star,* and the tabloid *Toronto Sun*—suffered financially as a result of Black's profligacy. He poached high-profile columnists from rival papers with hefty salary increases, stocked his pages with commentary from noted conservative thinkers, and authorized a huge editorial and travel budget.

It was a success by almost any measure except one: it lost money. Tons of it. By the time Black and Asper were deliberating, the *Post* had already cost Hollinger about $100 million in losses and start-up expenses, triggering a growing sense of concern among investors.[13] Black knew his retreat from the Canadian newspaper scene would be viewed as an ignominious withdrawal, a concession that he had lost the war. But the debt issue, compounded by the incessant nattering of investors, was too pressing to ignore.

In May, Asper sent Black a document outlining the terms of a proposed deal, which they had begun referring to as "A Canterbury Tale." The code name was a reference to Asper's vacation property on Canterbury Lane in Palm Beach, a home that Black had once occupied. It was here that Asper first began telephone negotiations with Black over a potential purchase of Hollinger International's newspapers. The two men were getting close to an agreement, but Asper still had a problem. Black had promised to provide management services to CanWest, essentially advising the company on newspaper operations, but he was demanding $12.3 million a year—roughly the same amount Ravelston had charged Hollinger International to manage these Canadian titles. Asper was mystified by the size of the sum and asked Black to explain why the management services contract was so expensive. But rather than provide a justification, Black quickly dropped his price to $3.9 million a year.[14]

Black had also begun warming to a compromise: he would give up all of his major city papers in Canada but would relinquish only half of his stake in the *Post.* In June, after many weeks of negotiations, the two men met in Belgium at a Bilderberg conference. They had arrived at the rough outlines of a bargain, which they sealed with a handshake at the luxurious Château du Lac Hotel, a restored castle in Genval, just south of Brussels. Lawyers on both sides would have to hammer out additional details, but a deal would be in place by the time Black arrived in Germany the following month to enjoy the opera.

———

On the morning of September 11, 2000, Thompson, Kravis, and Burt dialled into an audit committee conference call. The three audit committee members were charged with reviewing the "related-party" elements of the CanWest deal, which had been approved by the board a month and a half ago. Kravis, age fifty, a noted conservative economist from Montreal, was a senior fellow at the Hudson Institute, a right-wing U.S. policy think tank. Best known as the wife of legendary investment banker Henry Kravis, she sat on the board of the Canadian Imperial Bank of Commerce with Black and was also a director of Ford Motor Company. Burt, fifty-two, was chairman of IEP Advisers, Inc., a Washington, D.C., financial advisory firm. The well-connected former diplomat had also been the chief negotiator in the strategic arms reduction talks with the Soviet Union. Thompson, however, as chairman of the committee, was the leader of this triumvirate. The committee was responsible for everything from reviewing the company's financial statements and overseeing accounting procedures to inspecting major deals. But Thompson was the only one who typically met with Hollinger International executives to discuss the size of Ravelston's annual management services contract.

The sixty-three-year-old former governor of Illinois, whose bearish six-foot, six-inch frame had earned him the nickname Big Jim, had retired from government in 1991 after an unprecedented fourteen years in office and was widely regarded as a shrewd political operator with a knack for the common touch. Prior to running for governor in 1976, the young Republican had fashioned a reputation as a crime-busting U.S. attorney, targeting corrupt cops and shady city officials. He jailed more than fifty police officers during his tenure, according to one count, and put former Illinois governor Otto Kerner behind bars for bribery and mail fraud.[15] At the zenith of his career, in 1984, he had even been touted as a possible running mate for George H.W. Bush, but eventually decided not to toss his hat in the ring. Thompson was currently chairman of Winston & Strawn LLP, a large Chicago law firm, and had recently been named one of the one hundred most influential lawyers in America.

The primary task confronting Thompson, Burt, and Kravis that day was reviewing CanWest's management services agreement with Ravelston and the non-compete payments that would be delivered to company insiders. These crucial matters had to be approved before the companies could sew up their $2-billion deal. Radler and Mark Kipnis, Hollinger's in-house lawyer, were participating in the meeting by phone from their Chicago offices. The CanWest deal would not be finalized for several weeks, yet the mood within Hollinger International's executive offices was decidedly upbeat. The company's share price had mounted a steady climb since news of the proposed combination was announced in July, and the stock now hovered at just under $16—a 60-percent increase in just five months. When the transaction closed, Hollinger International would be able to virtually extinguish its $1-billion bank debt and, in the process, slice its overall debt load in half.

Before the meeting, Kipnis had delivered a memo to the directors outlining some extraordinary information. Company insiders—not the company itself—would receive $53 million for agreeing not to compete with CanWest. The memo said Ravelston was entitled to $20 million of this sum as a "termination fee" because it was reducing the amount of management fees it charged Hollinger International each year for managing its newspapers.[16] The remainder of the money would go straight to Black, Radler, and two of their long-serving associates: vice-president and legal adviser Peter Atkinson, and executive vice-president J.A. "Jack" Boultbee. The memo pointed out that Hollinger International had struck similar arrangements in previous newspaper sell-offs, but it failed to point out one significant difference: in these earlier cases, executives had never received any of the money.[17] Furthermore, the memo stated that CanWest was the one that had proposed the size of the non-compete payments to Black and the other executives.[18]

The only independent input on the matter was a document from KPMG LLP, the company's auditors, which could hardly be confused with serious analysis. KPMG provided a general, bullet-form summary of why media companies use non-compete payments, but the firm did not specifically discuss details of the CanWest deal.[19] Prior to the meeting, Thompson had asked KPMG and the company's law firm, Torys LLP, to look for other situations in which executives of public companies personally received non-competes. They could not find a single example. Torys, meanwhile, was in a very conflicted position, since it was representing Hollinger International and Ravelston at the same time. Representing both sides on a corporate deal is frowned upon in legal circles because it raises an obvious problem: if two sides have hired the same firm, how can each be certain it is getting the best advice?

Despite the appearance of multiple conflicts, and despite the fact KPMG could not find any precedent for similar payments to executives, Thompson, Kravis, and Burt unanimously approved the non-compete arrangements after a thirty-minute discussion. There is no evidence in records of the meeting that they asked why Ravelston, rather than Hollinger International, was entitled to receive $3.9 million a year for helping CanWest to manage its newspapers. The figure itself should have sounded an alarm, but no one appeared to raise the obvious question: why was Ravelston only charging CanWest $3.9 million, when in previous years it had demanded Hollinger International pay several times that amount for managing the same papers? The answer, perhaps, is that no one on the board ever did what Asper had done, which was ask Black to justify these fees.

Similarly, there was no indication that any of the audit committee members questioned why all of the $53 million worth of non-compete payments were flowing straight to Black, Radler, and other members of management, rather than to Hollinger International, which was the actual seller of the newspapers. Minutes of the meeting make no mention of any effort to seek an independent opinion on the fairness of the deal and the fees to company insiders, or to ascertain whether CanWest was the one that decided on the size of these payments to Black and his team. No one seemed to raise any concerns about the potential conflicts posed by Torys's multiple roles. Furthermore, there was no sign that the committee was upset by the fact that executives were bartering on their own behalf.[20] It was a remarkable display of passivity for a group of directors charged with safeguarding the interests of shareholders.

———

Immediately after the audit committee meeting was over, at around 11 A.M., Hollinger International held a board meeting. The attendance, given the gravity of the subject, was abysmal. Amiel, Andreas, Perle, Chambers, Taubman, and Wexner were no-shows, while Kissinger's name didn't even appear in the board minutes.[21] This wasn't altogether surprising. Chambers, Kissinger, Meitar, Perle, Weidenfeld, and Wexner—a group comprising more than a third of the directors—failed to attend 75 percent of the company's board meetings that year, a laughably poor record for a public corporation.[22] Many pension funds and institutional investors refuse to vote for directors who do not make at least two-thirds of a company's meetings. Odder still was the fact that Black himself was missing. While some of his directors were assembling to discuss a critical component of the CanWest deal, Black was on the company jet, flying from St. Petersburg, Russia, to Moscow for a meeting sponsored by the Russian Council on Foreign Defense Policy.

In his absence, Radler chaired the meeting and promptly called on Thompson to make a presentation to the other directors. The former governor had recapped his meeting earlier that morning and, repeating the memo's justification for the non-competes, explained that two previous sales conducted by Hollinger International had involved similar agreements. Although the board had never approved non-competes to individual executives before now, no one seemed to question the discrepancy. As with the audit committee before them, there is no indication that the remaining directors said much of anything. There is no trace in the meeting records that anyone asked why members of management were negotiating such rich fees for themselves. Nor was there any evidence that the directors requested an independent opinion of the fairness of these payments. The board quickly approved the deal, whisking through this and other business in a scant ninety minutes.

———

The fat non-compete payments to Hollinger International's top four executives might have remained hidden within the wood-panelled confines of Hollinger's boardroom, insulated from the inquisitive eyes of shareholders, had it not been for William "Bud" Rogers. A seasoned corporate lawyer with New York's Cravath, Swaine & Moore LLP, Rogers was advising Hollinger International about a planned debt refinancing in early 2001. When he began assembling company documents that would need to be reviewed as part of the refinancing, he noticed something unusual. Black and three other executives appeared to have pocketed tens of millions of dollars as part of the CanWest deal. It was a huge personal reward, and, more alarmingly, it had never been properly disclosed to investors.

He could see nothing about the payments in Hollinger International's latest annual report or the accompanying proxy circular in which public companies are required by securities laws to detail executive compensation. The only public reference to these fees that Rogers unearthed was tucked into a 111-page filing Hollinger had made with securities regulators in December 2000, just a month after the CanWest deal closed. And it didn't explain much. "Ravelston, Hollinger Inc., Hollinger [International], Conrad Black, David Radler, Jack Boultbee and Peter Atkinson shall each have executed and delivered a non-competition Agreement," the document stated. As Rogers dug further into the mysterious payments he found another discrepancy: the board minutes of the September meeting suggested Ravelston was receiving a termination fee, yet the transaction agreement with CanWest said that this money was in fact a non-compete payment.

When Rogers asked Hollinger International's managers why they did not reveal the prodigious rewards to executives, they explained that the company's law firm, Torys, had not indicated that the disclosure was necessary. Rogers disagreed. The $53 million of personal payments to company officials was extraordinarily large and had to be revealed to the company's shareholders, he insisted. Rogers's advice put Hollinger International in a delicate situation. His detailed review of the CanWest deal had turned up the awkward revelation that Hollinger International's directors had not been fully informed about the details of the non-compete payments when they approved them at the September meeting. If this wasn't corrected before Hollinger International filed its next financial statements, the company could run afoul of U.S. securities regulators for providing inaccurate disclosure.

Faced with this dilemma, Torys drafted a four-page memo to the audit committee, which was distributed by Kipnis, the company's internal lawyer, on May 1, 2001.[23] The missive contained a highly unusual request: Hollinger wanted the audit committee to reapprove the $53 million worth of non-compete payments to Ravelston and company insiders based on a different set of facts. "In a number of inadvertent respects the material reviewed in connection with the Sept. 11 meetings did not reflect the documentation for the CanWest transaction," the memo stated. For one thing, it revealed, CanWest had never determined how much of the non-compete payments should go to Black, Radler, Ravelston, Atkinson, or Boultbee. The memo didn't say who had established the size of these payments, but it didn't take much guessing: if it wasn't CanWest, and it wasn't the board, it must have been the executives themselves.

There was more. In the audit committee meeting the previous September, Kipnis and Radler had argued that Ravelston should receive $20 million worth of the non-compete payments as a "termination fee" to make up for the fact it planned to trim the amount of management fees it charged Hollinger International in 2000. Eight months later, however, one thing was clear: Ravelston never followed through on its promise to chop management fees. Did that mean, then, that Black's private holding company was no longer entitled to the non-compete payment? Not exactly. According to Kipnis's memo, the non-compete payments earmarked for Ravelston the previous September were legitimate, but were "incorrectly" characterized. Furthermore, Black's private company had received a larger amount than the committee had been led to believe when it signed off on the payments in September: $24.6 million.[24]

Kipnis's memo did not explain how insiders "inadvertently" mischaracterized these crucial details. Instead, it urged the audit committee to reaffirm its earlier decision and offered a fresh list of justifications for good measure. "The boards of directors and Audit committee are requested to conclude that the non-competition consideration was fair" for a number of reasons, the memo said. The non-competes had been "a critical condition of the completion of the corporation's sale to CanWest, which sale has been well received in the market place and was demonstrably in the best interests of all shareholders."

The memo was littered with red flags. It appeared that the records of previous board meetings contained serious errors and would have to be fixed. A landmark deal had been consummated with incomplete, and possibly false, information. Adding to the potential controversy was the fact that company insiders had been personally enriched.

———

On May 14, 2001, nearly two weeks later, the audit committee gathered on a conference call with Radler and Kipnis to discuss the alarming contents of the memo. But there was little deviation from the scripts of earlier gatherings. Just as they had done in September, the members of the audit committee appeared to have accepted advice from management without trying to confirm its accuracy.

It was disturbing, given the reputation of the independent directors. Thompson, in particular, was no stranger to boardroom predicaments.

Two years ago, in the fall of 1999, he and two other directors of Navigant Consulting, Inc. had ousted the company's management and formed a special committee to investigate loans to senior executives.

But the man who had locked up white-collar criminals as a crusading attorney and later led the boardroom revolt at Navigant appeared conspicuously quiet on this occasion. Once again, according to minutes of the meeting, there was no evidence the audit committee questioned why they had received inaccurate information in the September meeting. More shocking was that no one seemed to raise a fuss over the fact that Ravelston was receiving non-compete payments in addition to Black, Radler, Atkinson, and Boultbee. These very individuals were the principal owners of Ravelston, meaning they were, essentially, getting paid twice for doing the same thing.[25]

Despite all the warning signs, there was no indication the committee even revisited the need to get an independent fairness opinion—a logical step, given that the underlying justification for the related-party payments had suddenly changed.

Thompson later explained that he ratified the payments because the audit committee believed the CanWest deal was good for Hollinger International, and that even though some of the justifications had changed, the overall size of the payments to management had not. Yet if he and his fellow committee members thought to ask any questions about the highly unusual memo, they kept them brief. The conference call lasted just twenty minutes—and the changes were approved.[26]

———

The next day, May 15, 2001, Paul Healy, Hollinger's vice-president of investor relations, received a phone call from Laura Jereski. The Tweedy Browne analyst, known for her less-than-radiant disposition, was in a particularly bad mood. Earlier that morning, Hollinger International had filed its first-quarter financial results, and they were dreadful. The company posted a loss of $874,000, compared with a $28.1-million profit in the same period of 2000. The U.K. operations, which revolve around the *Telegraph,* had operating income of just $25.2 million, down almost $9 million. Chicago, meanwhile, lost nearly $3 million in the first three months of the year, versus a profit of $8.3 million in the first quarter of 2000. At the same time, CanWest's stock was tanking in the deal's aftermath, providing Hollinger International shareholders with another headache. As part of the overall purchase price, the company had received approximately $440 million in CanWest shares, valued at C$25 apiece. Now, however, those shares had sunk to about C$14.25, meaning Hollinger's proceeds—on paper, at least—had been substantially reduced.

Jereski was upset with Hollinger International's abysmal financial performance, but she could hardly have been prepared for what Healy was about to show her. On page eight of the news release, under a section titled "Sale to CanWest," the company had subtly slipped in details of the non-compete payments. This was the first time since the deal had closed the previous fall that shareholders got to see precisely how much money Ravelston, and individuals like Black and the other insiders, personally received from CanWest. The numbers looked exorbitant. Ravelston collected $26.4 million, while Black and Radler personally accepted $11.9 million each. Boultbee and Atkinson got a further $1.3 million apiece. All of this was "required by CanWest as a condition to the transaction," the filing explained. Healy, who had known about the $53 million worth of non-competes since the board meeting last September, had grown impatient with his company's lack of disclosure. He believed that the fees were material and thought they should have been published in the annual proxy statement that outlined executive compensation. He was also furious at the way the information was ultimately presented: it gave the impression that CanWest had made the payments directly to Ravelston, Black, and Radler, when in fact, as he knew, it had paid the money to Hollinger International, which then funnelled the money back to the executives. Furthermore, the filing implied that the non-compete fees were not included in the purchase price, when in reality, they were. In other words, shareholders were getting $53 million less for the newspapers than what they had assumed. Healy was in an awkward position. As an executive of Hollinger International, he shouldn't be publicly airing his frustration with management, much less inflaming the company's shareholders by steering them toward disclosure problems. Yet at the same time, he could no longer bottle up the anger he had felt for the past several months. Finally, he exploded. "Can you believe this?" he fumed.

CHAPTER FIVE

Act Like Owners

IF ANYONE WAS GOING to get to the bottom of the strange goings-on at Hollinger International it would be Laura Jereski and her sharp-eyed financial colleagues at Tweedy Browne. The New York firm has been a magnet for inquisitive, hard-working, and frugal professionals ever since it was founded as a brokerage in 1920 by Forrest Birchard Tweedy. Its early partners made their living hunting for bargains on the over-the-counter market, a disorderly bazaar where stocks of poky companies traded so infrequently that brokers had to hunt like detectives to find owners of the elusive securities. Tweedy's expertise in finding over-the-counter gems attracted Benjamin Graham as a major client. The stock guru, who died in 1976, was a Wall Street legend because of his knack for profiting from wallflower companies whose stock price traded at steep discounts to the value of assets or cash they owned. Warren Buffett, a disciple of Graham's so-called value investing philosophy, hired Tweedy in 1962 to track down and buy shares in Berkshire Hathaway Inc., today regarded as the world's most admired investment company.

Overseeing the Buffett account at Tweedy was Howard Browne, who joined the firm in 1945 as a trading desk partner. Taciturn, formal, and unflappable, Browne was as economical with his habits as with his money. For decades, the firm's six partners worked around a single table fashioned out of a large laminated board and knee-high filing cabinets. Browne was so obsessed with efficiency that when one of his four sons travelled with him on a commuter train, he demonstrated how to step off so that when he hit the ground, his feet were pointing towards the station's exit. Before and after work every day, Browne stopped in at Our Lady of Victory Catholic Church in the Wall Street district to say his prayers. When Buffett's partner Charlie Munger was once asked to describe Browne, he said "He never learned how to lie."[1]

A few years after Howard's son Chris joined the firm in 1969, the younger Browne lobbied Tweedy's partners to expand into money management so that the firm could earn fees by investing money on behalf of clients. By the late 1970s, savvy pension funds and government agencies were trusting Graham's and Buffett's little-known broker with a rapidly growing pool of money to manage. Tweedy stuck to its traditional analytical hunts for undervalued companies and, long before shareholder activism was a concept, the money manager learned how to fight with lawsuits and proxy battles to thwart acquirers who tried to buy out their neglected stocks on the cheap. When Tweedy confronted hostile management, its partners' rallying cry was "Act like owners."

In 1997 Tweedy parlayed its investment successes into huge personal fortunes for its partners when, in an estate-planning move, it sold a 70-percent stake in the firm to a subsidiary of Boston-based Affiliated Managers Group, Inc. Each of Tweedy's five managing directors signed long-term contracts to remain with the firm, and by 2001 it employed more than forty employees and managed close to $9 billion worth of assets through domestic and international funds. The more it grew, the more it invested in mainstream companies and the bigger its shareholder battles became.

Tweedy's newfound wealth triggered other changes. In the late nineties, Chris Browne, a white-haired man who looked more like an academic than the hardened Wall Street investor he had become, broke with family tradition and began to spend some of the fortune he had accumulated. He moved Tweedy's offices from its dreary midtown quarters on Vanderbilt Avenue to an airy, light-filled space on Park Avenue so he could be within walking distance of his new condominium, just up the street from Black's abode. Browne bought a home in L.A.'s affluent Bel Air community, and an eighteen-acre estate on Long Island, and began collecting such Modernist trophies as paintings by Willem de Kooning and Ad Reinhardt and Eames furniture. He also expanded his reach into America's establishment, serving as a trustee or adviser at a number of Ivy League universities, including Harvard.

In early 1998, Chris Browne had decided to invest in something else. That spring he hired Laura Jereski as a securities analyst to research some of the firm's stock investments. Jereski was a fifteen-year veteran of *The Wall Street Journal, BusinessWeek,* and *Forbes,* and in 1995 had been a recipient of the prestigious Loeb Award for business journalism.[2] As a journalist she had earned a reputation as a sharp financial analyst who dispensed withering criticisms of business excesses. Her frosty and guarded demeanour did not inspire warm conversations. Despite Jereski's chilliness, Browne liked the thirty-six-year-old because she shared his deep contempt for Wall Street's herd-like behaviour and she was a razor-sharp critic of such complex compensation practices as stock options, an executive perk she equates to "pick-pocketing." Jereski told Browne she wanted to start a new career as a financial analyst because she loved deconstructing corporate financial reports and, as a twice-divorced single mother of a preteen daughter, she needed to boost her income.

Jereski had another reason for switching professions. In 1997 a federal jury in Houston ordered *The Wall Street Journal* to pay the largest libel award ever for a damning article Jereski had written about shenanigans at a Texas-based investment firm. The company, MMAR Group Inc., collapsed shortly after the article was published in 1993. The jury found Jereski, who was mostly unapologetic during the trial, to have made some factual mistakes and she was ordered to pay $20,000 in punitive damages. The *Journal* was on the hook for more than $200 million. A federal judge would toss out the verdict in 1999 when he found that MMAR had failed to make required disclosures that would have supported the *Journal*'s defence. But for Jereski, the damage had been done. The gigantic libel award triggered an outpouring of negative stories about the media's lack of responsibility, with her case featured as a prime example. The worst was a lengthy story in *The American Lawyer,* which chronicled jurors' dismay over the lack of contrition she and a combative editor displayed during their testimony. "They needed punishing," one juror was quoted as saying.[3]

To Jereski, the punishment extinguished a passion for journalism, which had been so great that "it absorbed all of my emotional energy." It was time to move on. In May 1998, a year before the case was dismissed, Jereski quit *The Wall Street Journal* and joined Tweedy as an analyst. One year later the libel verdict was dismissed, but to this day Jereski still finds it painful to discuss her journalism career. "I was a reporter. I got sued. I lost a large case. It was extremely public.… I just don't think about it anymore." The experience may have closed the door on Jereski's journalism career, but it did not blunt her investigative fervour. If anything, it seemed to make her more determined to expose what she believed were dubious corporate practices.

––––––

Jereski looked at the small stack of envelopes for the last time. Months of research lay within the enclosed letters. She had scoured dozens of corporate documents and mined their buried footnotes and appendixes to make her calculations. She lobbied her bosses at Tweedy for permission to write the letters. She circulated draft copies to them, listened to their advice, and toned down most of her biting language. When the final copies were ready, she walked the letters around to three of Tweedy's five managing directors—John Spears, Chris Browne, and his brother Will—for their signatures. She hunted down the addresses and printed the envelope labels herself to ensure each would arrive at the correct destination. Now she was done. In a little while, a FedEx courier would mark them with the day's date, *October 16, 2001,* and launch them on their express journeys to Hollinger International's sixteen directors.

The analyst knew her way around corporate documents better than most securities lawyers and she was fluent in the mysteries of derivatives, stock options, and debt covenants. For all her experience, she had never fired off a letter quite like this one. Tweedy, one of Hollinger International's biggest investors, was about to tell the company's directors in writing that they were doing a lousy job. The money manager's complaint was that the board had approved more than $150 million in management services payments to Conrad Black's private holding company Ravelston since 1995. The annual payments had flourished substantially, while Hollinger International's profits had shrivelled. "We are writing to protest your role as a director in approving large-scale payments by our company to Ravelston," the letter began. At the receiving end of the finger-wagging were people who were unaccustomed to being lectured. How would Henry Kissinger, Richard Perle, James Thompson, The Limited's Leslie Wexner, and Sotheby's Alfred Taubman, to name a few, respond to the scolding?

Jereski had been studying Hollinger International since early 1999, when Tweedy managing director John Spears asked the experienced journalist to analyze the newspaper company. An office eccentric who was constantly hunting for stock bargains, Spears was so fixated on money that as a child he charged neighbourhood children five cents to ride on a hammock he built in the backyard of his family's suburban Chicago home.[4] The fifty-three-year-old rarely spent a penny on a stock unless he was convinced it was trading at a discount of more than 30 percent of its intrinsic value.

Hollinger International appeared to meet the discount criteria in 1999, when its stock price had slumped to a low of nearly $10 from a high of more than $18 a year earlier on the New York Stock Exchange. Like many companies, Hollinger International had become a market outcast during the dot-com bubble. It was an Old Economy stock whose core advertising revenue was being threatened by new internet classified-advertising websites. Jereski told Spears that the internet threat to Hollinger International's advertising revenue was overstated because the company had a large collection of profitable Canadian and U.S. community papers that were generating stable cash flows. The company had judiciously invested shareholder money by acquiring undervalued publications and turned them into cash cows through cost-cutting, thus breathing new financial life into newspapers that many investors had dismissed as relics. It was the kind of contrarian investment approach that mirrored Tweedy's. Furthermore, when Black first met Jereski and Chris Browne in 1999, he had presented himself as a shareholder-friendly CEO. He was so committed to boosting the company's share price that he had intimated he might buy back Hollinger's stock or take it private if he failed to enhance its market price.

Lately, however, it had dawned on Tweedy's partners that Black was not quite what he seemed. Tweedy's partners had given him the benefit of the doubt when Jereski grew concerned earlier in the year about the negative impact of the CanWest sale, the rising Ravelston fees, and the personal non-compete fees to which Healy had alerted her. The partners' initial response was to pursue a course of quiet diplomacy. Under the direction of managing director Chris Browne, a patient, long-term market player, Tweedy understood that it would never be able to outvote Black. Even though the press baron owned only about 30 percent of Hollinger International's equity, a special class of super-voting shares which he owned exclusively gave him a lock on about 70 percent of the company's votes. What they needed, Browne believed, was more information about the personal payments to Black and his team, and the only way they were going to get that was to keep up communications with Hollinger.

"Skip the accusations," Browne advised Jereski, who was becoming infuriated with Hollinger's scanty disclosure about the executive payments. "Once you start attacking people then they don't give you access."

Jereski and her bosses at Tweedy were betting the directors would not be pleased that a major Hollinger International shareholder was kicking up a fuss. If the board was smart, Tweedy calculated, they would move to avoid a public showdown by trimming the fat Ravelston payments. In the wake of the catastrophic crash of former high-flyers such as Texas-based energy giant Enron Corp. and the subsequent howls of shareholder and political outrage, directors were under heightened pressure to explain their actions. The scandals had made investors so cynical about the integrity of corporate officers and directors that federal politicians and regulators were preparing tougher boardroom standards to restore confidence.

Tweedy's letter should have been a wake-up call to Hollinger International's directors. One of the company's major shareholders had serious concerns about their stewardship, and if they didn't take steps to address the complaint, they could find themselves entangled in a nasty public spat. In her letter, Jereski had tried to make it easy for Hollinger International's directors to agree that they had erred by forking over so much money to Ravelston. What Jereski was able to calculate, she told directors in her letter, was that Hollinger International's annual payments to Ravelston had shown an astounding tenfold increase from $4.1 million in 1995 to $38 million in 2000. Tweedy hadn't complained about the Ravelston fees when it began buying Hollinger International shares in 1999, because up until that year the payments were small relative to the company's profits. By 2000, however, the $38-million payment looked enormous compared with Hollinger's net profit of $117.1 million. Given the decline in Hollinger's income, the letter demanded, "We would like to know how management's performance justifies the payments to Ravelston."

One of the reasons the Ravelston fees were costing Hollinger a bigger share of its income, Jereski believed, was that the company's celebrated deal to sell more than three hundred newspapers to CanWest in 2000 was beginning to look like a lemon. Black had hailed the sale as a corporate rebirth and the media trumpeted the sale as "a blockbuster media deal," Black's most "brilliant," "smartest," and "slickest" move since he purchased the *Telegraph*. But when Jereski crunched the numbers, the sale price wasn't worth nearly as much as the $2 billion that Hollinger initially boasted. To begin with, Hollinger had recently started selling at a loss some of the shares and debentures CanWest had paid the company as part of the newspaper purchase.

Making matters worse, Hollinger had sold CanWest newspapers that enjoyed virtual local monopolies and double-digit profit margins. With the loss of these money-makers, Hollinger was left with the *Telegraph*, the *Chicago Sun-Times*, and the money-losing *Jerusalem Post*, each of which had smaller margins to cope with a decline in newspaper advertising sales, the company's core source of revenue. Hollinger's vulnerability was exposed when advertising sales plunged in late 2000 in the wake of the technology stock crash. By the second quarter, ended June 30, 2001, Hollinger reported a jarring loss of nearly $16 million, its biggest quarterly loss *ever*.

Jereski believed it was only the beginning. Six weeks before Tweedy had sent its letter, terrorist planes toppled the World Trade Center, a seismic event that paralyzed many business activities, including advertising campaigns. Like most other media companies, Hollinger International was reeling from one of the worst advertising recessions in decades, sending its losses into orbit and its stock price into a tailspin. Against this troubling backdrop, Tweedy wanted the board to explain its benevolence to Black. In polite, but forceful language, Tweedy's letter invited Hollinger's directors to a meeting "to voice our displeasure and hear your remedies for our company's underperformance."

———

The next day a long letter rolled out of a fax machine in Tweedy's office. It was a reply to the firm's complaint, but not what the firm's partners had expected. The four-page letter was from Black at his *Telegraph* office. He was not amused. Mentored by the great nest-featherer Bud McDougald, Black was not disposed to tolerate complaints from shareholders about his lucrative compensation. When major shareholders lob serious criticisms at public companies, most chief executive officers at least go through the motions of appearing responsive. But Black was not most CEOs. His course that day was not to mollify but to insult. His rambling retort dismissed Tweedy's analysis of Hollinger's deteriorating financial condition as an "arithmetical travesty" riddled with "histrionic," "righteous," and "self-pitying" overtones. Sidestepping the concern that Ravelston's fees were consuming an alarmingly increasing share of Hollinger International's profits, Black lectured that the company's shrinking profits and stock price were merely a reflection of poor industry and economic conditions. "There demonstrably is no such underperformance as you claim." If Tweedy had a problem with Hollinger International's stock price it was because the firm was too myopic to grasp the ways of the market. "The stock market fluctuates and you did not buy an annuity when you invested with us." As for Tweedy's demand for a meeting with Hollinger International's directors, Black said:

I remain accessible to you as I have since you first invested with us, provided you are prepared to behave more civilly than the tenor of your letter implies. Our directors will obviously do what they think appropriate, but I will not recommend that they consent to be convened as you proposed.

Black offered Tweedy a carrot. He "might ask" Jim Thompson, chairman of the audit committee, to meet with the firm's partners and discuss the Ravelston fees. The message was clear: Black was going to obstruct one of the company's largest shareholders from communicating with directors if it continued to raise such hostile questions. The Ravelston fees, Black promised, were set to be reduced now that the company had become smaller in the wake of its various newspaper sales. Just when it seemed he couldn't be any more patronizing, Black concluded the letter to Tweedy with the following jibe:

Given your evidently aggrieved baronial references to me you will be relieved to learn that when I am inducted into the House of Lords at the end of this month I will not dilute my profound commitment to egalitarianism in shareholders as in other matters.

No other Hollinger International director replied to Tweedy's letter and the meeting with Thompson never took place. Hauled on the carpet, Hollinger International's board of prominent CEOs, former ambassadors, cabinet ministers, and lords chose to snub one of their company's biggest shareholders.

———

Shortly after lunch on Halloween Day, 2001, Conrad Black donned an ancient costume that had been the object of a long and tortuous personal quest. The worn, ermine-trimmed scarlet robe was the uniform of peers of the House of Lords, the centuries-old upper chamber of Britain's Parliament that is made up of more than six hundred hereditary and lifetime lords, bishops, and judges. Black had been vying for a peerage ever since his 1985 acquisition of the *Telegraph* granted him inside access to the upper echelons of the Conservative Party. He came within inches of his dream on June 14, 1999, when British Prime Minister Tony Blair advised him that his name had been put forward by Conservative leader William Hague for a peerage. Days later, the pending title was snatched away by Canadian Prime Minister Jean Chrétien, who invoked an eighty-year-old resolution restricting Canadian citizens from accepting foreign titles. Black thought he had surmounted the legal hurdle when he obtained dual status as a British citizen, a course that had been recommended by officials at the Canadian High Commission in London. But Chrétien, whose murky personal financial dealings had been relentlessly investigated by Black's *National Post*, was resolute. Canada opposed the peerage.

Denied his long-sought prize, Black did what he does best—he went on the warpath. "Do you know what that bastard has done," Black said to Ken Whyte, editor of the *National Post,* when he learned in mid-June 1999 that his name had been dropped from the list of nominations.[5] Later that week the *National Post* plastered its front and inside pages with news stories and features questioning the legality of the Canadian prime minister's action. Three weeks later, on August 8, Black filed a lawsuit against Chrétien for his "abuse of power" in blocking his nomination to the House of Lords. For the "considerable public embarrassment" he had suffered, Black claimed $25,000 in damages. His wife Barbara Amiel aided the cause with a column in the weekly Canadian magazine *Maclean's* that explained her husband "cares about policy issues and has a remarkable sense of history. Playing a role in the House where Lords Denning, Disraeli, and Carrington had spoken thrilled him."[6]

The public relations campaign, however, backfired. Competing newspapers and satirical publications in Canada and Britain found rich new fodder in the controversy and launched cruel new parodies of the wannabe peer. The long-standing media caricature of him as a kind of bombastic "Citizen Black" morphed into the more pitiful "Lord Nearly-Nearly" and "Lord Tubby of Fleet (Pending)." Canada's courts were also unsympathetic, dismissing Black's lawsuit in May 2001 on the grounds that it had no jurisdiction to second-guess the prime minister. Defeated, Black renounced his Canadian citizenship, casting his exit as part of the exodus of great Canadian talents who were departing a country mired in political treachery, "complacency," and economic "decline."[7] The man who had explained away his theft of private school exams as retribution against harsh teachers, who had justified his controversial Argus takeover tactics by casting aspersions on aging widows, and who had accused Dominion store employees of stealing when they protested his pension grab, was blaming Canada for his decision to renounce his citizenship.

And so on that Halloween Day, five months after he jettisoned his home country, Black stood in the House of Lords flanked by his two red-cloaked sponsors and loyal Hollinger International advisers, Lady Thatcher and Lord Carrington, and pledged his oath of allegiance to the Queen. Bowing slightly, Black stepped forward and shook the hand of the Lord Chancellor. As the peers in the chamber shouted "Hurrah,"

Black glanced up to the visitors' gallery. Sitting there was Amiel, now Lady Black, and more than a dozen of his closest friends and their spouses, including Hollinger directors Lord Weidenfeld, Henry Kissinger, and the *Telegraph*'s deputy chairman Daniel Colson. As Lord Black of Crossharbour made his way through the chamber, one of his guests whispered to visiting *National Post* columnist Linda Frum, "Take that, Mr. Chrétien."[8]

———

Conrad Black and Paul Healy pushed their way through the revolving door of a Park Avenue office tower and explained their destination to a waiting team of security guards, a fixture in most New York office buildings since the September 11, 2001, terrorist attacks. It was just before 10:30 on the morning of November 17, 2001, and the Hollinger International executives were headed for a meeting at Tweedy Browne's offices. Black was pumped. He had been furious when he dashed off his response to Tweedy's letter a month earlier, but now he was shifting into diplomatic mode. It was time to hose down the inflamed shareholder with a more conciliatory approach. Black had first met Browne and Jereski at his New York office two years earlier. He found Jereski a cold fish but immediately warmed to Browne's droll wit and expansive knowledge of politics, economics, and culture. Black knew just what to say to appease these disgruntled investors.

Tweedy's offices are as understated as the quiet, genteel partners who run the small firm. Its tiny reception area with its stone floor, cream walls, and faded historical prints of London and Wall Street are about as colourful as a dentist's office. Its boardroom is even more spartan, with bare walls, a plain wood table, and Styrofoam drinking cups. Browne met Black and Healy and escorted the pair to the boardroom, where he introduced two of his partners, John Spears and Thomas Shrager, and their analyst, Jereski. Uncertain about the etiquette of addressing British lords, Jereski asked Black what she should call him. In the United States, Black replied, he wanted to be known as Conrad.

Spears kicked off the session, asking Black about his voting power at Hollinger International. Adopting a polite tone, Spears reminded Black that Tweedy had bought into his company with the understanding that he would be looking out for all shareholders and not just himself. "It is important that we are all on the same side," Spears told Hollinger International's CEO. Assuming an equally respectful manner, Black assured Spears and his colleagues that he was on the same side of the table as all shareholders. To prove it, he promised, Hollinger would be reducing the fees to Ravelston in the future. Furthermore, he would make it his personal mission to restore Hollinger International's profits through cost-cutting and increased efficiencies. Good times were around the corner, he promised. Pouring on the charm, Black offered his insights into British politics in the post–September 11 era and shared some tales from his recent induction into the House of Lords. For extra measure, he even gave the firm a free subscription to *The Sunday Telegraph*.

———

Black was very pleased as he and Healy walked north along Park Avenue away from Tweedy's office. "The meeting went well," he told his vice-president. Tweedy's partners had listened thoughtfully to his comments and they had not made any demands. No tables were thumped, no threats or legal action were suggested. Always quick to claim victory, Black had somehow convinced himself that the flames of the shareholder revolt had been doused.

It is doubtful that the press baron realized that day that he was facing a group of partners who were wealthier than him, better connected to the U.S. business establishment, and more skilled than most investors at outmanoeuvring executives who endangered their investments. It was a surprising lapse for a man fond of comparing his corporate moves to famous military battles. Like Napoleon in his premature victory dance in Moscow in 1812, Black, an avid student of the French leader, seriously underestimated his formidable opponent.

CHAPTER SIX

Epidemic of Shareholder Idiocy

EVER SINCE one of John D. Rockefeller's partners built a fashionable hotel on a scrubby Florida sandbar in the 1890s, Palm Beach has been a winter playground for the super-rich. Morgans, Astors, Carnegies, du Ponts, Mellons, and Vanderbilts have been sunning themselves for generations on this sixteen-mile strip. For a few months of the year, the winter colonists flock to villas, mansions, and chateaus, attend a merry-go-round of charity balls and dinners, and shop for nine-hundred-dollar cashmere sweaters at stores like the unapologetically named Trillion.

Conrad Black fell in love with Palm Beach when he first visited in 1969 as a guest of Bud McDougald. McDougald had climbed to the upper rungs of Palm Beach society, serving as a governor of the exclusive Everglades Club and boasting such high-society neighbours as Marjorie Merriweather Post. To the budding aristocrat Black, Palm Beach's millionaire-studded island was paradise. "Some people are offended by the extreme opulence," Black told his biographer Newman, "but I find it sort of entertaining."[1] Black has been making the seasonal pilgrimage since 1978. Following in the footsteps of McDougald, Black spent part of the winter season negotiating deals under the palms and jetting between offices for business meetings. As well as forging friendships there with America's financial and political nobility, he also relaxed with his daughter Alana and sons Jonathan and James, and rode his bike daily along Lake Worth. It was here, in 1979, that Black first met his long-time ally Henry Kissinger.

By 1997, Black wanted more. He was the CEO of a thriving newspaper company that had moved its base to the United States following the 1994 purchase of the *Chicago Sun-Times,* one of the country's major city dailies. Along with owning the *Telegraph,* Black now had admired flagships on both sides of the Atlantic. In 1997, in keeping with his new stature, Black and Amiel purchased a $9.9-million, fourteen-thousand-square-foot mansion on Palm Beach's South Ocean Boulevard, known locally as "Billionaires' Row." Although small when compared with South Ocean Boulevard's castle-like residences, the Blacks' sprawling two-storey home resembled a small inn. An attractive jumble of slate-covered gables, white-columned balconies, and jutting wings, the house offered a gleaming, grey-blue marble lobby with a winding double staircase, an elevator, five bedrooms, nine washrooms, and a tiled underground tunnel to a private beach. If ever the Atlantic Ocean was in a disagreeable mood, the owners could relax by the pool surrounded by polished marble tiles, boxwood mazes, and swaying palm trees.

Thinking it nice, but not quite *there,* the couple hired New York architects Anne Fairfax and Richard Sammons, who, having finished a makeover of the couple's Park Avenue co-op, remade the beach palace with the traditional lines, classical columns, and spacious entertaining rooms that had come to define Black's residences. Also added was another six thousand square feet of space to accommodate a movie theatre, poolside cabana, two-storey guest house, and servants' quarters. The lobby-sized living room was crowned with crystal chandeliers. Beneath this bright sun, antique rugs, burgundy-and-cream chairs, wall-sized antique mirrors, photographs, and busts of historical figures fought for attention. Outside the home, a life-sized marble statue of Poseidon, the volatile Greek god of the sea, stood guard over a vast billiard-table-like carpet of grass. In a feature celebrating Palm Beach society, *Vanity Fair* ran a full-page photo of Black, seated, content and smiling, within a few metres of Poseidon's lowered trident. Amiel is closer and more deferential, curled up at Black's feet, looking every part the adoring wife.[2]

By early 2002, Black's life was anything but tranquil. His older brother Monte, who had been a reliable anchor in Black's tumultuous life, died on January 10 after a battle with bowel cancer. Although Monte had opted out of corporate life after he sold his Ravelston stake to Black in the mid-1980s, the brothers had remained close. Monte and his second wife June often wintered in Palm Beach, and Black had hired his older brother's stepson, Matthew Doull, to work as a Hollinger International executive.

Things were also bleak in his corporate world. Hollinger International had just finished the worst financial year in its history. It was losing money, it had looming debt problems, and shareholders were stepping up complaints about the flow of money to Black's holding company Ravelston. Removed from the fray at Palm Beach, Black buried himself in the writing of his Franklin Delano Roosevelt biography, a project that had consumed years of research. The conservative press baron had admired Roosevelt since his youth and, contrary to the views of his right-wing friends, he believed the liberal president was a misunderstood political genius who fixed a broken nation during the Great Depression.

Black was yanked out of his Roosevelt reverie in early March, when he met with one of Hollinger International's shareholders, Leon "Lee" Cooperman. The fifty-nine-year-old was a legendary Wall Street stock picker who in 1991, after two decades as a stock strategist at Goldman Sachs Group, Inc., had formed his own hedge fund, Omega Advisers, Inc. Cooperman's track record was impressive. Omega's funds consistently bested the market, even through the crash in 2000 and 2001, but by 2002 Omega was dragged into the bear market's maw. Pulling the fund down was a big bet on troubled conglomerate Tyco International Ltd., which was being rocked by a scandal about the spending excesses of its top executives. Another hot spot in Omega's portfolio was Hollinger.

Two years earlier, in 2000, Cooperman had first visited Black in London to get a better measure of Hollinger's CEO. Like Tweedy's partners, Cooperman is a no-nonsense long-time value investor who loves placing bets on unfashionable stocks trading at deep discounts. Curious that fellow value investors were buying Hollinger International, Cooperman considered the advice of one of his analysts who believed Hollinger International's stock was hugely undervalued. Less certain were the ambitions of its controlling shareholder and CEO Conrad Black. Was he committed to unlocking Hollinger International's buried value? Cooperman decided to check for himself and he arranged to visit Black at his London home.

When Cooperman rang the bell at Black's Kensington home, a huge mansion fashioned out of two townhouses, a butler in a dark black suit ushered him into a grand foyer. The hallway floor was decorated with inlaid marble tiles in a pattern similar to a backgammon board and its walls were dripping with art, including a portrait of Black. Cooperman, a self-made multi-millionaire who started life as a son of a plumber in New York's South Bronx, was not impressed. He thought, I'm worth a lot more than Conrad Black and *I* don't need a butler.

Black joined him in the library, a mahogany-panelled room crammed with hundreds of antique leather books and a bronze sculpture of Napoleon. After drinks were served, the two men sat down and Black told Cooperman what he wanted to hear. Hollinger's CEO confided that he was frustrated with his company's stock price, which that year had dipped below $10 a share. Steps, he said, were being taken to "create value." As for the company's dividend, Black reassured him, it was safe. Omega's funds later purchased more than one million Hollinger International shares.

Initially, Cooperman's investment blossomed, with Hollinger's stock price climbing to a high in 2000 of more than $17 on the New York Stock Exchange. But by early 2002, the stock had slipped to the $12 mark after record losses the year before. Another indignity came in February, when the company sliced the dividend that Black told Cooperman he would protect. Companies cut dividends to conserve cash, and Cooperman knew where some of the cash was going. The management fees to Ravelston were too much of a strain on Hollinger International—and they had to be contained. A month later, in March 2002, while wintering at his nearby Boca Raton home, Cooperman arranged to meet Black for lunch in Palm Beach. When they sat down at Amici's, a popular local Italian restaurant often flanked by Rolls-Royces and Mercedeses, Cooperman got right to the point.

"Conrad, I'm going to give you a piece of unsolicited advice. You are never going to get the respect of the market unless you get rid of the relationship between Ravelston and Hollinger."

The company was pumping millions of dollars of cash into Ravelston for management services, an expense Cooperman said could be sharply reduced if Hollinger International merely hired a few full-time executives to do the same work at a fraction of the cost. At the very least, he urged, Hollinger International should hire compensation experts who could analyze the payments and assure the company's shareholders that the Ravelston fees were justified. The cloak of secrecy had to be removed. Without more transparency, Cooperman said, investors would lose faith in the company.

Black nodded thoughtfully and told Cooperman his proposal was an "interesting idea." The good news, he told his lunch companion, was that Hollinger's performance was starting to improve. Costs were being cut and advertising revenue was improving. It wasn't out of the realm of possibility, he allowed, that Hollinger's operating income or EBITDA (a rough measure of cash flow known as earnings before interest, taxes, depreciation, and amortization) could hit $150 million in 2002, a threefold increase over the previous year.

Shortly after the lunch, Cooperman placed a call to Hollinger International's Healy, who was in Boston for a meeting. Cooperman told the investor relations executive about his meeting with Black and about the CEO's rosy outlook for Hollinger International's cash flow. Could Hollinger's EBITDA really crest $150 million in 2002? Healy did some quick mental calculations. He was used to this. Shareholders sometimes called him after a meeting with Black because the numbers didn't add up. Black had been known to confuse currencies, and other times he forgot to account for certain expenses. This time, Healy realized, Black had failed to deduct the more than $30 million Hollinger International would be paying Ravelston in management fees for 2001. "I think what our good chairman is forgetting is the allocation of Ravelston management fees for the year," Healy explained. Once again Black had painted a high-gloss sheen on Hollinger's performance.

———

A few weeks after Black met Cooperman, Hollinger International filed its annual report to the Securities and Exchange Commission on April 1. To a number of shareholders the eighty-eight-page report, known as a 10-K form, read like a bad April Fool's joke. Under a section called "Related Party Transactions," Hollinger International disclosed a series of deals that showed a trail of multi-million-dollar payments up to Black and his senior executives. Shareholders learned that Black, Radler, Boultbee, and Atkinson had received $21 million in special payments since 2000. Like the $53 million in CanWest payments, these new personal rewards were paid by various acquirers of Hollinger International newspapers to the executives in exchange for their promise not to compete against the new owners. Added up, the executives and their private company Ravelston had walked away with an incredibly large sum of $74 million in non-compete fees in three years. Almost as troubling was the fact that in previous years these large rewards had not been disclosed when Hollinger International announced the newspaper sales to a variety of buyers. The payments, the annual report said, had been approved by Hollinger International directors, but none of the company's previous press releases or regulatory filings had mentioned the lucrative personal rewards.

There were other startling revelations. According to the annual report, Hollinger International had transferred, for an undisclosed amount, two newspapers to Horizon Publications Inc., a company owned by Hollinger International executives. The only detail shareholders were given was that the papers had been sold for an amount equivalent to what the annual report vaguely described as "net working capital." There was more. The report highlighted the sale of four newspapers for $38 million in 2000 to a company named Bradford Publishing Co., which was also owned by Hollinger International officials. By the company's own admission, Hollinger International insiders were selling newspapers to themselves, and details were scarce.

The news in Hollinger's proxy circular, filed a day earlier, wasn't much better. Hollinger International had only reduced the annual Ravelston management fees by a few million dollars to about $31 million in 2001. Black had promised the fees would come down to reflect the company's reduced size, but relative to the company's profits, the fee was in fact substantially larger. In 2001, the $31-million Ravelston fee equalled a stunning 57 percent of Hollinger's reported $53.7 million worth of so-called EBITDA. In the previous four years the management fees had averaged 9 percent of Hollinger's EBITDA. Given Hollinger's sharply reduced earnings in 2001, the fat fees stood out like a pikestaff.

Something else screamed out in the proxy statement. Five months after Tweedy's October letter scolding Hollinger's directors, four members were stepping down from the board. Former U.S. ambassador to the Soviet Union Robert Strauss, Midland's Dwayne Andreas, New Jersey businessman Raymond Chambers, and Amiel's long-time friend and British publisher Lord Weidenfeld would not stand for reelection to Hollinger's board in 2002. Company officials privately explained that the advanced ages of three of the directors—which had not been an issue previously—was now a concern. Andreas and Strauss were eighty-three years old and Weidenfeld, eight-two. Chambers, fifty-eight, offered no explanation for his departure.

———

Tweedy Browne had had enough. Faced with the silent treatment from Hollinger's board and the disturbing revelations in Hollinger's annual report, the firm's partners agreed it was time to air their concerns in public on May 23, at the company's annual meeting. As a courtesy, Jereski sent an email to Healy late in the afternoon of Friday, May 17, to give him a heads-up on questions she and Chris Browne planned to ask at the meeting.

Tweedy wanted details of Hollinger International's management contract with Ravelston. How could the company justify the lavish fee when, by her calculation, the company had lost more than $280 million on sales of securities it had received from CanWest as part of the great newspaper sale in 2000? "Why is our company rewarding its management? What do you intend to pay yourself this year, and why?" Jereski asked of company executives in her email. As for the $15.6 million in new non-compete payments to Black and his team, she was unrelenting: "Why do you feel it was appropriate for these individuals to pocket that money, instead of our company?"

———

At 9:10 that evening, five hours after he received Jereski's message, Healy forwarded her email to Black in London. His boss's reply came to him a day later on Saturday at 7:05 P.M. and it was short by Black standards. The subject line was "Epidemic of shareholder idiocy."

I am assembling material to rebut these foolish questions. I don't think it will be particularly difficult to do so. I think it might not be a bad idea to offer to meet Laura and her overwrought friends on Monday afternoon (early). Even if they decline the offer, it will be seen as a conciliatory gesture. If they accept, it should defang this issue.

Black, the master tactician, was continuing to play chess with his major shareholders. At a time when he could have started appeasing powerful investors by addressing legitimate concerns about Hollinger International's lousy financial performance in 2001 and exorbitant executive payments, he instead chose to dismiss the complaints. Black was not going to let shareholders tell him how to run the company.

Tweedy declined Black's offer for a meeting. Their quiet diplomacy had failed to elicit any changes at Hollinger International, and now it was time to apply public pressure.

———

One hour before Hollinger International's shareholders were due to gather at the company's annual meeting at 11 A.M. on May 23 in New York's Metropolitan Club, two men entered an ornate room on the building's first floor. Eugene Fox and Robert Kirkpatrick, who were more comfortable wearing golf shirts and khaki pants than suits, had taken the train in from Greenwich, Connecticut, that morning. The men were managing directors with Cardinal Capital Management, a Greenwich-based money manager that had begun buying Hollinger International shares in 1997. One of the first of a small circle of value investors that saw potential in Hollinger International's depressed stock price, Cardinal had become concerned with the company's recent revelations about non-compete and management fees to Black and his executives. They had been asking a variety of Hollinger International executives for more details about the payments but hadn't learned much more than what had already been released in the company's quarterly report. Shortly before Hollinger's annual meeting, Cardinal got a message that Hollinger International president David Radler wanted to talk with them beforehand. Hollinger International was considering hiring the firm to manage some of its pension savings. The small firm, with about $700 million in assets under its administration, welcomed the news.

Standing in the Club's meeting room before the annual session was set to begin, Fox and Kirkpatrick saw Radler sitting at a table in the corner. Kirkpatrick had come prepared to make a presentation about Cardinal's investment record since it was founded in 1995. He spoke for about a minute before Radler waved him off. "All right, we'll give you a little money to just test you out to see how you do," he said. Although the pair was taken aback by Radler's abruptness, they thanked the executive. They were pleased with the new business, which would result in Cardinal managing about $2 million of Hollinger's pension funds, but the deal didn't detract from their concerns about the company's lucrative executive fees and worsening health. Their fears deepened during the annual meeting when Black became irritated with probing questions from Jereski, Browne, and Cooperman about the Ravelston fees and non-compete payments. They learned something new when Black told the meeting that he and Radler were only paid "a couple of million U.S. dollars" each, from Ravelston's annual fee. If that was all Black was taking home, then the compensation didn't seem too unreasonable, the pair thought.

When Hollinger International shareholder Shufro accused Black of being a thief, Cardinal's Fox threw the Hollinger International boss a lifeline by congratulating the CEO on his past business decisions. In gentle terms, he chided Black about the need for more openness to eliminate investor scepticism. Black thanked Fox for his comments and swiftly brought the meeting to a close. Fox walked over to Tweedy's Jereski and Browne to ask them about some of their questions, but they were interrupted when a fuming Black joined the group. He wanted reassurance that his other shareholders didn't agree with Shufro's wild accusation.

"I can't believe he suggested I was a thief," Black told Browne.

"I'm not ready to call you a crook, *yet*," Browne replied. "I'll keep an open mind."

———

Paul Healy had a difficult decision to make. He had been with Hollinger International since 1995, and the personable thirty-nine-year-old had loved the job of managing the company's relations with so many blue-chip investors. But now, in the spring of 2002, things were getting very bumpy. Shareholder outrage was mounting and Black was increasingly distant and irritable about the criticisms. Healy could see that if he stayed at Hollinger International, he would be caught between two high-speed trains moving in opposite directions. Shareholders were heading down the track of rebellion and Black was stubbornly pursuing his self-indulgent compensation practices. If Healy leaned too far to help either side he could be flattened.

Healy had initially turned Black down when approached to join the company in 1995. At the time, Healy was with Chase Manhattan Bank, specializing in structuring debt financing for media companies. Black's offer didn't interest him because his U.S. company, then known as American Publishing Co., was a ragtag collection of county papers anchored by the *Sun-Times*. He changed his mind in 1996, after Black said he was planning to roll all of his media assets, including the prestigious *Telegraph* and the prosperous Canadian chain of Southam newspapers, into one publicly traded company that would be called Hollinger International. Healy took Black's offer for two reasons. He found the Hollinger International chief executive and his circle of elite friends exciting and engaging. He also believed the Hollinger International makeover was a great story to sell in the exuberant 1990s, when soaring advertising sales were producing some of the fattest newspaper editions ever.

Initially, Healy's biggest challenge was counselling Black about his responsibilities to shareholders as the CEO of a United States–listed public company. Unlike the Canadian and United Kingdom markets, where a small number of dominant pension, insurance, and mutual fund investors tended to air their complaints behind closed doors, U.S. shareholders were much more outspoken. When companies sold new debt or equity, their top executives typically went on gruelling road shows to promote their securities to a wide variety of investors in different U.S. cities. Road show days started early with breakfast meetings and continued until dinnertime. The late-rising Black was inevitably tardy for the early meetings, ruining the company's carefully plotted schedule. Complicating matters, Black sometimes was less than precise with his numbers.

The other thorny issue for Healy was Black's wife Amiel. When Hollinger International was redecorating its offices under David Mlinaric's instructions in the late 1990s, Amiel frequently visited or called him to get updates on the progress of the renovation. Sometimes Black's wife was gracious and considerate when she visited Hollinger's offices in New York; at other times, she was cold and haughty. Once, the company's receptionists and secretaries were so busy fending calls that Amiel couldn't get through. When she finally got the receptionist on the phone, Amiel became so angry that she had the other woman in tears by the time she hung up. When Healy heard about the confrontation, he explained the situation to Black, who at the time was visiting the New York office. Black immediately walked over to the front desk to placate the receptionist. His wife, he explained, was a long-time sufferer of the painful muscular disease dermatomyositis and she was having trouble adjusting to new medication.[3] "Let's put a sunset on this," Black asked his staff.

It was the kind of cordiality that Healy most admired about Black. He treated his staff with respect and he was a master at smoothing ruffled feathers. Lately, however, there wasn't much evidence of Black's good humour. After his outburst at the recent annual meeting and his subsequent tirade when Healy had pushed to tell company director Jim Thompson about shareholder criticisms, Hollinger's vice-president began contemplating an exit. He was reluctant to leave because he had helped attract so many blue-chip investors to the company. If he left, he might permanently damage those relations or, worse, be tainted by the company's troubles. If he stayed, he was going to have to convince Black to respond to his shareholders' demands. It was the only way he could see to fix this mess.

Healy began the difficult high-wire act of balancing Black's directives against the growing demands of Hollinger's shareholders by sending a long email to his boss on the afternoon of May 25, 2002, two days after the annual meeting. The email urged Black to give more information to shareholders about the Ravelston fees. Shareholder rebellion would be unavoidable, he warned, if Hollinger International didn't start acceding to some of their wishes.

Black's email response was a jumble of defiance and responsiveness. Acknowledging Healy's concerns, he said that he and Radler, Colson,

Atkinson, and Boultbee had agreed after the tempestuous annual meeting "to clean things up" in the future.

> *The stance to take is that we agree to disagree about the non-competes but that is a thing of the past; we have agreed to the request for transparency to show there is nothing odd or bad about compensation levels, so everyone should be able to focus on real value.*

Despite the accusations and complaints at the annual meeting, incredibly, Black sought to convince Healy that he had won the day.

> *I thought the annual meeting went fairly well. There was no threat of litigation, the usual recourse in this country ... and we fought Browne and Cooperman to a civilized standstill.*

He became belligerent when he wrote about recent criticisms from financial analysts and investors. These rabble-rousers, he argued, were using shareholder activism as a Trojan horse to overtake the company and force it into selling the company or its assets.

> *We do not accept such comment as pressure and will pay no attention to it, other than to take steps to satisfy reasonable people that there is no cause for concern.... We may quickly reach a point where shareholders attempting to confect a moral or equitable argument for the purpose of shaming or bullying or aggravating us into a liquidation mode have to be dealt with extreme bluntness. I will not be found wanting for either task.*

The email concluded by asking Healy to help bolster employee morale about the company's poor performance. "Two years from now no one will remember any of this."

Heartened by Black's somewhat conciliatory tone, Healy sent a lengthy email response a few hours later, pleading with him to show more sensitivity to shareholders.

I know that you can appreciate how difficult my position is with regard to these issues and I'm doing my level best to deal with the present situation. I also know you appreciate the fact that I'm forced to walk a fine line given my responsibilities to the public shareholders and to you as my boss. I do agree that this will all pass into distant memory as we "put up" the numbers and take certain comprehensive steps to address these concerns in short order. To a large degree it is about the optics and we need to give credible evidence that we've listened and that we respect our partners.

Healy told Black that the pressure was mounting. Tweedy and Cardinal had advised him they would be sending letters next week with more questions and demands. Healy reminded Black how hard he had worked to attract these "pedigree" investors to Hollinger and urged his CEO to "make our company more transparent" by bending to the demands for information.

Though the last two months [have] been extremely difficult for me to stomach, you have my word that I will give every effort to support your vision for Hollinger and I stand ready [t]o support any of the initiatives to ameliorate the concerns we currently face. I am highly motivated to do so.

Touching on Shufro's accusation of thievery at the annual meeting, Healy chose to coddle rather than criticize Black for his angry retort. A little ego stroking could go a long way with Black, Healy had learned over the years.

I don't believe there is any Chairman of any other NYSE listed company that could have handled things the way you did with such incredible poise and dignity.... You handled him brilliantly.

Black emailed a reply to Healy's entreaties the next night, Saturday, at 8:59 P.M.

Rather than softening his position towards shareholders as Healy had hoped, Black had hardened. Like so many times before, he blamed others for his woes. If Hollinger International had a problem with its shareholders, it was because the shareholders were wrong or misguided. He reserved particular contempt for Jereski, "that barrel of laughs and great arithmetician," who had persisted with her negative evaluations of the CanWest sale. As for the "antics" from Browne, Cooperman, and Shufro about the management fees to Ravelston and the non-compete payments, Black wrote:

Don't be apologetic about any of it; the complaints are magnified for ulterior reasons and the real grievance of our questioners is that they know we are not under any real pressure to take them out, either by going private or selling the business.... They clearly do not enjoy their inability to challenge our control of the business, but they will have to live with it.

Looking ahead to the future, Black promised a Shakespearean plot for Hollinger International that would prove to be much closer to the mark than he had ever anticipated.

The drama will change from King Lear to Julius Caesar (minus the last act, one dares to hope).
So be good of heart.... Profits will rise, borrowings will wither and loyal shareholders will flourish.
Have a pleasant weekend and remember the Veterans of Foreign wars.
Regards,
Conrad

———

As Healy had predicted, the shareholder rebellion gained more steam after the disastrous annual meeting. Conrad's defensive stance and the lack of answers about the Ravelston management fees had only heightened their determination to push for changes. One of the first communications was from Cardinal. On May 30, Gene Fox sent an email to Healy, which he then passed on to Black.

> *I would not be an investor in Hollinger if I had any question as to the integrity of Conrad or any of the management team. Having said that, in light of the Enron scandal and controversy over business practices during the internet bubble, more scrutiny and greater skepticism exists in the market than ever. Companies have a choice: they can use these developments to their advantage or they can be penalized because they choose to fight them.*

Hollinger International could move out of the "doghouse," Fox suggested, if it made a number of changes, including providing more details about the terms of the Ravelston management fees and minimizing future non-compete payments. Cardinal also wanted Hollinger International to stop paying more than $30,000 annually in directors' fees to Black, Amiel, Radler, Colson, and Atkinson, who were already earning large salaries as company executives. It would also be nice, Fox added sarcastically, if directors attended their company's annual meeting.

––––––

More demands landed in Black's in-box on June 7. This time it was a letter from Tweedy's Chris Browne. Echoing Cardinal's Fox, he wanted changes at Hollinger. Browne had heard from Healy that Hollinger's top brass was considering a plan to make a regulatory filing, known as an 8-K, that would provide more details about how the Ravelston fees were calculated and divided among the company's executives. "I think he's getting it," Healy confided to Tweedy's managing director. Seeking to ensure that the 8-K included everything that Tweedy Browne had been demanding, Browne outlined the steps he wanted Black to take. It was time for the company to justify and detail past Ravelston management fees and freeze future non-compete payments and directors fees' to company executives. Failure to do so, Browne warned, would only result in investors growing more enchanted and trigger a further decline in Hollinger's stock price.

> We want to reiterate our request for greater transparency into our company's operations and expenses. In the current environment, public companies that are perceived as not completely forthright are penalized by the market. Hollinger presently falls into this category.

Black was also being pressured by someone else in the summer of 2002 to scale back the company's controversial perks and compensation. Black's long-serving Toronto lawyer and recently appointed Hollinger International director, Peter Atkinson, had been dismayed by shareholder grievances at the annual meeting. Atkinson had been a recipient of some of the controversial non-compete payments, but he grew concerned that Hollinger International was heading for a potentially disastrous battle with powerful shareholders. To head off such a confrontation, he had privately been urging Black to mollify shareholders by cutting back on the multi-million-dollar personal expenses and to reveal more information about these perks.

Black appeared to be listening to Atkinson's advice when he replied to Tweedy four days later in a letter dated June 11. The caustic denunciations of shareholder motives in his earlier email to Healy were not evident in this letter. Instead, Black was presenting himself as a responsive CEO who was willing to bend to their demands.

> I can assure you that we are preparing a comprehensive response to this problem which will be incorporated in an 8-K statement. I believe this will reassure all reasonable people on all legitimate matters that have

been raised.... The transparency you seek will not be long in coming and will not reveal anything startling or discouraging to any reasonable shareholder.

Within a few weeks, however, Black had slammed shut the promised window of transparency. It fell to Healy in early July to break the bad news to Tweedy's Jereski and Browne that Hollinger International would not be filing the pledged 8-K. Instead, he explained, the company would include a breakdown of the Ravelston fees in its forthcoming second-quarter results. It was unclear, Healy confided, how much detail would be included in the report. Jereski and Browne were stunned. Conrad was backpedalling on his word weeks after his written promise. They were not appeased when Healy added the small, good news that Hollinger International would stop paying directors' fees to executives who served on the board.

Chris Browne sent a letter to Black on July 11 in a last-ditch effort to convince him that it was vital for Hollinger International to be more forthcoming. If Hollinger's decision about the 8-K was final, Browne wanted Black to ensure that a number of their long-standing questions about the non-compete payments and management fees would be addressed in the pending quarterly report.

We are displeased by your decision not to file the interim 8-K regarding your compensation and other matters raised at the annual meeting.... We urge you further that you include not only how compensation has changed over time, but on what basis payments have been and are made—as you asserted you would do in your June letter to us....

We look forward to the transparency you have long promised us.

——

Cardinal Capital's Gene Fox and Robert Kirkpatrick were furious when Hollinger International released its second-quarter results on

August 6. While the report clearly showed the company's financial performance was improving with sharply reduced losses, Hollinger International had yielded very little new information about the Ravelston management fees. A footnote on page thirty of a statement filed with the SEC devoted sixteen lines to a discussion of Hollinger's management fees to Ravelston. The note provided a breakdown of how much money was allocated individually in 2001 to Black, Radler, Colson, Boultbee, and Atkinson, but the amounts, the report said, had not been "independently verified" by Hollinger. Also missing was any comparison to previous years or a discussion of how the payments were determined.

Fox looked at the numbers. Of the $30 million Hollinger International had paid Ravelston in 2001, $6.6 million had been allocated to Black and $3 million to Radler. This was substantially larger than the "couple of million U.S. dollars" that Black had described during the annual meeting. The shareholders had been misled.

We're not that stupid, Fox thought. We can add.

———

In private, Black's contempt for his rebellious shareholders was far greater than any of his shareholders could have imagined. In his mind he had magnanimously opened the window on the Ravelston fees and, instead of being grateful, investors wanted more. Black seethed about them in an August 3 email to two of his most trusted advisers in Toronto, long-time corporate counsel Atkinson and financial adviser Boultbee.

We now have an unsatisfactory situation where a number of the share-holders think we are deliberately suppressing the stock price, some others think we are running a gravy train and a gerrymandered share struc-ture, and we think they are a bunch of self-righteous hypocrites and ingrates, who give us no credit for what has been a skillful job of build-ing and pruning a company in difficult circumstances.[4]

By August, Atkinson's dismay about Hollinger International's pricy executive perks had begun to drive a rift between him and Black. In an August email he pled with his boss to drastically cut back.

The only real solution to our problems involves selling the jets, getting rid of unproductive assets, cutting costs and reducing personal expenses laid off on the subsidiaries. Band-Aids won't do it. Announce a cut in dividends and management fees and the problems will largely evaporate. I would be perfectly happy to take a compensation cut provided we all suffered proportionately. While you don't think cost-cutting is much of a panacea, there is so much we could do. Cut all the useless clubs, the unnecessary tables, the investments that are fun to be in but useless to the bottom line.[5]

Black responded to the email by conceding a twinge of guilt over the expenses, but the regret was fleeting.

There has not been an occasion for many months when I got on our plane without wondering whether it was really affordable. But I'm not prepared to reenact the French Revolutionary renunciation of the rights of nobility. We have to find a balance between an unfair taxation on the company and a reasonable treatment of the founder-builders-managers. We are proprietors, after all, beleaguered though we may be.[6]

Black went on to explain that his opposition to reduced expenses was based on his conviction that executives should not be second-guessed by overwrought shareholders.

My problem is not with drastic cost-cutting and my self-esteem does not depend on the perquisites of corporate office; it is with making excessive concessions to the Rod "Hysteria" school of corporate governance.

As private complaints from his biggest shareholders piled up in Black's letter box, Hollinger's CEO seemed to believe he could talk his way out of the crisis of shareholder confidence. He went on the offensive by holding a conference call with media, analysts, and investors on August 7, the day after the quarterly results were published. Hollinger International had reported improved results for the second quarter, and Black clearly wanted to continue building a good news story by publicly offering some concessions to shareholders. Hollinger, Black told listeners, was on a "holy crusade to banish from the minds of any shareholders the thought that our motives and objectives are in the slightest respect different from yours."

As proof of his commitment to investors, Black promised that the company's management would recommend to its board of directors in September that management fees to Ravelston be reduced.

We will be making an announcement in the second week of September that we are confident and determined will be pleasing to all of you and will eliminate any doubts that may linger in the minds of shareholders about whether we are all seeking the same goal.

In mid-August, Black sat down in his Toronto office with two share-holders who had kept quiet throughout the past several months. Mason Hawkins and Staley Cates had carefully analyzed Hollinger's financial statements and press releases, sought information from its executives, and listened to the various complaints of other shareholders. Hawkins, a polite Southerner with a dark slash of eyebrows and bone-white fringe of hair, was chief executive officer of Southeastern Asset Management Inc., a money manager he founded in 1975. Cates, another courteous Southerner, was Southeastern's president. Southeastern was yet another value investor that had been attracted to Hollinger International in the late 1990s. Significantly larger than Hollinger's other value investors, with $18 billion worth of assets under its administration, Southeastern liked to place larger bets on a smaller portfolio of companies that it believed were underpriced. It had placed a huge wager on Hollinger, buying 17 million, or 18 percent, of its shares outstanding, making it Hollinger's largest shareholder after Black.

Southeastern had been drawn to Hollinger International for two reasons. The money manager had profited from investments in a number of unfashionable Canadian stocks including Toronto conglomerate Brascan Corp., once owned by Peter and Edward Bronfman. Brascan had a long history of business dealings with Black, and when one of the conglomerate's executives suggested that Southeastern might find value in Hollinger's stock, Hawkins and Cates took a look. Like Tweedy, Cardinal, and Omega, they saw Hollinger International as a classic value investment with its stock price trading well below what its assets could fetch if sold. They had heard the market grumblings about the Black Factor, but when they did their research they concluded that Hollinger's management had shrewdly invested in unfashionable newspapers and turned them into stable cash cows.

Value investors are a tight circle and Southeastern kept close tabs on the investment activities of other major money managers, such as Tweedy, that followed Benjamin Graham's investment philosophies. The investors sometimes swapped notes on possible investments and exchanged ideas about misbehaving companies. They had heard the objections about Hollinger's non-competes and management fees to Ravelston, but instead of trouble, Hawkins and Cates saw opportunity. The pair had never been comfortable with Hollinger's Class-B supervoting shares, exclusively owned by Black, which enabled him to control close to 70 percent of Hollinger International's votes. If shareholders continued to push Black for change, maybe he would consider selling some of his shares.

When they met with Conrad at 10 Toronto Street, Hawkins and Cates outlined a complex share-purchase plan that they believed could accomplish two things. Southeastern would buy hundreds of millions of dollars' worth of Hollinger International stock from parent company Hollinger Inc., which was controlled by Black. In exchange for the cash infusion to the parent company, Black would agree over time to reduce the voting power of Hollinger International's Class-B shares that gave him control of the U.S. newspaper company. Under the plan Black could potentially pocket a fortune and his stake in Hollinger International would fall below 50 percent, giving shareholders more clout to correct the company's governance problems. It was a complex concept, but the Southeastern executives were betting that Black would be motivated to sell, to free himself of his shareholder troubles.

Black had always liked the polite Memphis money managers, but that day he was not going to give them what they wanted. He saw no need to yield any of his votes at Hollinger. The company may have had its problems with shareholders, but now, with improved profits around the corner, there was no incentive for him to sell. The answer, Black told the pair, was no.

———

Silence. No one was complaining.

By early September, there were no more protesting letters, emails, or calls from Hollinger's shareholders. No lawsuits had been filed and no one was pestering company officials about the controversial non-competes. The only remaining issue on the table was the Ravelston management fees, and shareholders were waiting for the promised announcement from Hollinger's board of directors later in the month. By Black's standards, this was victory. On September 6, in a confidential memo to Atkinson, Boultbee, Colson, and Radler, General Black trumpeted what he believed was a shareholder retreat.

[W]e have pretty well won the great battle over the non-competition agreements and a decent interval has passed....

Reflecting on the long history of executive indulgences at Hollinger's predecessor Argus, Black reminded his team of the entitlements they had enjoyed during their lengthy tenure at Hollinger. Shareholder activism meant the executives should show more restraint with company perks, but they needn't go overboard.

> *These companies have always been run in the Argus tradition of proprietary businesses where the controlling shareholders take reasonable steps to ensure their comfortable enjoyment of the position they, (we, in fact), have created for themselves. Care must be taken not to allow this to degenerate into decadence, as it did in the old Argus. But nor should we allow the agitations of shareholders, amplified by certain of our colleagues discountenanced at the performance of their stock options, to force us into a hair shirt, the corporate equivalent of sackcloth and ashes.*[7]

———

Hollinger's much-promised concession to shareholders was delivered September 11, when the company announced in a press release that after "extensive discussions" with Black, the directors had accepted a plan to reduce the Ravelston management fees. Hollinger International would pay $22 million to Ravelston for its management services in 2002. According to the press release, the new fee would shave $2 million off the $24 million that Hollinger International had originally planned to pay Ravelston that year. Two million dollars …

Black was throwing peanuts at his angry shareholders.

CHAPTER SEVEN

We Can Get Around That

IT HAD BEEN A YEAR since Tweedy began pressuring Black and Hollinger International's board to stem the torrent of money flowing to Ravelston, yet by October 2002 little had changed at the company. Another group, however, had found a way to dam the outflow. Banks and bond investors had an opportunity to tighten their grip on Black's group of companies starting in October, when the company began to refinance some of its debt and replace a loan that jittery lenders were not renewing to Toronto-based Hollinger Inc. Hollinger International's ongoing losses and low credit rating left it with few options but to sell a lowly form of corporate debt known as high-yield or junk bonds, which pay investors premium interest rates to compensate for greater credit risks.

Hollinger International turned to a team of high-yield team investment bankers at Charlotte, North Carolina–based Wachovia bank to sell its bonds and arrange its new bank loan. Wachovia banker Rick Fogg and bond specialist David Haase led the group. Joining them was Gordon Paris, a Wall Street junk bond specialist with Berenson Minella, who had previously advised the company. Black needed these bankers to raise new money. Now he was going to have to play by their rules.

Wachovia came up with a plan that called for a new issue of $300 million in junk bonds by a subsidiary and a new $310-million bank loan for various Hollinger International companies. Aware of the controversy over the fees Hollinger International paid to Ravelston and Black's team, Wachovia dispatched a team of investment bankers and lawyers to sift through the company's records and interview its executives. Known as due diligence, the probe is a typical protective measure taken by investment bankers to ensure that investors are adequately protected and informed about a company's financial condition. At Hollinger International, however, the due diligence was unlike anything the company had experienced before.

Wachovia's team conducted more than fifty conference calls with Hollinger International's New York executives over three months to unravel the company's complex business transactions. Throughout the due diligence process, the mantra of Hollinger's advisers became "Stop the leakage" of money to outside companies controlled by Black. Aiding the investment bankers were Hollinger International's company treasurer Robert Smith, its new chief financial officer Peter Lane, and Healy, each of whom was sympathetic to shareholder demands for more information. If Black wanted Wachovia's backing, there was not much he could do to stop them.

With the help of Hollinger International's New York executives, Wachovia's bankers hatched a plan to build a safety wall around the company that would make it harder for money to spill out to Ravelston and the senior executives. Applying unusually strenuous terms to the bank loan, the investment bankers severely restricted the company's ability to move cash to other Black companies and capped the annual management fee to Ravelston at $25 million.

Wachovia's probe uncovered a number of unreported transactions that had been beneficial to Black and Radler. One of the most unsettling discoveries was Hollinger International's $8-million purchase of a collection of Franklin Delano Roosevelt letters and memorabilia from the estate of the late president's secretary, Grace Tully. Although the

FDR artifacts were purchased in early 2001, shareholders had never been informed about the unusual and costly acquisition. The bankers understood the significance of the discovery immediately. Hollinger International had spent at least $8 million of shareholders' money on FDR artifacts at the same time that its CEO was writing a biography of the late president. The investment added nothing to Hollinger International's business, and indeed most of the memorabilia was scattered in Black's various homes. Wachovia's bankers added a line about the $8-million FDR collection to a schedule of Hollinger International investments that was included with documents for the bank loan.

The material was confidential, but it would not remain buried for long.

———

Conrad Black and Amiel greeted their guests in the spacious living room of their Palm Beach home at cocktail hour on March 28, 2003. They welcomed about forty Hollinger executives, Wachovia bankers, and lawyers who had contributed to the debt refinancing. It was an evening to celebrate, and Black, dressed in a blue jacket and khaki pants, was magnanimous, taking some of the bankers on a tour of his antique- and art-filled home. He explained that the framed American flag hanging at the top of the winding double staircase in the lobby had flown over the White House the day Roosevelt died. He then took them to his study, an oceanside room overflowing with photographs and letters from the late president. Nobody that evening was going to raise any concerns about his double role as a CEO and author, or about the corporate purchases of the Roosevelt artifacts. Debt had been sold and money had been made—it was not a time for questions.

In the ground-floor living room, Amiel, dressed in pale cargo pants and a russet top with a plunging neckline, mingled with guests as waiters wandered the room serving wine, vodka cocktails, and appetizers. Black's closest advisers were there, except Radler, who had chosen not to make the long trip from his Vancouver home. Radler's nemesis, Colson, the *Telegraph*'s chief executive officer, had driven in from his nearby winter spread in Highland Beach. Boultbee and his wife, Sharon, had flown in from Toronto. From New York there was Hollinger International's treasurer Smith and vice-president Healy. Atkinson had decided to come at the last minute with his wife, Stephanie, and his appearance cloaked an unsettling secret that might have torpedoed a $120-million Hollinger Inc. junk-bond sale led a month earlier by Wachovia. Frustrated with Black's refusal to reform his free-spending ways, Atkinson had penned a resignation letter on February 17, which stated, "I now find myself in a position where I completely disagree with your view that the old Hollinger philosophy and methods are an appropriate vehicle to deal with our problems." He changed his mind after one of the company's lawyers at Torys warned him that his departure might scuttle the junk-bond sale.[1]

After guests had finished their cocktails, a small squadron of rented cars and vans pulled into the Black's gravel driveway and ferried them to the nearby Ritz-Carlton Hotel for dinner. Hosting the evening were Wachovia's Fogg and Haase, who had overseen the Hollinger debt deals. The bank officials were happy to put the difficult assignment behind them. It had not been easy selling the Hollinger group's debt because of the growing controversy over management compensation, and, making matters worse, Black had been unpredictable with potential investors and the bank's chairman.

Black had startled potential bond buyers during a December lunch at the New York Palace Hotel when he promised that Hollinger International expenses would decline "once we are rid of superfluous people." At a Boston meeting that same month, one investor asked for details about the restrictions or covenants on the debt. When Hollinger's treasurer Smith began reciting the onerous financial terms, Black interrupted him and said, "We can get around that." His apparent willingness to sidestep the rules raised more than a few eyebrows. On December 16, one of the last days of the road show, five Wachovia bankers and Hollinger International executives had been forced to shuffle restlessly on the first floor of Black's New York co-op building as they waited for him to wake up. After two urgent telephone calls, Black had appeared more than an hour after the designated 6:30 A.M. departure time, making the group late for a meeting with investors in New Jersey. Black was also tardy for a private lunch in March with Wachovia's chief executive G. Kennedy Thompson at the bank's headquarters in Charlotte, North Carolina. When Black arrived forty minutes late for a one-hour lunch with the head of the United States' fourth-largest bank, he explained that British politics had held him up. "I was on the phone with Tony Blair."

To commemorate the closing dinner, Wachovia handed out small trophies and keys to an imaginary Wachovia city called Charlestonville. After dinner, the lights were dimmed so that guests could watch a short slide show prepared by Wachovia to revisit highlights of the road tour. Near the end of the show on that evening of celebration in March, a slide appeared on the screen with a five-word quote from Black that elicited howls of laughter from everyone, including Black.

"We can get around that."

———

When Hollinger International shareholders and analysts logged on to the website for the Securities Exchange Commission's electronic filing system, known as EDGAR, in early April, they got more than they bargained for. They were searching for Hollinger International's much-anticipated annual report, or 10-K. Those Hollinger International watchers that hit the print button would spend a good part of their morning replacing ink cartridges and adding paper to their printers. Depending on how it was formatted, the report was in some cases over eight hundred pages long, more than four times the length of any of Hollinger International's previous 10-Ks. The colossal document was not a sudden burst of corporate confession by reticent Hollinger International executives. As a horrified Black would later learn, it was a mistake. Somewhere between Ravelston, which prepared Hollinger's financial reports, and Bowne & Co., a New York–based financial printer that publishes and manages electronic filings of corporate documents, it appeared someone had accidentally added confidential debt schedules to Hollinger International's 10-K. The data that had surprised bankers and bond investors in the previous fall was now in the public arena. Waiting to be discovered in a schedule on page 633 was a one-line entry about the FDR collection.

———

In theory, Jereski should have been thrilled with Hollinger International's voluminous public filings in the spring of 2003. Tweedy's analyst loved combing corporate documents and these filings were a gold mine of new information about the company's inner workings. After sustaining investors for years with a miserly drip-feed of information, Hollinger International had finally opened the taps and unleashed a torrent of data. But Jereski was anything but happy.

The documents disclosed a number of shocking new details about special deals that had personally enriched Black and his senior executives. It was several weeks before she spied the $8-million FDR nugget, but there was enough other troubling information to keep her busy. What was so galling about the disclosure was that much of the new information involved transactions that had taken place years earlier. The outdated information reinforced Jereski's conviction that Hollinger International had little regard for shareholders' rights to timely and full disclosure. Underlining this was the boldface-type admission in the 10-K that had first been printed in the confidential bond memorandum the previous fall. "Lord Black is our controlling shareholder and there may be a conflict between his interests and your interests." Talk about the blindingly obvious, Jereski thought. This company is thumbing its nose at shareholders.

What the documents told Jereski was that, contrary to Black's promise in September, the Ravelston fees had been reduced only marginally in 2002. According to the proxy statement, Hollinger International paid Ravelston $21.4 million in management fees in keeping with the $22-million limit the company had announced in September. But when you added Ravelston fees paid in Canadian currency, separate management fees to Black's various private companies, and other bits of compensation, the number soared to $26 million. While the fee had shrunk from about $31 million in 2001, it was in effect $4 million higher than the reduced payment Hollinger International had promised in September. Included in the latest compensation was a $276,000 salary and bonus payment to Amiel, which she earned as an executive with the *Sun-Times*. Aside from the fact that the position and compensation had never been announced, no one at the Chicago paper could remember having seen her at their offices since a brief visit in the late 1990s.

In addition to the multi-million-dollar payments, Hollinger International was paying the costs of the Blacks' New York co-op and Radler's Chicago condominium, perks that were costing the company $122,000 a year. During the first six months of 2002, the document said, Hollinger International had paid $2.3 million to cover the cost of one of the two jets leased for Black and Radler. Hollinger International also footed the bill for Black's Bentley and driver in London, and Mercedes S-Class and driver in New York, and Radler's Jeep in Chicago. In addition, the company paid a "portion of the cost of [Black's] personal staff," but the costs were not broken down in the proxy. Lord Black was living like a king at Hollinger International's expense.

Of all the news the Hollinger International documents yielded, what surprised Jereski most were the terms of a debt agreement signed by the company's Toronto parent, Hollinger Inc., a month earlier in March 2003. The parent had sold $120 million worth of junk bonds to investors to replace a line of credit that was not being renewed by its long-standing banks, the Canadian Imperial Bank of Commerce, the Toronto-Dominion Bank, and the Bank of Nova Scotia. Incredibly, the junk bond deal included a pledge from Black that tied up most of his shares in Hollinger International as security for the parent company's loans. The pledge meant that unless Black somehow came up with the money to buy back the $120 million in junk bonds, he was prohibited from selling his U.S. subsidiary's shares. The other shocker was that Hollinger Inc. was in such weak financial condition that, under the terms of the junk bonds, Black's private company, Ravelston, had agreed to give the Toronto company millions of dollars in support payments.

Black, Laura realized, was being backed into a corner. His Hollinger Inc. holding company had a severe cash shortage and he had little freedom to sell his Hollinger International shares. Investors had always assumed that Black would sell or take private his newspaper empire if shareholder complaints became intolerable. Now Jereski understood that even if Black wanted to, it would be almost impossible for him to pursue such exit strategies. He was running out of options.

———

A green Ford Explorer nosed its way passed the mounds of garbage in Greenwich, Connecticut's town dump during the first week in April. When the large sport utility vehicle came to a stop, two men stepped out, opened the rear hatch, and began tossing garbage into a pile. Cardinal's Rob Kirkpatrick had asked his partner Gene Fox to accompany him during the domestic spring-cleaning chore so that the two could get away from the office and talk about something that had been bothering him for days.

Kirkpatrick had been dismayed by Hollinger International's 10-K and proxy. The self-dealing, exorbitant perks, and compensation smelled as rotten as the waste around them. He realized now that Black's so-called "holy crusade" to win back shareholder confidence had been little more than a public relations gesture. Even worse, the company's board of directors seemed indifferent to the mounting controversy. According to the 10-K, they had approved everything. Something needed to be done.

Nothing was going to be done at Cardinal unless Fox, its intense and gifted stock strategist, agreed. Fox had been the driving force behind Cardinal's initial investment in Hollinger International in 1997, and like a true value investor he believed that over time the company's deeply discounted stock price would rise to reflect its intrinsic worth. As pressure from shareholders mounted, Fox held on to the hope that Black would exit from the crisis by selling his shares or some of Hollinger International's assets. But as Tweedy's Jereski had discovered, Kirkpatrick and Fox now knew such a sale was unlikely because Black had pledged his shares to junk-bond holders. Kirkpatrick knew the best way to get Fox to focus on the issue was to pry him away from his cease-less stock research at the office. As they tossed garbage, Kirkpatrick asked, "What are we going to do about Hollinger? This has become distressing. Do we need to get someone outside involved?"

That someone, they agreed, was Herbert Denton. Since he founded Providence Capital, Inc. in 1991 in New York, the former institutional stockbroker had made a name for himself as one of corporate America's noisiest agitators. Denton attracts so much media attention to his corporate challenges that a *New York Post* headline once blared, "He scares CEOs."[2] Denton had helped mobilize shareholders against dozens of companies, from Time Warner Inc. to Walt Disney Company. It's easy to track his conquests because he likes to hand visitors bound copies of newspaper clippings chronicling his skirmishes.

To his detractors, Denton is a corporate governance gadfly who pounces on vulnerable companies with proxy battles and negative publicity for his own personal profit. To his supporters, he plays a helpful role as the public voice of aggrieved shareholders so that publicity-shy institutional investors who back him don't become directly entangled in the controversies. He makes most of his money when institutional money managers channel stock trade orders through him to a registered broker as a form of payment for the public pressure he can bring to bear in corporate standoffs. Dependent on a share of these commissions, Denton is always on the lookout for companies with what he calls "lousy" boards and "crummy" strategies.

Gene Fox gave Denton a new target when he called on April 3 to brief him about Hollinger International. Cardinal's managers had worked with the activist on previous shareholder uprisings. When Fox explained that Black controlled Hollinger International through multiple shares, Denton blurted, "Whoa, that's not good." Denton's main weapon in shareholder rebellions was proxy battles, a means by which shareholders can forcibly appoint new directors by casting votes in a special resolution. Such a proxy vote would be pointless at Hollinger International as long as Black controlled the majority of the votes. Undeterred, Fox told Denton: "Take a look at this and see if you can add any value."

On Sunday morning, April 20, a London paper had a huge scoop about a story that had miraculously stayed out of the press for more than a year. The story was about Black, his controversial personal payments from Hollinger International, and its restless shareholders. The paper was *The Sunday Times,* owned by Black's old nemesis Rupert Murdoch, the CEO of News Corp. A costly circulation war triggered by Murdoch's *The Times* in 1993 had eroded the *Telegraph's* profits and paid circulation for years. Now Murdoch's *Sunday Times* was dishing the dirt against his adversary. Under the headline "Black Against the Wall," the story by Paul Durman and John O'Donnell featured a photo of a smiling Black against a brick wall holding a chart tracking the steep decline of Hollinger International's stock price. The story had everything, except the FDR shocker, which still lay buried at the bottom of the 10-K filing. It highlighted the rich payments, perks, and related-party transactions and the financial restrictions imposed by Hollinger International's recent debt deals. It also featured Jereski, who was complaining publicly to the press for the first time about the colossal fortunes Hollinger International was bestowing on Black and his team.

> *This has been a lucrative enterprise for everybody but us. This company isn't run on behalf of its other shareholders, or with any sense of independence on the board. It abuses the rights of minority shareholders.*

With his knuckles publicly rapped, Black had an opportunity to defuse what would inevitably become a big story at a time when the media were preoccupied with corporate scandals. Yes, he could have said, shareholders had legitimate concerns that deserved to be addressed. Yes, Hollinger International would scale back the excesses. Yes, he would change his ways. But Hollinger International's boss was not willing to bend with the times. In an interview for the story, he came out charging against critics of his multi-million-dollar payments and fees.

> *I recognize that it seems to have scandalized a few people but I consider their opinions ludicrous.*
>
> *We are not running a Christian Scientists' meeting here where we all have to sing from the same hymn sheet. Anybody who complains about it can take a hike.*

The most remarkable thing about Black's over-the-top quote was that it was tacked on to the end of the *Sunday Times* story. For years, most features about Black had tended to focus on his reliably outrageous remarks or, in later years, his and Amiel's high-society lifestyle. Complaints, if any, about his corporate actions were virtually always off the record and, given Black's penchant for libel suits, the anonymous criticisms were rarely cited. Now, as the *Sunday Times* article demonstrated, something else was grabbing the media spotlight. That something was Jereski, a former business journalist who knew what the media needed to tell a story. Fed up with Black's lack of response to its demands, Tweedy was going to give Black a taste of his own medicine. The media would be its new weapon to pressure Hollinger International into responding to their demands.

Within days, other major business publications jumped on the story. In Chicago, London, Toronto, and New York, newspapers and magazines began publishing stories about Hollinger International's shareholder revolt, and many of them were bolstered with quotes from Jereski and her boss, Browne. Black gave the story legs by continuing to dismiss his critics in true Conradian fashion. "I'm sitting here in Palm Beach watching the majestically swaying royal palms in my garden and I do not feel cornered and I am not against the wall," he told *The Globe and Mail*'s Keith Damsell.[3] Any suggestion of financial distress, he continued, was "codswallop" and Standard & Poor's recent credit rating downgrade was "bunk."

If there was any "bunk," business reporters soon found, it wasn't coming from Hollinger International's critics. With Jereski's assistance, reporters followed the *Sunday Times*'s lead and detailed some of the disturbing revelations buried in Hollinger International's recently released documents. "Papers' Money, Lord Black's Loot" screamed a headline in *Crain's Chicago Business,* "Press Lord Pressed," said a *Forbes* article.[4] The facts were starting to speak louder than Black's words.

———

"These guys are going to hang," Denton told his young analyst Jay Hill. A former credit analyst with Bank of America, Hill had just completed an intense three-week analysis of Hollinger International's public financial documents. The twenty-eight-year-old, one of four employees at Providence Capital, had presented his findings in a nineteen-page report that morning in late April. Denton couldn't believe what he was reading. Hill's report showed that Hollinger International had paid its senior executives about $73 million in non-compete payments in recent years, and that many key details about the payments had been disclosed years after the fact.

Even more troubling were the asset sales to private companies owned by Black and his team. Since 2000, Hill's report showed, Hollinger International, with board approval, had sold more than thirty-seven newspapers to two private companies, Bradford Publishing and Horizon Publications, which were owned by Hollinger International executives. From the time the first Horizon sale was announced in 1999, Hollinger International had kept a tight lid on details. With each new annual report, it tossed a few more scraps of information to shareholders about the deals. After plowing through the voluminous annual report released a few weeks earlier, Hill had learned that some of the Bradford and Horizon deals had very sweet terms. Not only had Hollinger International sold papers to companies owned by its executives, but it had lent them more than $10 million to buy them. Bradford was lucky that its Hollinger International loan was interest-free and unsecured.

"How can this be?" Hill asked Denton. "These guys are buying papers from themselves, for themselves, and on top of that they are lending money to themselves. There is nothing good about this."

What was bad for Hollinger International's executives was good for Denton. The record of self-dealing and lousy disclosure that Hill had pieced together would be dynamite if Hollinger International's share-holders decided to band together to fight the company. It was time to make a few calls.

———

Denton's plan was a simple one. One look at Hollinger International's blue-ribbon board told him that none of these directors wanted to get caught in an ugly, public battle with shareholders. The minute investors turned on the heat, directors such as Kissinger, Perle, Thompson, and Kravis would take action to diffuse the crisis, Denton was convinced. All he had to do was elicit shareholder support for a public assault.

Cardinal had been pleased with Hill's analysis but told Denton it was not interested in a public campaign. As long as Black controlled the votes, all the proxy battles and negative publicity in the world weren't going to change things at Hollinger International. The only option left for Cardinal, Fox told Denton, was a lawsuit. The money manager was reviewing with its lawyers whether it made sense to sue the company and its directors for allowing Black to drain so much money and assets from the company.

Southeastern also took a pass. Compared with Hollinger International's other shareholders, the Memphis money manager was less troubled by the sky-high management fees and non-compete payments. To Southeastern these benefits were not much different than the fat bonuses executives at a number of public companies were pock-eting for orchestrating major transactions, such as the CanWest sale.

Like Cardinal, Southeastern didn't think it made much sense to mount a publicity campaign against Hollinger International as long as Black had voting control sewed up. "I think your chances are one in a million," Cates told Denton.

Denton also struck out with Omega's Cooperman. "I've got to pick my battles, and this isn't one of them," Cooperman told Denton. Omega's major preoccupation at the time was its investment in Tyco. Cooperman would later be a key witness for the prosecution against Tyco's CEO Dennis Kozlowski, who was charged in September 2002 with stealing $170 million from the company.[5] Tyco would give the emerging era of corporate excess its defining image when it was revealed that Kozlowski had lavished Tyco money on a Sardinian birthday party for his wife, an event that featured an ice sculpture of Michelangelo's *David* dispensing vodka from his penis.

Only Tweedy was left. The firm's partners had been so impressed with Hill's report that it would hire him as an analyst in August. What Tweedy didn't want, however, Browne told Denton, was to spend a lot of time and money fighting Black. There was an option, Denton explained. What if Tweedy asked Black to form a special committee to review shareholder complaints? If Black had nothing to hide, he would agree. If he opposed the request, Tweedy could be in a good position to sue the company. When Browne responded that he was interested, Denton told him he would find a lawyer.

———

Robert Curry, Jr. had been intrigued by the Hollinger International file ever since Bert Denton handed him Jay Hill's research in late April. After thirty-two years as a corporate lawyer for U.S. conglomerates and various boards of directors, he was well versed in the practice of non-compete payments and inter-company management services fees. He had never, however, seen anything like the Hollinger International payments. The Ravelston fees seemed unusually generous and the non-competes were even more alarming. In his experience it was corporations, not their executives, who were paid an inducement not to compete with a rival. Why would any executive have a right to help himself to what was traditionally regarded as a corporate right? Something, he believed, seemed wrong at Hollinger International.

Curry was a newcomer to shareholder activism. He saw growing investor outrage over corporate misdeeds as an opportunity for a new avenue of litigation for a lawyer versed in the legal duties of boards of directors. A year earlier in 2002 he had acted on behalf of a Ford Motor Company shareholder who had demanded that the company's board investigate a multi-million-dollar windfall to CEO William Clay Ford, Jr. The auto giant's long-standing banker Goldman, Sachs & Co. had, in 1999, allocated 400,000 shares of the firm's hot initial public offering to the executive. By the time of the complaint, Ford, Jr. had earned a paper profit of more than $4 million on the shares. The board rejected the shareholder's demand, but in February 2003, Ford, Jr. moved to quell the controversy by announcing he was donating his profits on the shares to charity.

Curry wanted Tweedy to consider a similar tactic at Hollinger International. On the morning of April 29, he and his partner Roger Kirby, along with Denton, met with Will and Chris Browne and Jereski in Tweedy's boardroom. Tweedy, he explained, had two choices. One was to write a formal letter to Hollinger International's board of directors demanding that they investigate the massive payments to Black and his senior executives. The board had blown Tweedy off before, but no thinking board was going to ignore a legal demand letter. If they did, the directors could be vulnerable to a lawsuit by shareholders on the grounds that their inaction could make them seem complicit in controversial payments to Ravelston and Black and his senior executives. And that, Curry said, was Tweedy's second choice.

Tweedy could sue the directors on the grounds that the directors had allegedly failed to make a good-faith effort to act in the best interests of all stakeholders by approving the Ravelston and non-compete fees. Curry advised that Wilmington, Delaware's Chancery Court—which served as the country's key commercial court system because most major publicly traded companies are incorporated in the state—had in the past been reluctant to question board decisions. But in the wake of such devastating failures as Enron, Tyco, and WorldCom, courts were showing signs that they favoured more legal scrutiny of boardroom conduct. For example, Curry said a Delaware court had recently allowed shareholders of the Walt Disney Company to apply to have their suit against the company's board of directors brought to trial. Shareholders were suing Disney directors to win back $140 million in severance paid to former president Michael Ovitz for only fifteen months of work. The decision on the Disney trial request was expected shortly, Curry said, and if the case was sent to trial it could open the door to future suits against directors.

The choices were stark ones for Tweedy. It had been a year and a half since the firm had sent the written letter to Hollinger International's board, and nothing had changed. Black's Ravelston continued to siphon large management fees from the company with board approval. Tweedy had threatened and sued a lot of companies over the years, but it had never taken on a power board like this. It was time to bail out of the stock, or step up to the plate.

———

This is friggin' obtuse, Browne thought as he read the letter. Tweedy Browne's managing director was holding a two-page letter from Nicholas Sleep, a portfolio manager with one of Hollinger International's shareholders, London-based money manager Marathon Asset Management. Sleep had sent the note to Black on April 29, the same day Tweedy's partners had met with Curry. Black had copied the letter to Hollinger International's major shareholders. In a maddeningly circuitous way, Sleep was warning Black that Marathon might sell its Hollinger International shares if the company didn't clean up the "pyramid structure ... [a] financial tautology" that allowed him to rule the company through super-voting shares. At least, that's what Browne thought Sleep was trying to say.

Black's response on May 6, which he copied to Tweedy, was much clearer. "No one in my position in his right mind could agree" to extinguish multiple voting shares, he wrote. As to shareholder complaints that were being aired in the media, Black offered:

I am conducting a peace process with Tweedy Browne … which I hope will bring an end to their unedifying practice of denouncing the company in the pages of our competitors.

Browne was not impressed by the dig. "Nice language, but what's the purpose?" he asked Black in a May 7 email. Although Browne lectured Black that "it is our right to speak freely about that to whomever we please," he offered that he might be "prepared to refrain from any conversations with the press" on one condition. Floating the recommendation from Denton and Curry to demand an investigation, Browne's email said his condition was that Black had to agree to appoint new independent directors to Hollinger International's board to review the Ravelston fees and other beneficial deals.

Black's reply landed in Browne's in-box at 12:49 A.M. the next day. The email began with a swipe at Marathon's Sleep, "as aptly named as most Dickensian characters, to judge from his letter to me." Having insulted one of Tweedy's fellow shareholders at Hollinger International, Black moved to Browne's request. He said he would be "happy to invite three new directors" to Hollinger International's board and he listed some potential candidates. The company had already targeted as a board nominee Gordon Paris, the investment adviser on Hollinger International's junk bonds. There would be limits, however, Black insisted of the review.

What we are talking about is a review of future compensation and related party transactions…. We will not accept a consequential review of past arrangements…. Neither new directors nor anyone else will have any license, and I trust none is requested, to rummage through the past.

The patient, unflappable investor was angry now. Black's dodge to keep a special committee from "rummaging around in the past" wasn't going to work. Browne's reply later that day was swift and direct.

If you are concerned that these transactions may not hold up under the light of day, then I am concerned.

Our purpose is in no way meant to impugn the integrity of the current independent directors. However, the facts known to us do not pass our smell test.

Browne had had enough. After months of correspondence and broken promises from Black, he doubted further discussions would accomplish anything. It was time to end the communications.

I regret we have come to this impasse and will discuss with my colleagues alternative courses of action that might provide the information we seek.

———

Tweedy didn't waste any time. The next day Browne and his partners met with Curry to give him their decision. Tweedy was going to send a formal demand letter to Hollinger International's board of directors that called for an investigation into the executive non-compete payments. As Curry and Denton advised, Tweedy was going to make its demand public through a regulatory filing, known as a Schedule 13D, that would include much of the research Jay Hill had compiled a month earlier. The board would not be able to ignore Tweedy this time. The so-called "talking 13D" would draw media scrutiny for the first time to the role played by Hollinger International's high-powered board in the controversial payments. "This is a straightforward rifle shot at the board," Curry told the Tweedy group. "They will have to clean up their act or they are going to be sued."

CHAPTER EIGHT

"There Has Been a Sighting"

BY EARLY MAY, some of Hollinger International's directors were starting to get nervous. Leading U.K. and North American newspapers were writing numerous reports quoting some of the company's angry shareholders about Black's corporate extravagances. Most of the directors had continued to loyally support Black, but a May 7 newspaper story put a dent in their confidence. That day the *Los Angeles Times* published a front-page article about Hollinger International director Richard Perle and his potentially conflicting roles as an adviser to the Pentagon's Defense Policy Board and as a venture capitalist seeking to invest in high-growth firms. The article explained that Perle, a leading supporter of the war in Iraq, had formed a fund called Trireme Partners to raise money for investments in such businesses as security companies. One investor who had contributed $2.5 million to the fund was Hollinger International.

The news put Hollinger International's board in a very awkward position. A newspaper company with no connection to the defence industry was giving money to a private company run by one of its directors. Making matters worse, neither the company's board nor the audit committee had ever approved the investment. James Thompson was furious when he joined a May 14 meeting of the audit committee. Management never should have made the investment without the consent of the board, Thompson told fellow members Marie-Josée Kravis and Richard Burt. The time had come, they finally agreed, to question the practices of the company's management. Thompson designated Hollinger International's chief financial officer Peter Lane to investigate the unusual payment to Perle's company. The audit committee also agreed to hire James McDonough of Gardner Carton & Douglas of Chicago as legal counsel to advise it during the potentially thorny investigation.

———

As Hollinger International's corporate governance troubles neared the crisis stage, Kravis, one of Black's oldest friends, began to take a closer look at shareholder complaints. That spring she had phoned Healy at the New York office and asked him to send her a summary of the issues that were being raised by company shareholders. When Black heard about the request, he told Healy to send him the summary first. He would edit it and send it on to the board's audit committee himself.

On May 11, Black sent a confidential seven-page report to the audit committee that was a remarkably thorough synopsis of shareholder complaints—filtered through his own prism. He spelled out the concerns about management fees, Horizon and Bradford newspaper purchases, Black's personal expenses, and the $53-million non-compete payment from CanWest. For each criticism, he offered the board explanations—many of which would fail to stand up to scrutiny. The Ravelston fees, he said, had undergone a "sharp reduction" of $2 million, for which neither he nor the board had "received much credit." His and Radler's companies, Horizon and Bradford, had received loans to buy Hollinger International newspapers because "there were no other buyers for these assets at sensible prices." He attached a vaguely worded note recently sent from CanWest CEO Izzy Asper that, according to Black, proved the Aspers had insisted that the Hollinger International executives personally sign the lucrative non-compete agreements.

Moving to Christopher Browne's request for new directors to investigate the controversial payments, Black cast himself as an obliging CEO who was faced with an unreasonable shareholder.

He wishes to introduce new directors unknown to us with an unlimited mandate to engage lawyers and accountants at the company's expense and conduct a forensic investigation into the entire recent history of the company....

Christopher Browne reached a very agitated condition before it became obvious that he had launched a systematic campaign of denigration against us in the international financial press and among institutional shareholders....

It was obvious that I was dealing with someone who would grasp at anything to find evidence of sinister practices....

Black told the board he would invite new directors of "high and unquestionable reputation," but there had to be limits to their review.

There is no moral imperative to accept and no sane person would, that we should bring in complete strangers with an antagonistic brief to apply contemporary standards to past actions that were judged appropriate and fully disclosed at the time.

———

On May 19 Tweedy caught Black off guard by publicly issuing a demand letter for a special investigation three days ahead of the company's 2003 annual meeting. The stunning hardball tactic unleashed a torrent of negative media stories, which only added pressure on Hollinger International's board of directors to launch the wide-ranging investigation Black had tried to head off. Tweedy's 13D filing had laid out Hill's research and included a letter to Hollinger International's board that

117

demanded a special committee of directors investigate and take "corrective" action in relation to the total $73 million in non-compete payments paid to Black, Radler, Atkinson, and Boultbee from a variety of newspaper sales including CanWest. Failure to take action, Tweedy's letter warned, "would constitute a failure to act independently" and therefore free shareholders to launch a lawsuit against the board.

Tweedy's hostile missive would likely whip shareholders into a fury at the annual meeting if Black didn't do something to divert their attention. The something, he decided, was the complex share-purchase plan that his major shareholder Southeastern had proposed nearly a year ago in Toronto. Southeastern's Hawkins and Cates had called Black on a number of occasions to urge him to reconsider their plan to buy a larger stake in Hollinger International and ultimately phase out his super-voting shares. As Tweedy's demands escalated in late April and May, Black began preliminary discussions with Hawkins and Cates. He pursued the talks in earnest after the demand letter was published. By May 21, Black was ready to do a deal, and Cates and Hawkins flew to New York to meet with him the day before the annual meeting.

After hours of negotiations, the two sides reached an agreement at 2 A.M. on May 22. Under the plan, Southeastern would buy as much as $116 million worth of Hollinger International's shares from Black's Toronto holding company, Hollinger Inc. In exchange for the money, Black would agree to convert his super-voting shares over a four-year period into ordinary one-vote shares. To Southeastern's top executives, the deal meant that they could eventually emerge as Hollinger International's largest shareholder, a position that would enable them to resolve the corporate governance issues that were suppressing the company's stock price. They were set to buy Hollinger International's Class-A common stock for $11.60 a share, a price they believed was well below its intrinsic value of about $18.00 a share. It was a terrific way to make money from a distressed company.

For Black the deal offered more than money. It would be a surprise development that would help distract the media and shareholders from

Tweedy's demand for an investigation. If he was lucky, no one would notice that he had little to show for the Southeastern agreement. The two sides had not signed anything in writing. Indeed, the pact was so hastily arranged that no lawyers or advisers had been present. The only thing sealing the deal was an early morning handshake.

———

The next day, May 22, 2003, one hour before the annual meeting, Hollinger International's audit committee gathered in a small anteroom in the Metropolitan Club. Thompson, Kravis, and Burt understood that Tweedy's 13D had forced their hand. If they did not take steps to investigate shareholder complaints, the directors could be vulnerable to a lawsuit. They were savvy enough to recognize the impending calamity. Over a few cups of coffee, they quickly decided they would recommend that the board form a special committee to look into Tweedy's allegations.

They agreed that investment banker Gordon Paris, who was due to be nominated as a director at the pending annual meeting, should be chairman of the new committee since he was the only outside Hollinger International director who had not approved the controversial deals that were being challenged by Tweedy. Other outside directors would have to be recruited and they would have to be impartial and respected to convince the company's rebellious shareholders that the company was launching a serious investigation. When the meeting concluded, Burt slipped out and pulled Healy aside. "Paul," he said, "here's Richard Breeden's number. Call him and see if he can meet tomorrow."

Healy made the call, and Breeden asked him to send a copy of the Tweedy filing. The former chairman of the Securities and Exchange Commission was emerging as a leading corporate-governance hired gun as a result of his ongoing work at WorldCom, a bankrupt telecommunications company whose boardroom failings he documented in a 150-page report that condemned the "nearly imperial reign" of the company's CEO Bernard Ebbers. Breeden told Healy he was busy, but he would take a look at the filing.

———

Healy had been in a tizzy all morning. He had only heard about the Southeastern deal less than two hours before the annual meeting was due to start at 11 A.M. That had given him mere minutes to call the New York Stock Exchange to request a halt in the company's stock before the exchange's opening bell rang. Companies are required to request halts during trading hours when major news is pending, to ensure that the news is disseminated at the same time to all shareholders. He couldn't tell the NYSE much about the halt because the company's lawyers had only that morning been informed of the agreement with Southeastern. They were racing to hammer out details and write a press release in time for the annual meeting. Half an hour before the meeting, Healy had another problem on his hands. The Metropolitan Club's security was not letting reporters into the private sanctuary. Facing more than two dozen irate journalists who were being shut out of a newspaper company's annual gathering, Healy told the reporters to hide their microphones, take off their press badges, and discreetly slip into the stream of shareholders who were heading into the meeting.

Standing outside the door of the main meeting room, Healy could see that most of the reporters had found their way into the room, along with about 150 other people. The room was packed with investors, analysts, and onlookers who, in the wake of numerous stories about the shareholder revolt, had come to see Black face the firing squad. Healy could also see Barbara Amiel approaching him in a blue-grey jacket and dark pants.

"Don't worry, Paul, everything will be fine," she told him. A few minutes later, Amiel slipped her arm into Black's and the two made their entrance into the buzzing room. They waved to friends, and spotting New York showman Donald Trump, stopped to exchange kisses with the developer and his girlfriend, model Melania Knauss. Armed with the Southeastern agreement in his back pocket, Black began his annual speech by coming out charging at his critics. The speech was filled with the usual withering attacks on his detractors and rosy depictions of Hollinger International's performance. Though he must have known that Browne was in the room, he engaged in a bit of historical revisionism about his relations with Tweedy. He cast himself at the meeting as a responsive CEO who had made "a very comprehensive effort" to placate Tweedy, despite its managers' habit of "garrulously defaming us" in the media. He gave the impression that it was his idea to invite independent directors to Hollinger International's board, and suggested the peace process had failed because Browne wasn't responding to his emails.

Near the end of his half-hour speech he pulled two rabbits out of his hat. The first was the news that a special committee would be formed to investigate Tweedy's concerns. The committee would find little more than a public relations problem, he assured, because compensation scandals were the lot of affluent people whenever "small amounts [are] dispersed … that [seem] … absurdly self-indulgent." The other rabbit was the Southeastern deal, which he explained would ultimately reduce his voting stake in the company from 70 percent to 35 percent. Shareholders should have nothing to worry about, he said, with a special committee being formed and Southeastern due to play a bigger role in the company.

———

Black's deal with Southeastern bought him some time. Newspapers and press reports for the next few days focused largely on Southeastern's planned new investment. Hollinger International's major shareholders, however, weren't buying it. The sophisticated investors knew from the parent company's recent junk-bond issue that Black would have a lot of difficulty selling his shares to Southeastern because he had pledged them as security for the Hollinger Inc. bonds, an obstacle the Memphis money manager appeared to have overlooked. Unless Black came up with more than $120 million to repay the notes at a premium, which seemed unlikely, he would not be selling his shares to Southeastern. "That deal is never going to fly," Browne told Curry and Jereski when they heard the news at the annual meeting.

Browne's suspicions about the viability of the Southeastern deal were reinforced a few days later on May 27, when Black visited him at his office. The feisty, ebullient CEO who had been on stage at the annual meeting had been replaced with a quieter, much less confident man. Speaking hypothetically, Black outlined a scenario in which he might be able to offer Tweedy a large block of Hollinger International shares priced somewhere between $17 and $19 each.

"Would Tweedy be interested in such a block?" Black asked Browne.

Browne was flabbergasted. Five days after announcing the Southeastern deal, Black appeared to be offering his control block to Tweedy. "No, Conrad, I would not be interested. We invest in newspaper companies, we don't operate them." Sensing that Black wanted out, Brown then asked, "What are you going to do if you sell your newspapers?"

"There are lots of things I can do," he responded, without offering details.

Shortly after that, Black departed.

Browne was left wondering, What was that all about?

———

On June 3, Paul Healy had lunch with the enemy.

That day he joined Bert Denton at Michael's Restaurant, a popular midtown hangout for New York media executives. The shareholder activist had requested a get-together to discuss a recent legal breakthrough that might affect Hollinger International. Healy advised Black that he would be having lunch with Denton, whom the press baron had added to his list of opponents after the activist was quoted in a number of press stories as criticizing the company's management. If Black wanted to stop the lunch, there wasn't much he could do about it. By the spring of 2003 Healy was openly supporting shareholder demands for change, winning him the trust and backing of the company's biggest shareholders and bankers. Any move to corral or eject the investor relations executive would only incite further investor fury.

Denton did most of the talking during the meal, outlining for Healy the seismic impact of a May 28 decision by a Delaware judge to allow shareholders of Walt Disney Company to proceed with a lawsuit against the company's directors for their "ostrich-like" approval of an astonishingly rich executive-severance package. The Delaware move opened a new avenue of shareholder attack that could be applied against Hollinger International's board, Denton warned. When Healy and Denton were finished, they walked towards the exit together. Hearing his name, Healy turned to see Barbara Amiel at a table with *Vogue* editor Anna Wintour. His face breaking into a grin, Healy told Denton to follow him to the table, and as the men approached, Healy heard Amiel boast to Wintour, "This is one of my husband's most important executives."

Healy bowed slightly and introduced Amiel to Denton. Recognizing Denton's name from negative media stories about Hollinger International, Amiel blanched. As the two men walked towards the exit, Healy turned to Denton and whispered, "Watch how quickly she reaches for her cell phone." Denton turned to see Amiel rummaging through a large leather Hermes purse.

Shortly after Healy returned to his office, Black came rushing through his door.

"There has been a sighting," he said, explaining that Amiel had called in an agitated state about the rendezvous with Denton.

"But, Conrad, I told you that I was lunching with him," Healy said.

"Yes, I know." Black winced. "But I neglected to tell my wife."

———

As Denton had predicted, Delaware's sanctioning of a shareholder lawsuit against Disney's board of directors opened a new front in the revolt against Hollinger International. Leading the charge this time was

Cardinal Capital. In early June the Greenwich money manager quietly served notice on Hollinger International's lawyers that it was demanding, under Delaware law, the right to review the company's boardroom minutes and records. Such demands are typically a prelude to a lawsuit. As lawyers for Hollinger International and Cardinal argued over the summer about how much data the money manager would be entitled to review, Gene Fox and Rob Kirkpatrick began to joke about the anticipated information. "Did the tractor-trailer show up with the documents yet?" Fox would ask.

In late September, Cardinal's receptionist called Kirkpatrick in his office to tell him there was a delivery for him. When he walked to the front door he saw a single document box. It was the minutes and records of Hollinger International's board. When he opened the box he saw that it wasn't even half full. Records for years of boardroom deliberations about the multi-million-dollar management fees to Ravelston and the non-compete payments to Black and his executives added up to a stack that measured a few inches high.

Kirkpatrick phoned Fox, who was out of the office. "Gene, it's a really small tractor-trailer," he explained.

CHAPTER NINE

The Executioners

THE FATE OF CONRAD BLACK was sealed on the top floor of a restored dairy barn in a leafy residential neighborhood of Greenwich, Connecticut. At a casual glance, the building might be mistaken for a bed-and-breakfast: a quaint, two-storey, white clapboard structure with cedar-topped gables and green shutters, framed by a manicured garden. A narrow brick path, hemmed in by rows of neatly trimmed boxwood hedges and blooming rhododendrons, winds its way under a trellis and into a circular courtyard. The only thing belying the pastoral nature of this setting is a small white business card taped to a window pane on the side door: Richard C. Breeden, Chairman, Richard C. Breeden & Co.

The fifty-four-year-old former chairman of the Securities and Exchange Commission, now head of his own consulting firm, was chatting with colleagues at his office that morning, preparing to welcome a handful of visitors. It was August 4, 2003, about a month and a half since he had been hired to advise the special committee of independent directors investigating alleged misconduct at Hollinger International. Until quite recently, this "committee" had consisted of just one person, Gordon Paris, an investment banker who lived a train stop away from

Breeden in the neighbouring hamlet of Harrison, in New York State. The two had worked closely together for several weeks, gathering evidence, lining up interviews with Hollinger International executives, and scouring the company's complex financial statements.

Today they were welcoming a pair of new committee members into the fold, both of whom had been sworn in as Hollinger International directors at a special board meeting the previous week. Raymond Seitz, a career diplomat and one-time U.S. ambassador to the United Kingdom, and Graham Savage, a Toronto money manager who had spent several years as chief financial officer at Rogers Communications Inc., Canada's largest cable company, had each been nominated to the special committee with Black's personal endorsement. Seitz, who had previously sat on the board of the Telegraph Group, had initially aroused some suspicion. Part of the crisis at Hollinger International, as far as Breeden and Paris could tell, stemmed from the fact that Black had populated his board with hand-picked lackeys, and the last thing they needed was one more. The two men had several phone calls with the former diplomat to make sure he was suited to the task, and they were eventually satisfied. In retrospect, there would be little cause for concern. Black, the devoted student of military history, a man who could dazzle with his near-perfect recollections of battle campaigns and the commanders who waged them, had made an unthinkable tactical error. He had unwittingly appointed his own executioners, and today would be their first meeting.

———

Six months earlier, just minutes after a February board meeting, Black, Colson, Radler, Atkinson, Boultbee, and Peter Lane, Hollinger International's chief financial officer, had strolled down the hall to Paul Healy's office. Black, the last one to enter, shut the door behind him and leaned against the jamb. The audit committee had just urged them to nominate another director to the board, one with sound financial expertise, and the executives needed a recommendation.

"Do you know of anyone we can recruit?" Radler asked. Healy, who was seated at an antique desk in the back left corner of a spacious room, didn't hesitate. As head of investor relations and corporate development, he maintained an extensive network of contacts on Wall Street, but one name came immediately to mind. "It's obvious," he replied. "Gordon Paris is the one."

Healy had hired Paris and his investment banking firm, Berenson Minella, to advise Hollinger International on a $300-million note offering in late 2002. Paris had been working in finance for a dozen years in a variety of jobs. He ran a junk-bond operation at Lehman Brothers in the early 1990s, before jumping to Credit Suisse First Boston to lead its leveraged buyout business. He began dealing with Black in 1996, after he joined TD Securities Inc. as a managing director. The New York–based investment banking unit of the Toronto-Dominion Bank was one of Hollinger International's primary lenders, and Paris had played a key role in helping the company raise money through bond offerings and other financings.

Paris, forty-nine, was known for his bulldoggish determination and no-nonsense demeanour. He was both tough-minded and analytical, and his blunt approach could be prickly: as one colleague put it, "he has a sense of humour, but he has to be reminded of it every so often." Healy respected his financial talents, but perhaps more than that, he admired Paris as one of the few bankers willing to stand up to Black. In March, Black approached Paris and asked him if he would consider becoming a Hollinger International director. It was a highly unusual recruiting move for Hollinger International's CEO, since Paris was neither a close friend nor someone who could be reliably counted upon to toe his corporate line, but times had clearly changed. Black had been buffeted by an escalating barrage of shareholder complaints, and now that the audit committee was clamouring for some financial help, he needed to foster the perception that he was taking these concerns seriously. Black told Paris that if he took the job, one of his first tasks would be to mount an independent analysis of the tens of millions of dollars in fees collected by Ravelston each year. Paris didn't immediately bite. But after thinking the offer through, he eventually agreed to stand for election to the board at Hollinger International's annual shareholders' meeting in May. Although he had counted on some measure of controversy, he could never have anticipated just how ugly the assignment would become.

———

Richard Breeden would not have been Black's first choice as an adviser to the special committee. Renowned for his tenacious pursuit of white-collar criminals, Breeden epitomizes the role of the enforcer, an image that is only strengthened by his imposing stature and the gleaming black Hummer hulking in his driveway. He ticks off the number of enforcement actions he launched as a regulatory chief (1,208) like notches on his belt and has stationed an SEC flag beside his desk as an out-sized reminder of his former position.

The son of a greeting card salesman, Breeden graduated from Harvard Law School and joined the storied legal firm of Cravath, Swaine & Moore LLP in the 1970s. Not long after he began his private practice, the lure of politics pulled him to Washington, D.C. He campaigned for Ronald Reagan in 1980 and then went to the White House as deputy counsel to Vice-President George H.W. Bush. Under Bush, Breeden helped to shape financial policy on Wall Street and had a hand in mopping up the carnage from the thrift industry crisis in the 1980s, when the savings and loans business imploded. He also made a powerful ally.

Less than a year after Bush succeeded Reagan as U.S. president in 1988, he appointed Breeden chairman of the SEC, where Breeden remained until 1993. It didn't take long for Breeden to cultivate a reputation as an intelligent and pugnacious stock market cop. He went after corporate thieves relentlessly, often forsaking settlements in favour of court battles. Once, when he was just a few months into his mandate, Breeden privately told SEC staff that a lawyer who had been accused of insider trading "should be left naked, homeless, and without wheels."[1]

He was ambitious, a self-styled perfectionist who could also be abrasive, and, according to some of his critics, downright arrogant.

(Tibor Kolley, The Globe and Mail)

Conrad Black, shortly after he seized control of Argus Corp. Ltd. in 1978, holds his other trophy, his 743-page biography of former Quebec premier Maurice Duplessis.

(CP Photo/Blaise Edwards)

Hollinger International director and former U.S. secretary of state Henry Kissinger chats with Conrad in 1989, a happier time for the two friends. Black would later accuse Kissinger of betraying him.

Before they were enemies: Black and former Canadian prime minister
Jean Chrétien join Queen Elizabeth II at a veterans ceremony in London
in 1994. Five years later, Black would unsuccessfully sue Chrétien
for blocking his attempt to accept a British peerage.

David Radler, NYSE chairman Richard Grasso,
and Black were smiling when Hollinger
International was listed on the exchange
in 1996. By 2003 each was being sued
for controversial compensation.

Since Conrad Black inherited an eleven-acre estate from his parents in Toronto's Bridle Path, he has made numerous additions, including a library with fifteen thousand books and a copper cupola.

"A glowing and opulent stage" is how London designer David Mlinaric described his renovation of the Black's London home in Kensington, which included such flourishes as a two-storey dining room.

"I feel like I'm a court painter living in Versailles," said an artist who spent months hand-painting walls at Black's palatial Palm Beach, Florida, residence. The oceanfront mansion was briefly put up for sale—asking price US$36 million— before Black changed his mind and pulled it off the market.

Long-time Black loyalists William F. Buckley, Jr., with his wife, Pat, and Fredrik Eaton with wife, Nicky, at a Hollinger International dinner in Chicago in 1995.

Hollinger International director Lord Weidenfeld, his wife, Annabelle, and director Alfred Taubman at the 1995 Chicago dinner.

A Lord at last. Flanked by fellow peers and former Hollinger advisers, former British prime minister Margaret Thatcher and Lord Carrington, Black was introduced to Britain's House of Lord's on October 31, 2001, as Lord Black of Crossharbour.

Former business journalist Laura Jereski was one of the first shareholders to question Hollinger International's rich executive payments. Her persistence prompted Black to call her a "Rottweiler."

Tweedy Browne Company's senior managing directors John Spears, Christopher Browne, and his brother Will Browne stuck to the firm's motto "act like owners" in their long and tortuous struggle against Black.

Cardinal Capital's partners Gene Fox and Rob Kirkpatrick pose with the half-filled box of Hollinger International documents that formed the basis of their lawsuit against company directors and executive.

Black's right-hand man, David Radler, whispers a few words to the press baron before a shareholders meeting in 2000. A special committee investigating the Hollinger scandal singled out the long-time colleagues as "truly bad actors."

Associates say the Hollinger saga took a heavy toll on Peter Atkinson, the only member of Black's inner circle to reach a settlement with the company over allegations that he pocketed improper payments.

Daniel Colson (middle), CEO of Hollinger International's *Daily Telegraph,* and Jack Boultbee, Black's top financial executive, listen to Black speak at a 2002 annual meeting of Hollinger Inc. The two executives were later pushed out and sued by Hollinger International for allegedly taking improper payments.

Stuck between feuding shareholders and Black, his unyielding boss, Paul Healy quietly worked behind the scenes to help investors gather information about their company's irregular payments to executives.

Black's wariness of Richard Breeden, left, a past chairman of the Securities and Exchange Commission, was one of the main reasons he agreed to step down as CEO of Hollinger International without a fight. Gordon Paris, right, headed up the special committee investigating the corporate scandal and eventually took Black's job.

Raymond Seitz was a voice of moderation on the special committee probing Black and his associates. The former U.S. ambassador to the United Kingdom used his diplomatic finesse to win the support of other directors, including Kissinger.

Graham Savage took the precaution of transferring most of his assets to his wife before joining a special committee charged with investigating lavish payments to Black.

Surrounded by bodyguards, Conrad Black and Barbara Amiel head for the Toronto annual meeting of Hollinger Inc. in May 2002, a time when shareholders had begun questioning huge payments to Black and his lieutenants.

One day after he was forced out as CEO of Hollinger International, Black boasted to reporters at a Toronto book-signing, "I made $50 million bucks today" when the company's stock soared on news of the press baron's departure.

The billionaire Barclay brothers, a pair of reclusive British twins who live in a castle on one of the Channel Islands, bought the *Telegraph* from Hollinger International last summer. Reporters joked that the only way to tell them apart was by their hair: Sir David parts his to the right, Sir Frederick parts his to the left.

Disgruntled employees, who resented what they viewed as his imperious approach to management, began referring to him out of earshot as "King Richard." Both personally and politically he was conservative, although he allowed himself the occasional flamboyant indulgence, including a red Porsche with his initials stamped on a personalized licence plate.[2]

If Breeden had a rallying cry throughout his tenure, it was disclosure— the fuller the better. His crusade to make companies accountable in the eyes of shareholders could not have been a source of comfort to Black, for whom transparency was the corporate equivalent of a hair shirt. Indeed, Breeden's reputation on this point had only grown since he left the SEC. In the summer of 2002, he became the court-appointed monitor for WorldCom Inc., which had teetered into the biggest bankruptcy in corporate history. His job description was exceedingly broad: ensure evidence is not destroyed, stamp out any lingering instances of impropriety, recover stolen money, and essentially oversee everything from accounting and compensation issues, to executive hires and governance.

Breeden's tight control of the WorldCom purse strings, coupled with his insistence on being personally involved in all aspects of corporate decision making, earned him praise in financial and regulatory circles. Within WorldCom, however, his hands-on style quickly garnered him another sobriquet: "Dr. No." He accepted the WorldCom job even though recently he had been diagnosed with colon cancer and had begun to undergo chemotherapy. He was receiving his final treatments when Paris and others approached him about the advisory role at Hollinger International.

The job immediately appealed to him. The Tweedy letter had catalogued a host of alleged abuses, each grave in nature and scope, while the various high-profile players involved added an extra measure of intrigue. The only thing that puzzled Breeden was why Black had not attempted to block him from assisting the special committee. A collision between the two men was inevitable.

———

Peter Atkinson pulled Graham Savage aside and asked if he could spare a few minutes. The two had just concluded the June 2003 board meeting of Canadian Tire Corp., the iconic Toronto retailer for whom they both served as directors, and Atkinson tossed out a proposition: Would Savage be willing to join a special committee at Hollinger International?

Savage was intrigued. Although he ran his own merchant banking firm, Callisto Capital LP, it was fairly routine work, and he was restless for a new challenge. Seven years ago, he had retired as chief financial officer of Rogers Communications, the Canadian cable empire founded by legendary mogul Ted Rogers, and set out on his own. Savage had helped Rogers raise a small fortune in the 1970s and 1980s, when cable companies were still viewed as speculative investments, and in the process became regarded as one of the pioneers of Canadian junk-bond financing. He even did deals with Drexel Burnham Lambert and its notorious junk-bond king, Michael Milken, who was forced to pay $1.1 billion in penalties and serve two years in jail after Breeden and the SEC prosecuted him for a raft of securities violations.

Money was no longer a concern for Savage, and neither was time. He had known Atkinson for nearly thirty years, and valued their friendship, but he needed a few more days to consider the offer in detail. Atkinson emailed Black in London that night and told him about the exchange. Black responded immediately: Savage, he said, would be a "perfectly acceptable" candidate.

Savage, however, was torn. He wasn't intimately aware of the issues at Hollinger International, but he had a rough idea. Atkinson was a close friend, and Maureen Sabia, a fellow Canadian Tire director, was on the board of Hollinger International's Toronto-based parent company. Having run in Canada's top financial circles for much of his life, Savage was no stranger to Black and his Byzantine corporate dealings. He thought of Black as both pompous and patrician, but he also respected Black's ability to fashion one of the world's largest media companies out of guile and gutsy manoeuvring.

As Savage reviewed the Tweedy Browne allegations, it occurred to him that this formation of a special committee could turn out one of three ways, each of them equally unpleasant. The committee could discover that Conrad had done some unsavoury things, which would not be good; it could uncover evidence that the high-powered directors themselves were at fault; or, the investigation could turn up nothing, in which case the committee would be vilified by shareholders as nothing more than a group of minions.

As discomfiting as these options were, Savage was slowly won over by the prospect of working with such a fascinating collection of people. It was not every day that one had a chance to rub shoulders with the likes of Breeden, Kissinger, and Perle. But if he waded in, he would need protection. Savage phoned his friend Jay Swartz, a lawyer at Davies, Ward & Beck LLP in Toronto, and asked him for advice. The two men quickly agreed that Savage would need to shield himself if he joined the board, given Black's well-known fondness for spraying his foes with lawsuits. Swartz set up a trust fund for Savage's four children and transferred his home and other financial assets to his wife's name.

Ten days after he had been approached with the offer, Savage phoned Atkinson and accepted, but with one caveat: "I want you to know I am not going to be your whitewash guy," he said. "I won't be someone who gives you the answer you want."

For Raymond Seitz, July 10 had started off much like any other day in the summer of 2003. He woke up at the crack of dawn, as is his custom, read the papers, and smoked a cigarette, and then joined his wife Caroline in their ongoing project: the renovation of a 180-year-old plantation home nestled on an oak-studded hill overlooking the harbour in Charleston, South Carolina. Before long, his work was interrupted by a phone call. It was Conrad Black, and he needed a favour.

Seitz, then sixty-two, had known Black since 1991, when he became the first career diplomat to be appointed U.S. ambassador to the Court of Saint James in London. Tall and angular with narrow, deep-set eyes, a fringe of close-cropped silver hair, and impeccably tailored suits, Seitz cut a distinguished figure. His speech is measured and deliberate, and his listeners get the impression he is weighing each word before dispatching it with equally considered enunciation. He had spent twenty-eight years in the foreign service, including stints as the U.S assistant secretary of state for European and Canadian affairs, and before that as executive assistant to Secretary of State George Schultz in the Reagan administration. In England, particularly, Seitz was treated like a native son: when he was wrapping up his term in 1993, one British paper ran a profile of him under the headline "Yankee Don't Go Home."[3] *The Economist,* meanwhile, implored President Clinton to "leave America's man in London alone."

A history major at Yale, who once taught school in Texas, Seitz embodied diplomatic finesse: he was erudite, no question, but he also possessed the sort of self-effacing humour and understated charm that would not go unappreciated among habitués of the London establishment. At the same time, part of his appeal rested on his ability to forge a number of strong relationships with British political, corporate, and media leaders, the latter of which, not surprisingly, included Conrad Black.

In the mid-1990s, Black approached Seitz to join the advisory board of the Telegraph Group Ltd., which housed the flagship newspaper, the *Telegraph*. Seitz, who had left his ambassador's post, was primarily working as a vice-chairman at the investment bank Lehman Brothers, and sat on a few corporate boards. He accepted Black's invitation, which essentially required him to have lunch and conversation twice a year with a coterie of influential power-brokers that included Sir Evelyn de Rothschild, Rupert Hambro, Lord Carrington, and Canada's Paul Desmarais, of Power Corp.

Seitz had stepped down from the board some time ago, so he was only vaguely aware of Hollinger International's scrapes with shareholders when he received the phone call that afternoon. Black quickly filled him in on the demand letter from Tweedy Browne and asked him if he would become a member of the special committee. Seitz, not one for rashness, demurred. But at Black's urging, he promised he would call a few of the central players to get a better sense of the proposed assignment. He had a few conversations with Atkinson, and then learned more about the special committee from Breeden and Paris. The calls merely confirmed his initial reluctance. Seitz knew Kissinger and Burt from his political days, and to a lesser extent, he regarded Barbara Amiel and Dan Colson as social acquaintances. Like Savage, he initially saw the offer as a no-win situation: if he dug up evidence of fraud or abuse, he would be persecuting people he knew; conversely, if Black and his company were given a clean bill of health, Seitz would be viewed as part of an old-boys cover-up.

Faced with this conundrum, he phoned Atkinson and Paris and politely declined the invitation. But Black was desperate. A few days later, he called Seitz and pleaded with him to reconsider. He was having a difficult time finding independent directors whose reputations would pass muster with shareholders and the special committee. Just to make sure there were no misunderstandings, he pledged his full co-operation with the internal review and appealed to Seitz once more to accept the offer as a personal favour.

What the hell, thought Seitz, relenting. I'll do it.

———

At about 9.30 A.M. on August 4, Seitz and Savage arrived at the refinished barn, about a five-minute drive from downtown Greenwich, for their inaugural meeting with Breeden and Paris. The location was intentional: although Breeden had another office in Washington, D.C., he wanted to meet in a neutral zone, one where the committee members ran little risk of bumping into the power set that occupied Hollinger International's board and executive suite.

Linda Hudson, Breeden's secretary, welcomed the men at the side door. A large, ersatz Chippendale dining room table occupied the middle of the ground floor. The walls near the entrance were adorned with Breeden's credentials, including an SEC plaque commemorating his term as chairman, framed appointment certificates, and pictures of him with President George Bush, Sr. On the opposite wall were numerous photographs of sailboats and schooners, including three shots of Breeden aboard *Bright Star*, the seventy-five-foot sloop he races to Bermuda each year.

Hudson directed the men to a spiral cast-iron staircase tucked in the left-hand corner, which they climbed to a spacious second-floor loft. There Breeden was discussing the Hollinger International file with three lawyers: Norman Harrison, whom he worked with in Washington, and two lawyers from the firm of O'Melveny & Myers LLP, Jonathan Rosenberg and Andy Geist. The latter two had been hired as counsel to Hollinger International's special committee. A quick round of introductory handshakes ensued, and each man helped himself to a cup of coffee from a Thermos on the nearby credenza. The atmosphere was casual: ties were loosened and suit jackets were doffed as they seated themselves around a large rectangular conference table.

The purpose of the meeting was mainly educational, since Seitz and Savage were joining a work very much in progress. Breeden began by updating them on what the committee had been doing for the past several weeks. He and Paris, with help from the legal team, had begun compiling company documents, requesting email records, and conducting interviews with a few Hollinger International employees. Breeden then dispensed a series of three-inch-thick black binders, each containing a twenty-page report titled "Briefing of the Special Committee."

The report, outlining the committee's mandate, was daunting in scope, and closely paralleled Tweedy Browne's complaints. There were two main tasks: investigating the roughly $220 million[4] that Hollinger International had paid to Black's private holding company, Ravelston, for management and advisory services over the past seven years, and probing the tens of millions of dollars'[5] worth of non-compete fees that had flowed to Black, Radler, and two related companies: Ravelston and the Toronto parent, Hollinger Inc. This would require a forensic examination of every Hollinger International sale over the past several years, from the blockbuster CanWest deal to the sell-off of tiny community newspapers in the United States. Then there was a myriad of smaller matters: the $8 million Hollinger International had shelled out for FDR memorabilia while Black was penning a biography of the former president; the company's investment in Trireme Partners, a venture capital firm operated by long-time Hollinger International director Richard Perle; the millions of dollars that had been lavished on corporate jets, apartments, butlers, and chauffeurs, all for the benefit of either Black or Radler; and a string of "related-party" deals between Hollinger International and two companies— Horizon Publications Inc. and Bradford Publishing Co.—that were owned by Black and Radler. It was dizzying to contemplate.

The men were also reminded of the special committee's wide-ranging powers, bestowed by the Hollinger International board in June: the committee could demand documents and whatever other information it needed, and if its investigation uncovered any evidence of wrongdoing, it had the authority to take legal action. Rosenberg, a former U.S. attorney in his early forties, prepared an eight-page memo explaining Delaware corporate law and the so-called "entire fairness doctrine," which holds controlling shareholders to a higher standard when they are forging deals with related companies. The memo also touched on the landmark Disney ruling of May, whose reverberations were still echoing on Wall Street. A judge had ruled that Disney's shareholders could push ahead with a lawsuit against the company's directors for signing off on a $140-million severance package to president Michael Ovitz, who was fired fifteen months into the job.

The Disney decision had clear implications for Hollinger International. First, it gave both the special committee and investors reason to believe they could be successful pursuing Black in court, assuming it came to that. Second, it raised serious questions about the vulnerability of Hollinger International's board of directors. Boards have historically been protected by something known as the "business judgment rule," meaning that as long as the directors made decisions in good faith and with proper care, they would be shielded from litigious-minded shareholders. Yet this defence didn't work in the Disney case, where shareholders argued that the board breached its "duty of care" by approving the obscenely lucrative compensation during a hasty meeting. If the special committee's probe discovered that Hollinger International directors were rubber-stamping payments to Black and others, or failing to gather enough information to make an informed decision, the board could find itself in deep trouble.

Finally, Rosenberg put the financial implications of their assignment into stark relief. First he illustrated the convoluted relationship between Hollinger International, its Toronto parent Hollinger Inc., and Ravelston. Next he presented a rough estimate of how much money Hollinger International's controlling shareholders had sucked out of the company in the form of management fees, non-compete payments, salaries, bonuses, and other perks between 1997 and 2003. Black, both personally and through his private holding company, Ravelston, along with Radler and other executives, had pulled hundreds of millions of dollars out of Hollinger International since 1997.[6] The company's reported profit during that time, after all this money was shelled out, was just $155 million. The numbers were staggering. It looked as though the majority of the company's profit over the past seven years had gone straight to Black, his private holding company, and his closest colleagues.

No one was quite ready to hang Black or any of his associates. At least, not yet. The board had approved many of the payments, including the ones to Ravelston for management services, albeit in apparently cursory fashion. But to experienced financial hands like Breeden, Paris, and Savage, things just didn't look right. The sheer scale of funds flowing to Black, the numerous examples of self-dealing, the absence of any sort of precedent entitling executives to non-compete fees—all of these pointed to something unpleasant. Untangling this knot of inter-company dealings and related-party transactions was a daunting task, but Breeden offered some helpful advice. An early lesson he learned at the SEC, he told his troops, was that when faced with such a complex case, investigators should begin their work by trying to figure out one thing: who got the money.

CHAPTER TEN

Follow the Cash

LUKE CATS CLIMBED the stone steps of 10 Toronto Street at 6:45 P.M. on Wednesday, August 6, 2003, and approached a pair of tall, black wooden doors. The beefy ex-cop was a vice-president at the New York forensic technology firm Stroz Friedberg, LLC, which had been hired recently by the special committee to assist with its probe. Earlier that day, he and a colleague had boarded a plane armed with a delicate assignment: they were to visit the squat, temple-like edifice that doubled as corporate headquarters for both Hollinger Inc. and Ravelston, Black's private holding company, and copy the emails from their computer servers.

Cats had spent fifteen years with the New York City Police Department, the last four as part of a computer investigations unit. He had received the Chief of Detectives Award for three consecutive years between 1997 and 1999 and had performed more than 250 examinations of seized computer equipment. Even though he was a veteran, this job was proving to be complicated. His travelling companion that day, Richard Molnar, had attempted to clone the emails at Hollinger Inc.'s Toronto office in late July but had been turned away because the process was taking too long. Currently, there was a dispute over whether the special committee had a right to take these emails, since many of them belonged to Ravelston, and Hollinger Inc., the parent company. Until the skirmish was resolved, Ravelston and Hollinger Inc. agreed to a compromise: Cats and Molnar would be allowed to copy the contents of the servers onto another hard drive, but they could not take the copies with them back to New York. Instead, the hard drive would be sealed in Hollinger Inc.'s offices until lawyers for Black and the special committee could resolve their dispute.

Andrew Booker, a technology employee with Hollinger Inc., greeted Cats and Molnar when they arrived. The two men were whisked past the security guard in the front foyer and led to the cellar, where the computer servers were housed. At 7:45 P.M., after installing some special software, the men began copying the information. Six and a half hours later, the duplication was completed. At 2:17 A.M. on Thursday, Booker placed a hard drive containing the copied emails into a tamper-proof police evidence bag and locked it in his office. A few minutes later, Cats and Molnar filed out of the building.

Now it was up to the lawyers to decide when—or if—Hollinger International could take possession of the hard drive and its trove of emails.

———

If there was an early voice of conciliation among the members of the special committee, it belonged to Ray Seitz. He had attended the first meeting at Breeden's with a dispassionate view of Tweedy's allegations, and he still held out some hope of settling things amicably. The email situation was a case in point. Lawyers were already squabbling over the committee's request for the corporate emails at the parent company, Hollinger Inc., and now Black was balking at the prospect of giving up personal emails stored on his home computers. Savage, who was angry over what he viewed as a stalling tactic, harboured a hawkish attitude. He favoured a stern response and suggested they forcibly compel Black to give up the emails, possibly with the threat of legal action. But Seitz, ever the diplomat, had another idea.

In early September, following a Hollinger International board meeting in New York, he approached Black with a proposal. A lawyer for the special committee and a lawyer for Black would sit side-by-side and sort through the emails, casting aside whichever ones were not relevant to the probe. If there was a disagreement over whether a particular piece of correspondence was admissible, the contested email would be brought to Seitz and Black, who together would be the final arbiters. It was an elegant gambit, and it worked. Black, who said he did not want outsiders to comb through emails between himself and his wife, some of which contained medical records and other private information, still trusted Seitz more than he did other members of the committee, and agreed to the arrangement.

As a matter of courtesy, a Hollinger International official sent an email to Black and his wife on Friday, September 19, advising them that a group of people would be visiting their homes in London and New York the following week at 6 A.M. to copy their hard drives and retrieve emails. The entire procedure, he informed them, would take about eight hours.

Amiel was livid. It was one thing to be the brunt of countless newspaper articles, many of which took a voyeuristic pleasure in juxtaposing her personal extravagances with Black's mounting woes. But this was a physical invasion of her property. The barbarians were literally at the front gate. "No one is cloning my personal mail and I will kill them first," she fumed in a terse email reply. "The board can take a running jump into well." It's not clear whether she meant to type that the board could go to "hell," or jump into "a well," but in either case, the thrust was essentially the same. She didn't want anyone laying a finger on her private correspondence. Black was also miffed at the idea but knew he had little choice but to honour his promise. A couple of days after

Amiel's outburst, he sent a sarcastic-sounding email to Seitz, explaining that he would provide "technical observers" for the process to ensure the special committee was taking only Black's emails and no one else's.

Could you invite your paramilitaries to reformulate a plan that does not transgress what we agreed? ... You can also assure [special committee lawyer Jonathan] Rosenberg that there is no necessity to come to London; his legions will be hospitably received in my homes in Toronto or Palm Beach or even New York.... I hope, after all their histrionics, these people will not be too crestfallen when their research produces nothing even slightly controversial.

The two sides agreed to copy the emails at Black's New York residence on Thursday, September 25. As irritated as he may have been, Black did not neglect his responsibilities as a host. He told a Hollinger International official to make sure that the proper people were there, including his driver Gus, who would "keep an eye on everything and take care of anyone's needs, as I promised a reasonable level of hospitality—these people are not enemies and they are performing a useful service." Added Black: "The visitors should be treated cordially but their purpose is a narrowly defined one."

Just after noon on Thursday a group of men arrived at Black's home, a posh co-op that occupied the entire third floor of a stately, pale brick Park Avenue low-rise. Cats and Edward Stroz, a former FBI agent who had founded Stroz Friedberg, were joined by John Cary and Ian Robinson, two technology employees from Hollinger International. Gus ushered them in and told them that Black and his wife were out for the day. About twenty minutes later, Jesse Finkelstein, Black's Delaware lawyer, and Rosenberg, counsel to the special committee, joined the group. Gus led the group into Black's book-lined study, where a Compaq computer sat on an antique desk cluttered with photos and other knickknacks. Like many men of his generation, Black's relationship with the internet age was an uneasy one. In the mid-1990s, when he was grudgingly learning how to use a computer, he tossed one machine into the trash in a fit of exasperation. Months after the investigation, he may have wished he had done the same with this one.

Cats explained to the group what he planned to do and reassured Finkelstein that he was going to be copying only emails from Black's personal computer. Finkelstein and Rosenberg each insisted that they receive a copy, so Cats made a total of three, the last of which would be placed in a safe at the Hollinger International offices in New York. For what seemed like an interminable time, Cats painstakingly copied the information while the men peered in vain over his shoulder at a blank computer screen. Gus flitted in and out, sometimes to bring coffee and cold drinks, and other times just to observe.

Nearly three hours later, when the work was finally over and the men began to make their way out, Finkelstein pulled one of the Hollinger employees aside. The lawyer was clearly upset with the way things were unfolding. "I can't believe this is happening to Conrad," he muttered incredulously. "It's unfortunate that we have to get to this point."

――――

When the special committee began combing through Black's huge cache of correspondence, which spanned more than sixteen thousand emails, they were stupefied. Black may have promised that the search would yield "nothing even slightly controversial," but the special committee members begged to differ. The emails had presented them with a startling portrait of executive entitlement, one in which Black was dismissive of minority shareholders and seemingly unrepentant about his lavish compensation and perquisites. Shareholders who dared question the flow of money to Black's private holding company, Ravelston, were described in emails as "self-righteous hypocrites," tolerable only as a source of money to fuel his corporate ambitions. There was almost a blithe refusal to acknowledge that shareholders, too, were owners. "We have said for some time that [Hollinger International] served no purpose as a listed company, other than relatively cheap use of other people's capital,"[1] he wrote to Atkinson and Boultbee in the summer of

2002. In other emails, he extolled the privileges that should rightfully accrue to himself, as a proprietor, and to his inner circle at Ravelston. It was difficult to read through his private musings without concluding that here was a man who did not grasp the responsibility of running a publicly traded enterprise. Black appeared to have slipped into the persona of another legendary newspaper tycoon, the late William Randolph Hearst, of whom he once admiringly wrote: "Hearst had a conviction, often outrageous but sometimes magnificent, that the rules that applied to others didn't apply to him."[2]

———

Black wasn't the only Hollinger executive who had a penchant for playing by his own rules. During the late summer, David Radler was quietly negotiating to buy a new crop of publications for Horizon, the Marion, Illinois–based company that he and Black owned. Incredibly, he was attempting to forge a deal in the midst of the special committee probe, which was looking into Horizon after shareholders raised suspicions about the company. According to a memo Radler had submitted to Hollinger International's board in August, Horizon had lined up a deal to buy from a competitor $100 million worth of small newspapers in Ohio, Georgia, North Carolina, Oklahoma, Kentucky, Tennessee, and West Virginia. Close to half of the money would be lent by Wachovia— which happened to be one of Hollinger International's primary banks.

Radler had not been in the habit of seeking board approval for his Horizon deals ahead of time, but in the wake of the special committee investigation he wanted to make sure the directors were onside. When Radler flew to New York to make his pitch for the acquisitions at a September 8 directors' meeting, he discovered a board that had been utterly transformed. Galvanized by Breeden and the special committee, the directors were suddenly asking a number of questions. When they finished, they asked Radler to leave the room, a standard boardroom precaution against management conflicts that had rarely been followed within the company. After the meeting concluded, Black presented

Radler with the verdict: the board was opposed to further side deals by its top executives, and if Radler wanted to pursue the Horizon acquisition, he would have to quit.

Radler was clearly upset when he returned to the *Sun-Times* offices in Chicago. He complained bitterly to his managers that he was unfairly being forced to give up a legitimate business transaction and he portrayed himself as a victim of a witch hunt. Radler initially told some fellow executives that he planned to leave Hollinger International but, shortly after, was forced to scrap his planned deal when Wachovia's bankers told him that they were reluctant to provide the loan. Radler remained with the company but his complaints grew louder and more self-serving. On one occasion after the deal had fallen through, he muttered darkly to some *Sun-Times* managers: "They always go after the Jew first."[3]

For the special committee and its team of lawyers and advisers, it had been a summer of grunt work: collecting evidence, negotiating access to documents, interviewing various executives and directors, and, in general terms, simply trying to unravel the extraordinarily complex web of financial relationships among Hollinger International, its Toronto parent, Hollinger Inc., and various related companies including Ravelston.

The early focus of the investigation had been on Hollinger International's deal with CanWest, a logical starting point given both its sheer size and the prominent part it played in Tweedy's formal complaints to the board. The deeper the committee delved into that deal, the more concerned it became. First, it appeared that CanWest had never insisted on paying non-compete fees to Black or any other individual—contrary to what Hollinger International executives told the audit committee when they pitched the arrangement, and contrary to what was implied in the company's public filings with regulators.[4] Second, it looked as though CanWest had never determined the size of these fees: originally they had been pegged at just under $38 million, but just days before the deal closed, according to information compiled by the special committee, it looked as though Black, Radler, and others had successfully pushed to increase that figure to $53 million.[5] There was another stinger: it appeared CanWest had intended to pay these fees directly to Hollinger International, but Black had evidently decided the money should instead go to Ravelston, his private holding company.[6]

One of the main justifications for these payments was a memo Kipnis had sent to the directors in September 2000, reminding them that similar non-compete arrangements had been struck prior to the CanWest deal, when Hollinger International was selling off its smaller U.S. community newspapers. Naturally, this made the special committee curious. Just how forthright had executives been when they presented these earlier deals to the board?

At the beginning of the probe, Breeden had assembled a group of professionals at his firm, including lawyer Norman Harrison and investment banker Steve Quamme, and instructed them to follow the cash. They were to build a chart of all the money flowing in and out of Hollinger International, including the management fees that went to Ravelston and any non-compete payments that went to executives or other parties. Their assignment was to find proof that every payment leaving the company had been properly authorized. When the investigators began to slice their way through the financial underbrush, they realized this was a much more difficult job than they had expected. For a public company, Hollinger International's record-keeping was incredibly shoddy. When they asked Kipnis why the company had not originally disclosed the non-compete payments that Black and other executives received from the CanWest deal, he explained that Hollinger International's law firm, Torys, had insisted it was unnecessary. Even though this was crucial legal advice, Kipnis could not produce a written document to substantiate his claim. Instead, he offered up a transcription of a voice-mail message left on his phone by Darren Sukonick, a lawyer with Torys, who said the firm had "canvassed internally" before concluding the payments would not have to be disclosed in the company's proxy circular, where details of executive compensation are released every year.

"We agree that they do not have to be disclosed in that manner," the transcript stated. "They are payments that went directly from CanWest to the individuals, and did not run through Hollinger [International]." This last bit, of course, was wrong. The payments went to Hollinger International first and were then redirected to Black, Radler, Atkinson, Boultbee, and to Ravelston. Curiously, Torys didn't seem to be aware of this, even though it represented both Hollinger International and Ravelston in the deal with CanWest.

As the investigators pressed on, this began to look like a relatively mild example of Hollinger International's sloppy corporate culture. The bigger problem was the lack of documentation surrounding a number of deals in which the company sold off its U.S. community newspapers. By religiously following the cash, Breeden's team had ended up at the doorsteps of Black, Radler, Atkinson, and Boultbee—a group the special committee referred to as "The Big Four"—as well as that of the parent company, Hollinger Inc. A thorough review of Kipnis's archived files had produced a worrisome discovery: the Big Four and the parent company had received millions of dollars in non-competes from the U.S newspaper sales, yet the investigators could find no evidence that the board had approved the payments. In some cases, the payments had not even been publicly disclosed to shareholders. When they brought their findings to Breeden, his first instinct was that they had missed something. It didn't seem conceivable that so much money could be paid to executives without the board's authorization. He told his team they weren't searching in the right places and urged them to look harder.

Once again they sifted through the company's paperwork, and once again they came up empty-handed. By mid-October, the investigators had uncovered eight deals in which Black, Radler, Boultbee, Atkinson, as well as Hollinger Inc., the Toronto parent, had received a total of $32.15 million in non-compete payments, and nowhere was there any indication that the board had given its approval. At this point, Breeden realized something was terribly wrong. These findings had called into question the integrity of Black and fellow members of management and raised the ugly spectre that executives were surreptitiously diverting money from the company. Even Seitz, who had maintained a sceptic's cool throughout the ordeal, admitted the evidence looked damning.

In various transactions between 1998 and 2000, it appeared that Black and Radler had arranged for Hollinger Inc., the Toronto parent, to collect $16.55 million in non-compete payments. In practical terms, it was difficult to fathom: why would U.S. newspaper buyers demand non-compete agreements with a Canadian holding company that didn't actually operate any publications and clearly was not much of a threat? The short answer, as far as the special committee could tell, is that they never made such a demand. There was simply no apparent rationale for Hollinger Inc. to be collecting this money.

In February 1999, for example, Hollinger International sold forty-five U.S. papers to Community Newspaper Holdings Inc. (CNHI) for $472 million, a figure that included $50 million in non-compete fees. Three days before the sale was finalized, Radler added the Toronto parent, Hollinger Inc., to the non-compete agreement so that it could collect $12 million. He also signed the agreement on Hollinger Inc.'s behalf. According to the special committee's review, CNHI never asked for a non-compete arrangement with Hollinger Inc. There was no evidence that Radler mentioned this when he proposed the newspaper sale to Hollinger International's audit committee, which believed the company was getting the entire $50 million worth of non-competes.[7] The special committee discovered five other deals in which the parent company received non-compete payments. In each case, there was no evidence the fees were approved or reviewed by Hollinger International's board, and none of the payments were publicly disclosed to regular shareholders.[8]

The more the special committee probed, the more brazen these arrangements appeared. Evidence suggested that the executives had begun adding their own names directly to the non-compete agreements. In November 2000, around the same time Hollinger International sold off its Canadian papers to CanWest, the company agreed to sell another $90 million worth of U.S. papers to CNHI. The original agreement called for just $3 million worth of non-competes, split between Hollinger

International and its parent company. But documents showed that just before the deal closed, Radler instructed Kipnis, Hollinger International's lawyer, to create a new non-compete agreement so that $9.5 million worth of the proceeds would go to himself, Black, Boultbee, and Atkinson. Black and Radler received $4.3 million apiece, while Atkinson and Boultbee each got $450,000. Kipnis, meanwhile, received a bonus of $100,000. Once again, the special committee could find no record of these payments ever being approved by Hollinger International's board.[9]

There was more. In February 2001, the four executives received $5.5 million for agreeing not to compete with American Publishing, a Hollinger International subsidiary that was essentially dormant. This was the most dumbfounding of all: the executives were getting paid for agreeing not to compete with themselves. Not that there was much to compete with. American Publishing, by this point, had disposed of virtually all of its newspapers. Nevertheless, Black and Radler were each paid $2.6 million, while Boultbee and Atkinson each received $137,500. Oddly, even though the cheques were issued in February, the special committee discovered they were backdated to December to make it look like the executives were paid the previous year. Again, the board was left in the dark: there was evidently no review and no approval.[10]

By now an unmistakable pattern had emerged. The details changed from deal to deal, but the essential form remained the same. As the special committee would later allege in a lawsuit, it looked like Black and his closest allies had systematically "looted" the company by arranging lucrative payments to themselves.[11]

When the committee's lawyers interviewed Radler in Chicago, a session that spanned twelve hours over two days, they found him less than helpful. Radler, known for his meticulous attention to detail and his almost photographic recall of past business dealings, had suddenly gone amnesiac. He would often just shrug and say, "I don't know," or "I don't recall." At other times, he would instruct the lawyers to "Talk to Crossharbour," a cynical reference to Black's highly prized peerage. Radler admitted there were some details he could not recall about the payments. However, he defended his poor recollection by pointing out that the special committee and its legal counsel had asked him before-hand not to refresh his memory by reviewing company files or speaking with other officials at Hollinger International.

In late October, the special committee convened at Breeden's for one of its weekly meetings. Savage had flown in from Toronto, while Seitz had made his way from Hong Kong, where he had been attending a board meeting for a local telecommunications company. They were greeted by a new series of black binders on the U.S. newspaper deals, and the contents were ominous. Sceptical committee members could no longer dismiss the unusual payments to Black or his associates as freak occurrences or the products of some kind of administrative bungling. Everyone agreed that the problems that had been unearthed pointed towards something far more sinister. It was difficult to come to any conclusion other than that executives at Hollinger International were purposely siphoning money from the company. Things had reached a turning point.

Originally, the committee estimated that it would issue just a single report after the investigation was wrapped up, likely in January or February 2004. But the discovery of these suspicious non-compete payments had effectively killed that timetable. As Breeden reminded everyone at the table, the discovery meant that Hollinger International's financial statements would have to be corrected before the company issued its quarterly report the following month. That, in turn, meant the special committee would have to go public with some of its findings, even though it was only partway through its probe. The battle plan was etched in marker on a large board in the centre of Breeden's office. The special committee would have to take immediate steps to recover the money. They would have to force a number of executives to resign. And, barring some sort of miraculous explanation that would account for this mess, they might even have to fire Conrad Black.

The stage was set for a showdown. But the special committee knew they would need some allies on the board if they wanted to stand any chance of winning.

One of the biggest sources of consternation for the special committee as its investigation advanced was the seeming lassitude of Hollinger International's directors. At the centre of the scrutiny was the trio of Thompson, Burt, and Kravis, who collectively made up the audit committee. In deal after deal after deal, it looked as though they were giving their endorsement without a moment's hesitation. They seldom hired their own financial advisers or sought independent fairness opinions and failed to prevent Hollinger International executives from negotiating lucrative non-compete payments on their own behalf. Even when it appeared they had been misled, as in the CanWest sale, there was no indication they asked the sort of probing questions that might have uncovered what was really going on.[12]

In the case of the management fees Hollinger International paid to Ravelston each year, totalling more than $220 million since 1997, the audit committee never hired an outside expert to determine whether the agreement was fair. Instead, they negotiated the fees in a less formal manner: once a year, after consulting with Black and Boultbee, Radler would tell Thompson how much money Ravelston wanted and the fees would often be agreed upon over lunch in a quick and cursory fashion.[13] The audit committee never received any justification for the fee, or a breakdown of how the proceeds would be used, but that didn't deter the directors, who invariably conferred their blessing. It was like clockwork.[14]

But the problem wasn't just the audit committee. Other directors on the board seemed eerily quiet in the face of problematic issues. Richard Perle, nicknamed the "Prince of Darkness" during the Cold War for his opposition to nuclear arms reduction, was a prime example. The special committee learned he had received $300,000 a year to head up one of the company's subsidiaries, Hollinger Digital, but the salary had never been disclosed publicly. In addition, Hollinger International had invested $2.5 million in Perle's venture capital company, Trireme Partners, which invests in homeland security firms.[15] The committee discovered that Black and Kissinger also served as advisers to Perle's company, adding to the possible conflicts of interest.

It was not the sort of thing that inspired confidence in the board of Hollinger International.

As a member of the executive committee with Black and Radler, Perle frequently signed off on transactions before they even went to the board for approval. For example, the executive committee had authorized Hollinger International to buy the $8 million worth of FDR memorabilia in early 2001. However, they waited nearly two years before informing the board and presenting the matter for retroactive approval. The complete disregard for corporate protocol, and the rather unseemly coincidence of Black's biography of the late president, hardly seemed to register. The board had signed off on the acquisition in December 2002, and the special committee could find no indication that anyone raised concerns about the matter.

Although Jereski and other major investors had discovered the suspicious-looking acquisition, the public did not learn about the FDR papers until August 17, 2003, when the special committee was in the early stages of its investigation. Stephanie Kirchgaessner, a reporter with the *Financial Times*, published a story on the newspaper's website that day after stumbling over a brief mention of the acquisition buried deep within Hollinger International's annual report. Even though Black had just completed a book on FDR, he was remarkably indifferent to any appearance of conflict. The company had spent the money, he explained, because "$8 million was not something I was prepared to spend."

Newspapers around the world jumped on the story. Unlike the shareholders' complaints about Black, which tended to involve complicated business language and arcane issues like "non-compete" payments, the FDR purchase was something that virtually any reader could grasp. The "Roosevelt papers" became the enduring symbol of Black's financial shenanigans at Hollinger International, much as the infamous vodka-squirting ice sculpture of Michelangelo's *David* had come to represent the executive excess at Tyco International, another company engulfed by scandal. Either unable or unwilling to comprehend the public's intolerance for corporate greed, Black sought to quell the growing uproar by explaining, in a letter to the *Financial Times*, that the FDR collection was simply a shrewd corporate investment that had already appreciated in value. "I do not believe this is a matter of legitimate controversy," he said.[16] Once again, instead of trying to placate investors with an apology and take responsibility for his actions, Black refused to acknowledge that he had done anything wrong.

———

The special committee members were in a tricky position. On the one hand, they believed the company's directors had been shockingly blind to Black's behaviour and ineffectual in carrying out their responsibilities. On the other, they needed Thompson and Burt's cooperation if they were going to confront Black. Kravis, the third audit committee director, had resigned suddenly in the first week of October, telling Black that she chose to step down because her husband, Henry Kravis, was preparing some newspaper bids that might place her in a conflicted position. She made no mention of the fact she was on the board a few years earlier when one of her husband's companies was negotiating a newspaper deal with Hollinger International.[17]

Some members of the special committee, like Savage, warned that the committee could not become too friendly with the other directors, because at some point it might have to take action against them for their poor performance. But Paris insisted they should be pragmatic: Black and the other executives were the primary targets here, and in order to get Hollinger International's money back—and to effect any kind of management changes—they needed to have a majority of directors on their side.

At the end of October, the special committee contacted Thompson and Burt to explain what it had found. Both men had shrewd political instincts, and they proved ready allies. They knew by then which way the wind was blowing. If they sided with Black when the special committee released its explosive report, it might look as if they had colluded with executives to bilk the company. Clearly, it wasn't much of a choice: they would cooperate with the investigation. The committee figured it could count on the support of Thompson, Burt, and Shmuel Meitar, the Israeli businessman. They weren't so sure about Kissinger and Perle, both of whom had close ties to Black. But if things degenerated into a brawl, and Black attempted to shut them down with a vote, they felt that at least they had a fighting chance.

———

Black had been busy while the special committee was conducting its investigation. He was preparing for an international book tour to accompany the fall launch of *Franklin Delano Roosevelt: Champion of Freedom,* his voluminous 1,280-page biography of FDR. The book was a sore point for investors, and not just because Hollinger International had dumped millions of dollars into FDR collectibles that were scattered throughout Black's homes. Investors raised the rather obvious question of whether the CEO of a billion-dollar media company could justify handsome financial rewards and perquisites if in fact he was spending his waking hours on political scholarship rather than newspapers.

Unbeknownst to the special committee, however, Black was dabbling in some other extracurricular activities. He was quietly scrounging for money, or even a possible buyer, to bail out Hollinger International's cash-strapped parent, Hollinger Inc., whose financial condition had been steadily weakening. The company had averted a looming crisis in March, after borrowing $120 million to repay its bank debt—but meeting the payments, based on a near-usurious interest rate of close to 13 percent, was proving to be a challenge. Ravelston, Black's private company, had promised to help with the payments by passing along some of the rich management fees it received from Hollinger International, but Black could see where things were headed: the special committee was investigating those fees at the moment, and there was a decent chance they might begin to dry up, if not disappear altogether. After Hollinger Inc.'s annual meeting in Toronto in June 2003, he had hired Westwind Partners, a small Bay Street investment banking firm, to help.

In an interview later that summer, Black cast the looming cash crunch at the Toronto parent as a temporary obstacle that had been triggered by misguided shareholder attacks on both him and Hollinger International. "It is a liquidity problem only because the corporate governance terrorists in the United States have stirred up such a fuss …" he claimed.[18] Regardless of the truth of this statement, one thing was undeniable: Black needed cash to meet an interest payment on the loan, and he needed it by the spring.

While the special committee was turning up signs of the suspicious non-compete payments, Black was holding talks with sixty-one-year-old billionaire and Palm Beach neighbour Nelson Peltz, whose Triarc Companies, Inc. controls the Arby's fast-food chain. The roast-beef king, who made a small fortune by selling the rights to Snapple fruit juices, was one of several high-profile financiers sniffing around Black's newspapers. Some viewed Black's troubles as an easy way to seize control of well-regarded newspaper titles like the *Telegraph* and *Chicago Sun-Times,* while others were considering pumping money into Hollinger Inc., the parent company, in exchange for an ownership stake. Even Hungarian philanthropist George Soros, one of the world's richest men, contacted Black about Hollinger Inc.

The most ardent suitors, however, continued to be the Barclay brothers, a pair of wealthy and reclusive British twins. Sir David Barclay had sent Black a letter after Hollinger International's annual meeting in May, stating that he and his brother were interested in buying Black's controlling stake in the company. Black quickly replied that neither Hollinger International nor the *Telegraph*—the true object of the Barclays' affection—was up for sale. Now, in late October, Sir David was at it again, reiterating his desire to scoop up the company. Black may have needed financing, but the situation was not yet so dire that he was ready to part with the very newspaper that had brought him both title and influence. Exasperated, he sent another letter, urging the brothers to quit pestering him.

You have made your desire to buy the Telegraph *abundantly clear. You may recall that when we actually met we agreed I would be mad to sell it. In the unlikely event that my views on this subject change, I will not forget your interest. Please keep in mind how tiresome you would find it if every time I saw a negative article about you in the press I wrote of my unquenchable desire to buy an asset of yours that is not for sale. I'm happy to hear from you, but not on this subject again, please. Regards, Conrad Black.*[19]

On October 30, 2003, Atkinson, Boultbee, and Creasey phoned Black at Hollinger International's Manhattan office with deeply disturbing news. Kipnis, the company's in-house lawyer, had been reviewing financial statements for an upcoming financing and could not find any audit committee approval for two sets of non-compete payments. As Black could well anticipate, the special committee would take swift action if it believed that millions of dollars of Hollinger International's money had been funnelled to executives without the board's consent. From his office, he launched a flurry of calls and emails to gather more information. Kipnis was not much help. He told Black that he had given all of his records to the special committee and hadn't made any copies. Black then asked his assistant at Hollinger Inc. to begin sorting through documents at 10 Toronto Street for some evidence that these payments had actually passed through the proper channels.

Atkinson, meanwhile, had launched his own probe into the non-compete payments on behalf of the Toronto parent. The balding lawyer had joined Hollinger Inc.'s board in 1996 after leaving his private practice to become the company's general counsel. He had been elected to Hollinger International's board eighteen months earlier, when he was promoted to executive vice-president. Although he had been with the Hollinger group for only seven years, Atkinson had done work for Black's companies since 1979 as a lawyer with Aird & Berlis LLP. Regarded as a tough and intelligent litigator, in the 1990s he actually spearheaded a number of Black's libel suits against Canadian newspapers.

Of all the members of Black's inner circle, the special committee believed, Atkinson was the most penitent about receiving the non-compete payments. In his private emails to Black, he appeared conflicted about the arrangements, and in some cases he urged Black to scrap lavish indulgences like the private jets and cut the management fees to Ravelston.[20] In the first week of November, Atkinson met with the audit committee at Burt's office in Washington, D.C., and agreed to repay the $600,000 in non-compete payments he had received. Atkinson was supposed to pay 10 percent of this amount by the end of the year, but within a few weeks, he had sent Hollinger International a cheque for $350,000. As Burt later recalled in a court deposition,

It was very sad.... He was very contrite. He said that he had been asked to lie, cover up. There were these documents that were postdated. And it was essentially he described a conspiracy. He was clearly a kind of broken man.[21]

A few days after this meeting, on Thursday, November 6, the special committee sprang into action. It sent a letter to Black, Atkinson, Radler, and Boultbee, explaining that they could not find any board approval for the non-compete agreements, and demanded the executives provide a written explanation for the payments by the following Monday at noon.

In public, Black did an admirable job of maintaining a calm exterior. On Thursday evening, after he received the unnerving letter from the special committee, he travelled seven blocks north of his Park Avenue condo on the Upper East Side to the Council on Foreign Relations, where he was scheduled to begin his book tour with a presentation to a small, invitation-only crowd of about fifty people. The lavishly restored Harold Pratt House, home to the Council, was, when it was built in 1919, one of the city's most celebrated mansions. A gently curving marble staircase, bordered by an iron balustrade, occupies the main foyer and whisks guests into a series of interlocking rooms filled with chandeliers, oriental rugs, and fabric-panelled walls.

Tonight, however, Black was speaking in the newly designed Peter G. Peterson Hall, a large, modern-looking space with bleached hardwood floors and an arched ceiling. For two hours, Black sat next to moderator Harold Evans, the former president of the Random House Trade Group and husband of well-known New York media celebrity Tina Brown, and held forth on numerable aspects of Roosevelt's life, from his decisions on foreign policy to his apparently mirthless relationship with his wife, Eleanor.[22] Black, outfitted in a dark blue nailhead suit and striped tie, was at his charming best, displaying a deft command of historical detail one minute and engaging the attendees with humorous yarns the next. No one in the crowd could have guessed that earlier that day he had received a letter that might spell the demise of his once-prodigious empire.

No one, that is, except Paul Healy. Healy regarded Black's performance with a mixture of awe and admiration. Everything that had drawn him to Black in the beginning—the charisma, the fierce intelligence, the playful wit and imposing presence, all stripped of pretension—was on full display. After Black finished his talk and began mingling with the guests, Healy strolled up and offered his congratulations. The two men shook hands, and a glowing Black told his vice-president how much he appreciated his presence at the reading. Healy thanked him and quickly headed for the exit. A lump had formed in his throat, and as he walked out into the chill Manhattan night, he found himself on the verge of tears. It had been almost possible tonight, for a fleeting moment at least, to forget about the shareholder siege and the special committee investigation. But in his gut, Healy knew how things were going to turn out.

Black would soon be in the fight of his life.

CHAPTER ELEVEN

You Want to Fight?

AFTER YEARS OF SHAREHOLDER COMPLAINTS, and four months of internal investigation, the noose had finally begun to tighten around Black and his clan of insiders at Hollinger International. No one knew this better than Black himself. Directors like Thompson and Burt, whom he had personally recruited to the company's board and regarded as friends, had evidently turned against him and were now working closely with his opponents on the special committee. Black had always shown a remarkable ability to deflect criticism, as was apparent when he casually dismissed any notion of impropriety involving the FDR memorabilia—but this time was different. Taking company money without proper approval was the equivalent of a mortal corporate sin, and unless he could convince Breeden and the others that there had been some sort of honest mistake, he would be crucified. His control of the Hollinger group of companies, which he had painstakingly assembled over the past twenty-five years, was hanging in the balance.

Black's most pressing difficulty was time. The internal probe had proceeded in a slow, deliberate fashion through much of the summer and fall, but now events were unfolding with alarming speed. The special committee had written Black a letter demanding that he explain why he and other executives had received non-compete payments without the board's approval. He was no longer dealing with a group of disgruntled shareholders who could be appeased temporarily with promises. The special committee wanted answers, and it wanted them now. Black would have to scramble.

———

Cornered, and increasingly isolated from his allies, Black retreated to his Park Avenue home on Sunday, November 9, 2003, where he began crafting his response to the special committee. The luxurious co-operative, which occupies the entire third floor of a thirteen-storey brick building on one of the most expensive stretches of real estate in New York, was acquired by a Hollinger Inc. subsidiary in 1994 for about $3 million. Black and Amiel purchased the home from the company in 2000, but paid $2.5 million less than its market value.[1] The couple had made extensive renovations since then under the guiding eye of David Mlinaric, the same designer who had overseen the refurbishments at their homes in London, Palm Beach, and Toronto.

Amidst this opulence, Black made one last desperate effort to stave off an ugly collision between him, Breeden, and the special committee members. He had authored an eight-page letter (written in the third person, since it would technically be signed and delivered by his recently appointed Delaware lawyer, Jesse Finkelstein),[2] attempting to justify the payments he and other executives had received. The general tone of Black's response was a mixture of confusion and disbelief. He admitted the committee's findings were "disappointing and disconcerting" and promised that "the absence of evidence of approval by the audit committee is mystifying to everyone." If board approval was lacking in some instances, it was probably just the result of "innocent mistakes" or procedural errors. In Black's opinion, this had all been an unfortunate misunderstanding, a little local difficulty that could be satisfactorily swept aside without much fuss and which certainly did not require the involvement of securities regulators.

Black said he had conducted "extensive research" into the allegations since learning of the problems a little over a week earlier, including discussions with some of his fellow executives, and he then proceeded to offer up some unconvincing explanations for just about every one of the special committee's concerns. Broadly speaking, there were two main issues: the $15.6 million in non-compete payments that went to Black, Radler, Boultbee, and Atkinson; and the $16.55 million worth of payments that went to Hollinger Inc., the parent company.

The first matter was easy enough to explain, Black wrote. In one instance, Radler mistakenly believed that the company's lawyer, Mark Kipnis, had received the audit committee's approval to pay $9.5 million in non-competes to Black and the other executives. In the so-called "sham" deal with American Publishing that had raised the antennae of investigators—since it was a Hollinger International subsidiary—Black offered a more convoluted explanation: the $5.5 million in non-competes that he and the other officials had received from American Publishing were not really non-competes at all, but management fees that had been reclassified in order to give the executives beneficial tax treatment. Because of a mix-up, Hollinger International was not told of the arrangement and thus failed to deduct this amount from the annual management fees it sent to Black's private holding company, Ravelston. It was all very confusing.

Next, Black tackled the $16.55 million in non-compete payments to Hollinger Inc. This situation was a little different, in that none of these payments was ever disclosed publicly. However, Black had a ready scapegoat. In each of these cases, Black said, Radler had assumed Kipnis would bring these payments to the audit committee for approval. For whatever reason, Kipnis did not, something that Black "reluctantly considers to be negligent on Mr. Kipnis's part."

In characteristic fashion, Black was shifting the blame to underlings. After chiding Kipnis for being "so unenterprising and lacking in thoroughness," Black took a swipe at KPMG LLP, the company's auditors.

His letter stated that the "failure of the auditors to raise a single question about any of these payments in the last four years is not a flattering reflection of their thoroughness," and that one of KPMG's partners, Marilyn Stitt, had notes indicating that the non-compete payments had been discussed by Hollinger International's audit committee. "She has stated that these payments were approved," the letter continued, referencing a discussion Ms. Stitt had with directors at the parent company, Hollinger Inc.[3]

Even the audit committee was singled out for its lack of attentiveness. Some of the non-compete payments to executives had been publicly disclosed—albeit very late—in regulatory reports that the audit committee had reviewed and approved. If the committee had never signed off on the payments, why hadn't the independent directors sounded an alarm when the reports were published? And why had Thompson, Black asked, assured lawyers in a meeting in the spring of 2003 that all of the approvals outlined in the company's previous filings were accurate? Black had a ready answer:

The only plausible explanations ... of the state of the documentation are that either the discussions of these matters at the Hollinger International Audit Committee concluded by approving the payments without, by an oversight, a formal resolution, or that the company secretary inexplicably omitted to record the resolution.

So that was that. Kipnis had been irresponsible, the auditors were napping, the audit committee may have been forgetful, or the company secretary failed to take decent notes. The only person not personally accountable for these unseemly dealings, according to Black, was Black himself—the very person on whose watch they occurred. Rather than express contrition, Black insisted there was a "collective responsibility for a regrettable lapse and for the failure for several years to detect and correct that lapse when it would have been easy to do."

These sorts of tortuous explanations occupied nearly six full pages of the letter. Although Black was trying to cast doubt on some of the special committee's allegations, it seemed like a halfhearted response; his writing was curiously devoid of the indignation and combative spark that one had come to expect from him when he was under attack. As surprising as this may have been to the members of the special committee, it paled in comparison to the bombshell Black casually dropped at the end of the letter: he was prepared to put his beloved newspaper titles on the auction block in an attempt to quell the controversy.

He conceded that he had been holding intensive negotiations for the past five months to fix the "relatively minor" financial problems at Hollinger International's Toronto parent, but his progress had been hampered by the uncertainty stemming from the special committee's investigation. As a result, he suggested the company publicly announce that it was considering the sale of some or all of its assets—a "painful course," but one Black predicted would "break the informal cartel" of potential investors who were too nervous to get involved with Hollinger International. As the letter stated,

> *The timing and circumstances of a possible sale are not fortuitous, but the indefinite continuation of the present conditions, deliberately misreported by some of the company's competitors, is … intolerable.*

On the surface, it looked like a bewildering capitulation. Only days earlier, Black had told the Barclays he had no interest in relinquishing the *Telegraph,* the paper that had jump-started his ascension to the House of Lords and ushered him into some of London's most exclusive circles. Yet upon further reflection, it made a certain degree of sense. Black would rather rescue his reputation by exiting the company through asset sales than risk becoming embroiled in a regulatory investigation. The conclusion of his letter was particularly telling. In a rather deferential tone, he asked the committee to use its "undoubtedly decisive influence" to "avoid premature and unjustifiably damaging disclosures." Black, fearing that Breeden still exerted influence at the SEC, was prepared to do almost anything to discourage the regulators from becoming involved. Perhaps a sale of the company would keep them away.

In an email to Atkinson, his long-time legal adviser, Black predicted his letter of response would help to smooth over the current turmoil. It didn't exactly proclaim victory, but it left the indelible impression that Black had somehow managed to avert a disaster. He predicted,

> *I think my (technically Jesse Finkelstein's) letter, setting out a possible road map to a satisfactory end of the immersion in this quagmire, has had some effect.*

———

There was no shortage of suitors for Black's media assets: powerful investment funds, media companies, and independent financiers had shown a willingness to invest in his newspaper titles. But none had proven as persistent as the Barclay brothers. The sixty-eight-year-old identical twins, who controlled a diversified empire of shipping interests, London's prestigious Ritz Hotel, casinos, and regional newspapers including *The Scotsman,* zealously guarded their privacy. They so rarely appeared in public or granted media interviews that when they were knighted in 2000, reporters quipped that the twins could only be distinguished by their hair (Frederick parts his to the left and David to the right). Adding to their mystique, the pair seclude their families in what has been described as a "mock-Gothic fortress" on a 160-acre Channel island called Brecqhou, which they purchased in 1993.[4]

No one understood the Barclays' desire for the *Telegraph* better than Black. On Tuesday, November 11, 2003, just a day after he had sent his response to the special committee and reluctantly proposed a possible sale of Hollinger International, he sent the brothers a letter and scheduled a meeting.

> *I have had a thought that may be worthy of discussion, based on our previous correspondence. Could you tell me how I might telephone you Wednesday, November 12, at between 5 and 7 London time, or suggest a couple of other times that might work and I will try to hit one of*

them? I wouldn't want you to think I was trying to avoid you, but I have not, until now, been able to think of a suitable subject for a talk.[5]

Not long afterward, Black received a confidential email from David Barclay. He and his brother Frederick had been so delighted by Black's about-face on the potential sale of the *Telegraph* that David's son Aidan was rushing to New York for a hastily convened conference with Black. David wanted Hollinger International's CEO to know that if he consummated a deal with the Barclays he could remain an investor in the prized London newspaper. "I believe we can find a way of working together," he said.

There was one other person Black had to contact now that an auction of Hollinger International appeared inevitable. Like the Barclays, Bruce Wasserstein, head of the New York investment banking firm Lazard Frères & Co., had also been dogging Black for months in hopes of landing a lucrative assignment. Wasserstein, a pudgy mergers and acquisitions specialist, had long been regarded as one of Wall Street's most famous deal-makers. Nicknamed "Bid-'em-up Bruce" for his ability to wrangle top dollar from buyers, he had assisted Henry Kravis's leveraged buyout firm, Kohlberg Kravis Roberts (KKR), in its 1989 takeover of RJR Nabisco and later advised internet titan AOL on its merger with Time Warner. Wasserstein had visited Black in May at his ornate London townhouse to see if there might be a role for Lazard in helping Hollinger International attract investors or orchestrate a sale. Black, however, wasn't ready to formally hire an investment banker, and he rebuffed Wasserstein much as he had initially dismissed the Barclay brothers. Wasserstein and his colleague Louis Zachary nevertheless kept in regular contact with Black throughout the summer, as he was courting investors to help ease the financial burden at Hollinger Inc., the Toronto parent.

Eventually their persistence paid dividends. On the same day that he wrote the Barclays to arrange a meeting, Black sent a brief email to Jim McDonough, the Chicago-based lawyer for Hollinger International's audit committee. He told McDonough that he planned to call a board meeting later that week so that Lazard could be hired to explore a "recapitalization of the group, a sale of some assets, and an outright sale of the company."[6] Wasserstein had finally gotten his assignment.

———

The following day, a Wednesday, Black boarded Hollinger International's Gulfstream jet and flew to Washington, D.C., for another leg of his book tour. He was one of seventy authors, including General Wesley Clark, who had descended that afternoon on the National Press Club, just a few blocks' stroll from the White House, for an annual book fair. Hundreds of people packed the club's Ballroom, a huge, flag-filled, blue-carpeted space where a lacquered wooden ceiling cuts a zigzag pattern eighteen feet above the floor. Black, dressed in a charcoal-grey suit, pale grey shirt, and a tie flecked with red and navy blue, glad-handed with the other authors and signed copies of his new book for autograph seekers. He even good-naturedly huckstered the weighty biography to prospective buyers: "A bargain at twice the price," he shouted out as passersby filed past his table.

Yet he was not nearly so cheerful with the throng of reporters who had braved the rain in order to pepper him with questions on his way into the fair. "Wait for it. Call me on Friday," he snapped to one reporter, who inquired whether Nelson Peltz, the financier, was preparing to make an investment in Hollinger Inc. Asked whether the company would announce a refinancing by the end of the week, Black responded icily: "That's a reasonable surmise."

In fact, Black had emailed Thompson earlier that day and told him that Lazard should be hired to assess the company's strategic options. Thompson replied with a request: would Black be able to meet with him and Paris at Hollinger International's offices tomorrow? There was something they needed to discuss. Black said he would be there. This already hectic week was about to become even more frenetic, and the next three days would prove to be the most pivotal in Black's career.

———

At 1:00 P.M. on Thursday, November 13, four men walked into the sumptuously appointed boardroom at Hollinger International's Fifth Avenue offices—the one decorated with FDR memorabilia—and shut the door. Black was waiting for them, alone. He had been expecting Paris and Thompson, but did not know that Breeden and McDonough would also be attending the meeting. The visitors seated themselves around the large mahogany table, while Paris quickly got to the point.

The special committee members had received Black's letter of response just three days earlier, but after reviewing its contents in detail, they remained unmoved: as far as they were concerned, there was still no evidence that the $32.15 million in non-compete payments to executives and Hollinger Inc. was approved. The full amount would have to be repaid, including a 10-percent down payment by the end of the year, and Black was expected to use his clout to ensure that Hollinger Inc. also turned over the money it had received.

But the special committee was not content merely to recover this money and sever the prodigious stream of management fees that flowed to Black's private holding company, Ravelston. It wanted an overhaul of Hollinger International's entire front office, including the removal of Black. Paris did not mince his words. He told Black he would resort to "draconian measures," including possible legal action, if Black did not resign as CEO and cease acting as the public face of the company. Furthermore, Radler would be asked to step down from the board, relinquish his executive titles, and resign as publisher of the *Chicago Sun-Times*. Boultbee would be asked to go. Atkinson would be forced off the board but could maintain his management title for a six-month transition period. Black was told that if he did not co-operate with the special committee's requests, Hollinger International would immediately cut off the management fees to Ravelston and forward the entire matter to the SEC.[7]

Black was shell-shocked. He remonstrated against being removed as CEO and insisted it would be "too humiliating" if he were replaced by Paris, a man with no newspaper experience. Black wasn't accustomed to being bullied, and his normal instinct would be to fight back, yet this last threat had struck a nerve. Sitting across the table from him was Breeden, the former head of the SEC. Black harboured little doubt that if the conflict escalated, Breeden had the power to incite a regulatory investigation into Hollinger International and the allegations of improper payments to executives. This was a ghastly prospect, and one that Black wanted to avoid at almost any cost.

He leaned over to Breeden and, maintaining his innocence, asked whether the SEC would stay out of Hollinger International's affairs if he co-operated with the committee's demands. "You're the former chairman of the agency," Black said. "Surely they listen to you."

"Yes, but that doesn't guarantee you anything," Breeden replied.

Black pressed on. If he agreed to the special committee's demands, he wanted to be sure that Breeden would vouch for him with the SEC and hopefully persuade the regulator not to launch its own investigation. "But you'll at least tell them about the agreement we reached?" Black asked.

Breeden felt that Black was trying to put words in his mouth. Black seemed determined to cling to the belief that Breeden could somehow dictate which cases the SEC decided to pursue. "Yes, I will represent and describe this process as it happened," he said. "[But] I'm not promising that I have any special influence with the SEC."

Black had good reason to be fearful of regulatory scrutiny. More than twenty years earlier, he had endured a frightening run-in with the U.S. regulator. In November 1982, Norcen Energy Resources Ltd., a company controlled by Black, had acquired a small stake in Hanna Mining of Cleveland, Ohio. Norcen made a filing with the SEC saying it was a passive investor, but Hanna, convinced Black was trying to mount a hostile takeover of the company, launched a lawsuit and demanded to see Norcen's internal documents. What they found looked damning. According to records of a board meeting two months earlier, Norcen had made the investment "with the ultimate purpose of acquiring a 51-percent interest" in Hanna, which, if true, appeared to contradict Norven's earlier filings with the U.S. regulator.

Just as he had blamed Kipnis for not getting the non-compete payments approved, Black had blamed the Norcen fiasco on one of his subordinates. In a high-profile trial in Ohio, during the spring of 1983, Black insisted he had mistakenly signed off on the SEC filings without reading the board minutes closely enough. In the end, Black did not admit any wrongdoing, but he was forced to sign a so-called "consent decree" with the SEC, essentially a strict promise never to run afoul of U.S. securities laws again. These decrees are like court orders: if you violate them, even through a minor infraction, you automatically open yourself up to potential criminal prosecution.

Black's relatively controlled response to the special committee's demands had caught his visitors off guard. They had expected a violent reaction, but instead he seemed distracted and repeatedly excused himself from the room. At one point he wandered down the corridor to his office to chat with David Boies, a lawyer he had hired only days earlier. Boies was a legendary litigator, having served as a special trial lawyer for the U.S. Department of Justice in its successful antitrust suit against Microsoft Corp. He had also represented former U.S. vice-president Al Gore in his challenge of the Florida vote recount during the 2000 election campaign against George W. Bush. The sixty-two-year-old was arguably just as famous for his unconventional attire, including a penchant for blue-striped shirts and cheap department-store suits, which he often wore to court with a pair of black sneakers. So great a legal celebrity was Boies that in 1999 he was inducted into the *Vanity Fair* Hall of Fame along with the cast of *The Sopranos* and Tour de France champion Lance Armstrong. It was a little late in the game for Black to be hiring new lawyers, but he needed all the legal firepower he could get.

Boies remained in Black's office while his client concluded the meeting with Paris, Breeden, Thompson, and McDonough. The two sides had not been able to come to an agreement, and it was clear that Black resented the special committee's demands. Yet in a baffling gesture, Black invited his adversaries for dinner that evening at Le Cirque, the fashionable and expensive Manhattan restaurant. The four men were mystified, but they accepted the offer before walking the short distance to the Citigroup Center, a hulking aluminum and glass skyscraper, where they were scheduled to hold a meeting at O'Melveny & Myers with the special committee's lawyers.

———

Paris kicked off the meeting at O'Melveny at about 4 P.M. by recapping the meeting with Black earlier that afternoon. He was joined at the table by Breeden, Thompson, McDonough, and Savage, who had just flown in from Toronto. Jonathan Rosenberg, the special committee's lawyer, was in attendance, and Seitz, who was in Hong Kong, listened in by phone. The group discussed its options and quickly agreed on continuing their current course of action: Black and other executives would have to be removed, the non-competes would have to be repaid, and the management fee contract with Ravelston would have to be severed eventually. All of this would have to be done on an urgent basis, so that Hollinger International could file its quarterly financial statements in a timely fashion.

That was only part of the work that lay ahead of them. Originally, the special committee had been created with a fairly straightforward mandate: investigate Tweedy Browne's allegations and, if necessary, take appropriate action to remedy the situation. But Black's recent letter had suddenly presented Paris, Seitz, and Savage with added responsibilities. As directors of Hollinger International, they would now have to help oversee the sale of the entire company, or various of its newspaper titles. It was a distraction, one that would almost certainly delay them in completing their investigation.

After the meeting ended, Paris, Breeden, and Savage moved into another room and phoned a handful of independent directors, including Henry Kissinger, who was in Beijing. They quickly briefed the former secretary of state on their conclusions and their plan to unseat Black as head of the company. Kissinger, one of Black's closest friends on the board, said very little, but did have one question. "What does Raymond think?" he asked in reference to Seitz, the one member of the special committee he knew personally. Paris gave Kissinger Seitz's number in Hong Kong and suggested the two men discuss the matter directly.

In the middle of the night, Seitz was awoken by a phone call. For several days he had gotten virtually no sleep: he would join Hollinger International teleconferences at about 11:00 P.M. Hong Kong time and often remain on the line for four or five hours. Tonight was the first time he had retired at a decent hour, and now Kissinger was calling in a flustered state. He had been surprised by the gravity and breadth of the special committee's findings, and he wanted to know whether Seitz supported the decision to unseat Black from Hollinger International's executive suite. Seitz confirmed that yes, he did support the move, and spent some time walking Kissinger through the results of the investigation. In the end, however reluctantly, Kissinger accepted the special committee's conclusion.

Paris, Thompson, Breeden, and Savage, meanwhile, left to meet Black at Le Cirque.

———

Black, who had successfully wined, dined, and flattered so many power-ful people over the years, appeared to be making a brazen attempt to do the same with the special committee. Located in the historic Villard Houses on Madison Avenue, Le Cirque is a mishmash of Renaissance and modern design: carved walnut walls, gilt wainscotting, elaborate chandeliers, and marble fireplaces are juxtaposed with purple mohair chairs, blown-glass clowns and strongmen, and vividly coloured carpets. The bar is located in a high-arching two-storey room, decorated almost entirely in gold, that features a painted mural at either end.

Black quickly got to business. One of his gravest concerns, he told his dinner guests, was the precarious financial health of Hollinger Inc., the Toronto parent, which relied almost exclusively upon Ravelston for its income. If Ravelston was no longer allowed to collect management fees from Hollinger International, the parent company would be unable to pay back its debt. Normally, Black would have tried to refinance the company with outside help, but he believed potential investors were being scared off by the special committee's investigation and the firestorm of media scrutiny it had generated.

The Hollinger International directors knew this was a problem and weren't totally unsympathetic. Over dinner, Thompson told Black that even though the Ravelston payment would be diminished, a large part of it could be paid up front to help the parent company survive until the investigation was finished. It was an olive branch of sorts, but not enough to make Black capitulate. Black, meanwhile, admitted to the group that he—not his lawyer Finkelstein—had been the principal author of the letter he had sent to the special committee earlier that week. After a wide-ranging conversation, which even included a chat about opera, the group disbanded and agreed to meet the following day, after the scheduled board meeting to hire Lazard. Hollinger International picked up the bill.

———

Bruce Wasserstein arrived at Hollinger International's offices the next morning, Friday, November 14, armed with a three-page report explaining how Lazard intended to market the company to suitors: the "strategic process." A week earlier, he had received an email from his partner Zachary, explaining how they should promote themselves to the Hollinger International directors. Even experienced bankers found the structure of Black's various companies incredibly complex.

> *Pitch is we know newspaper sector and buyers better than anyone else (both sides of the Atlantic), know [Hollinger International's] screwed-up structure and issues better than any other potential adviser given dialogue of the last five months, know special committee members well (especially Breeden and Paris), senior attention led by you.*[8]

Wasserstein unveiled an ambitious plan: they would contact prospective buyers by November 24, just ten days away, and distribute offering materials on December 8, with an eye toward having an agreement in place to sell some or all of Hollinger International's assets by March 1. If things went well, they might even be done by mid-February, but Wasserstein insisted the process would run smoothly only if Lazard was solely in charge of the auction. The investment bank did not want Black or the other executives confusing the process by attempting to seek out buyers on their own. The board agreed on the aggressive timetable, and Black voiced his support, although he made no mention to the board of his overture to the Barclays.

After the board meeting concluded, a small group of directors stayed behind and met with Black in the boardroom. Paris, Breeden, Thompson, and Savage were there, as was Meitar, the Israeli business-man, who had flown in that day. Black's mood that day had been oscil-lating between conciliation and defiance. While he had informally agreed to pay back any money that was improperly collected, he remained steadfastly opposed to the planned management changes. It was hard enough to step down from the top executive post and leave the day-to-day business operations in the hands of Paris. But the idea of turfing Radler, his staunch ally and a business partner since his earliest days as an entrepreneur, was too painful to contemplate. Black's anger, for the most part sublimated over the past several weeks, finally boiled over into a nasty tirade. This was what everyone had been expecting.

"If you want to fight, I'll fight," he snarled. "You can't push me around."

The members of the special committee had anticipated some sort of resistance and remained quiet until Black had exhausted his tantrum. Then Savage got up from the end of the conference table, walked toward Black, and took the seat beside him. In a stern but measured voice, he reiterated the committee's position: they were not going to back down on their demands to remove Radler immediately; they were not going to continue paying management fees to Ravelston after June; there would be one official process to seek out potential buyers for Hollinger International, the "strategic process"; and Lazard would effectively report to Paris and the as-yet-to-be-formed executive committee, which Black was welcome to join. All of this would be enshrined in a proposed restructuring agreement that the special committee wanted Black to sign.

Black was still not ready to commit to the bargain, but his almost chronic worries about the SEC's involvement suggested he was leaning toward co-operation. Once again, at the end of the meeting, he said he assumed that Breeden would let the SEC know that everything was being taken care of. And once again, Breeden told him he couldn't control the SEC. The awkwardness of Black's request was not lost on the other members of the committee. The securities watchdog had opened a file on Hollinger International after Tweedy's letter in May and had already made informal contact with the committee and its lawyers in the early fall. That very day, in fact, the company made a brief filing with the SEC explaining that the special committee had uncovered non-compete payments that were not publicly disclosed. "The Committees' investigation has determined that there are inaccuracies in prior public filings of the Company involving the amount, authorization and purpose of such payments, among other things," the filing read. As ominous as this sounded to investors, it was merely the beginning. The group agreed to hold yet another board meeting the next day, Saturday, to hammer out a resolution.

Black, meanwhile, believed his strategy was working. In an email that day to Boultbee, one of his right-hand men at Hollinger International, Black predicted that by striking an agreement with the special committee he could "head off" an SEC investigation. Boultbee was outraged at the suggestion he had done anything wrong by collecting non-compete payments, but Black assured him that an agreement was in everyone's best interests.

I agree with everything you wrote. I did my best for all of us and made it clear I had no authority to speak for anyone else. I tried to send you the term sheet. The only advantages of what is proposed are that it seems to head off a real investigation and we get the financial condition of [Hollinger Inc.] stabilized to June 1 and Breeden says he intends to finish his process by June 1. Of course it's a smear job, and the Audit Committee wriggles out by joining in the assault on us on these issues. However, when the smoke clears we should still have either a functioning business or a good deal of money. We can pick up the pieces then.[9]

———

On Saturday morning Black exchanged emails with McDonough, the audit committee's lawyer. The men were still haggling over the wording of the restructuring agreement, which was scheduled to be presented to the Hollinger International board that afternoon. Black had an objection: the seventh item listed on the email was designed to prevent him from interfering with Lazard's search for buyers. The original version read like this:

I will not support a transaction involving ownership interests in [Hollinger] Inc. if such a transaction would negatively affect [Hollinger] International's ability to consummate a transaction resulting from the strategic process.[10]

As far as Black was concerned, this was far too restrictive. The parent company, Hollinger Inc., was in poor financial condition, and he needed the flexibility to seek out financing that would keep it afloat. Black responded by email to McDonough and managed to win a key concession: he would not support a transaction that would "negatively affect consummation of a transaction resulting from the strategic process *unless* a Hollinger Inc. transaction is necessary to enable Hollinger Inc. to avoid a material default or insolvency (emphasis added)." In other words, Black could potentially seek out his own buyer or investor for Hollinger Inc., but only if he could demonstrate that the parent company was on the verge of financial collapse. The revised agreement also promised that in any event, Black would have to provide Hollinger International with as much

173

advance notice as reasonably possible if he ended up pursuing such a deal.

The board meeting, which was to be held by teleconference, had been scheduled to begin at 10 A.M., but Black wasn't quite ready, so it was delayed until 3 P.M. However, with directors waiting on the phone line, Black failed to appear for the 3 P.M. call as well. No explanation was given, but the board was told to stand by for further information. Finally, at 6 P.M., Kipnis contacted directors and told them the meeting was about to start but neglected to inform Savage, whom he believed would attend the meeting in person at Hollinger International's offices. Savage, however, was in Toronto and had decided to go out for dinner. He brought his cell phone with him, expecting that someone would call him when the teleconference was about to start, but nobody did. He missed most of the meeting.

The meeting was strained, even though Black and the committee had already discussed most of the issues relating to the payments over the past several days. At one point, Thompson disputed the suggestion he had ever approved the non-compete payments to executives and Hollinger Inc. Black, who was participating by phone along with Andrew Hayes, a lawyer from Boies's firm, seemed to agree, acknowledging that the payments he received "were unauthorized by the board" and "improperly disclosed" in Hollinger International's financial statements.[11]

His wife, however, was not so pliant. Amiel, normally a reserved presence at these meetings, was unusually vocal on the teleconference. She repeatedly interrupted, demanding that the board explain "why they are doing this" and scolding them that Black did "not have to go along with what they're saying." But she was the only loyalist to voice her objection. Thompson and Burt had given their allegiance to the special committee. Radler and Atkinson were about to be removed from the board. Colson could not do much if he wanted to keep his job at the *Telegraph,* and Kissinger, Perle, and Meitar had already been briefed on the investigation and wanted to avoid a nasty dispute.

The tension was momentarily broken when the line went dead, the blinds closed, and the lights went out. Someone had forgotten to unplug an automatic shut-off timer in Hollinger International's boardroom, leaving the group of lawyers in total darkness. But the disruption was only temporary. When the meeting resumed, Black ignored his wife's last-ditch attempts at persuasion. He had decided, however ruefully, that his best course of action was to bow to the special committee's demands and resign as CEO of the company he had built and controlled. As painful and humiliating as that might be, Black must have surmised that it was better to step away rather than risk inflaming Paris, Breeden, and potentially the SEC. He promised to repay the $7.2 million in non-compete payments he had received, and agreed to sign, the following day, a restructuring agreement filled with a number of measures, including the termination of the annual management fees to Ravelston and the removal of Radler and Boultbee, who were among his closest friends.

After a whirlwind week, just six days after he had written a letter of explanation to the special committee that he had hoped might scuttle this sort of confrontation, Black's reign was over.

He would be allowed to remain as chairman, a role in which, he pledged, he would devote his time and energy to helping Lazard with the strategic process to sell the company. What he didn't tell the board, however, was that he had already initiated private negotiations with a possible buyer, the Barclay brothers.

———

Shortly after lunch the next day, a Sunday, Black opened a hidden compartment behind a bookshelf in the office of his Park Avenue co-op and turned on his fax machine. He was there with his wife, Amiel, who had protested so vehemently against his capitulation the night before. But Black had followed through on his promise to sign the restructuring agreement, and he was sending a copy to the board. He would officially resign as CEO on Friday, November 21. All but ousted from the executive suite at Hollinger International, his influence sharply curtailed, he would turn his attention to the parent company, which he continued to rule with an iron fist.

At 4 P.M., he picked up the phone and dialled into a board meeting for Hollinger Inc. in Toronto. He announced to the company's directors that he had stepped down as CEO of the U.S. operating company and conceded that "it now appeared that certain inadvertencies may have taken place."[12] Black explained that there was allegedly no approval for the $32 million in payments to himself, Radler, Boultbee, Atkinson, and to Hollinger Inc.[13] Furthermore, the gravy train of annual management fees that Hollinger International had paid Ravelston over the years was halted. This was exceedingly bad news, since Ravelston routinely forwarded some of this money to Hollinger Inc. to help the parent company with its debt payments. There were tentative discussions to replace the annual fee with a monthly stipend of about $100,000 a month for its services, Black told the directors, but this was only a tiny fraction of the $2 million in monthly installments that Ravelston typically received.

The Hollinger Inc. directors, many of whom, like Fredrik Eaton and Douglas Bassett, lived in Toronto and had known Black for years, were not accustomed to seeing Black retreat. But it wasn't long before he provided them with a sliver of insight into his peaceable resignation. "Mr. Breeden will emphasize in discussions with the SEC that Hollinger International had co-operated fully with the special committee and complied with its requests."[14]

That same evening, Black's long-time deputy, David Radler, was also breaking the news to his subordinates. He placed some calls to his top editors at the *Sun-Times* from the tarmac of Chicago's O'Hare Airport, where he was waiting for Hollinger International's jet to fly him home to Vancouver. "I'm outta here," he told the editors. A major reorganization would be announced at Hollinger International the next morning, Radler said, and he was resigning as president of the company and as publisher of the *Sun-Times*. He instructed them that if they planned to write a news story on his departure, it should say that he was leaving to focus his attention on smaller, community newspapers. One of Radler's last orders to his *Sun-Times* editors was to leave his office untouched. He would be back, he explained, in a month or so.

Once Black signed the agreement, a team of lawyers, Hollinger International executives, directors, and public relations advisers went to work in Richard Breeden's converted dairy barn in Greenwich. Thompson and Paris made their way up the cast-iron circular stairway at about 5 P.M. for the inaugural meeting of the new executive committee, which had been formed that afternoon. This committee had been dominated by Black and Radler since the company's inception, but would now be populated by a majority of independent directors. Savage, who was participating by phone, had burst out laughing when he received a fax of the press release announcing the members of the reconstituted committee: Lord Black, former governor Thompson, Ambassador Burt, Ambassador Seitz, and him. "Well, we got two ambassadors, a governor, a lord, and this flunky Graham Savage," he joked with his wife Elise. "I need to get myself a title."

The first order of business for the executive committee was to approve the management changes following Black's departure. Paris, the investment banker who had been approached personally by Black to join the board less than a year earlier, was named CEO, while Colson, an experienced newspaper hand and the last remaining member of Black's old executive guard, would act as chief operating officer. Colson's appointment may have seemed unusual, given his ties to Black, but he had never received any of the allegedly improper non-compete payments. These two men would oversee Hollinger International's strategic review, which could include the sale of one or more of its remaining newspapers, including the *Telegraph,* the *Sun-Times,* or *The Jerusalem Post.*

The management changes were the easy part. Far more complicated was the task of winning Black's approval for the press release that would announce his fall from grace. Black, who was flying to Toronto from New York that evening, was on the phone with Breeden incessantly, requesting amendments that invariably pushed the news about the $32 million in unauthorized payments toward the bottom of the three-page press release. The first page announced the potential strategic sale of Hollinger International's newspapers and the resignations of Black, Atkinson, Kipnis, and Radler, who "has indicated to Lord Black a desire to work on privately held newspaper interests." These men and Hollinger Inc., the release said, would collectively return the $32 million. As for Boultbee, he had been "terminated" after the company "failed to reach agreement with him on several matters."

In newspaper parlance, Breeden and his team had "buried the lead." Yet they agreed to the artful arrangement of the announcement because they knew the facts would tell the story, regardless of the order in which they were placed. Black may have been attempting to save face, but the media tycoon was about to become the new poster boy for corporate excess. At about 1:30 A.M., Breeden took his last call from Black and ran the proposed revisions by Rosenberg, Geist, Harrison, and Quamme before taking the changes downstairs to a first-floor office where Molly Morse, a public relations adviser with Kekst and Company, was preparing the release.

When Morse finished editing the final draft, at just after 2 A.M., she hit the send button, dispatching the press release to the world's major media outlets. In less than half an hour the news would be public.

CHAPTER TWELVE

Gotcha

GENE FOX COULDN'T SLEEP. A few hours before dawn on Monday, November 17, Cardinal's managing director gave up his restless tossing and got out of bed. He had just returned to his Greenwich home from a weekend in Phoenix and it wasn't jet lag that was interfering with his slumber. He and his partner Kirkpatrick had been hearing rumours for days about pending changes at Hollinger International. All he could catch were fragments from company and industry sources. Lawyers had been spotted going into Hollinger International's offices and there had been lots of board meetings. Something big was brewing.

Like most investors, Fox hated uncertainty. He had talked to Hollinger International officials over the weekend and all they would say was that an announcement might be pending. When was it going to be released? Shortly after 3 A.M., Fox sat down in front of his home computer to check his email and found a press release sitting in his in-box. It was from Hollinger International, which automatically sent news releases to investors, analysts, and reporters. Fox scrolled down the announcement, stopping when he hit the revelation about the non-compete payments to Black and the three executives. It was unbelievable. The company's board had never authorized the controversial fees revealed in Hollinger International's annual report. The annual report had misled shareholders. The significance of the other news began to sink in. Black and his core executives had been jettisoned even though the press lord had a hammerlock on Hollinger International's voting shares. More surprising, Black was supporting a new strategy to potentially sell major assets, a plan he had resisted for more than a year. The news was going to send the company's stock price into orbit.

Fox couldn't wait to share the news with Kirkpatrick, but he checked the impulse to call his partner because he knew Kirkpatrick was asleep in Palm Springs, enjoying his first holiday with his wife since their second child was born a year earlier. The best Fox could do was send a copy of the release to Kirkpatrick's Blackberry. He scoured the internet for more stories, and when he found them he attached them to emails to Kirkpatrick.

A little while later, Kirkpatrick was woken in his Palm Springs hotel room by his humming Blackberry. The hand-held device vibrated when there was a new email and it was shuddering across his nightstand. He got out of bed and switched on a light in the corner of the room to read the small screen. He quickly scanned the press release and called Fox. His partner picked up the phone right away and the two men began speaking in hushed tones to avoid waking their sleeping wives. But Kirkpatrick couldn't contain himself for very long, blurting to Fox, "Ding dong the wicked witch is dead."

———

Laura Jereski's email in-box was clogged by the time she logged on to her office computer on Monday morning. The overseas press had been working for hours on the blockbuster Black story by the time she arrived at work, and British and Australian journalists had emailed scores of questions. She wouldn't have long to read them, because her phone was ringing. Dozens of reporters wanted to reach her and Chris Browne.

One journalist even barged into Tweedy's lobby to request interviews. How did she feel? Was she thrilled? Was she celebrating?

The seasoned journalist knew the media wanted to portray Tweedy as the victor in Black's downfall, but she was not in a celebratory mood. Hollinger International's unrelenting critic didn't think that the special committee had gone far enough. She was dismayed that Black still remained as non-executive chairman in the face of such serious allegations, telling *The Globe and Mail* it was "a disgrace" that Black would remain on the board and continue to collect management fees through his ownership of Ravelston. "Why are we paying him one more dime?"[1] Why weren't regulators investigating these serious allegations? she said in a quote printed by the *Australian Business News:* "How much money has to leave the company before someone calls the cops?"[2] Black's silver-lined departure, she told the *New York Post,* was further evidence to her that Hollinger International's directors were spineless. "This board is a disgrace."[3] With Black ejected, Tweedy's acerbic analyst was now aiming her barbed criticisms at the special committee.

Jereski's boss Chris Browne was more willing to savour the moment. When he walked down the hall on his way to his office that morning he was stopped by a co-worker bursting with news about Black's improper payments. As he listened, the taciturn money manager broke into a big grin and said, "Gotcha."

Southeastern's president Staley Cates felt ill when he saw the news on his computer in his Memphis office. He and his boss Mason Hawkins had been wrong about Black and they had been wrong about the impossible odds they had said Tweedy would face if it opposed the press lord. Thanks to Tweedy's demand for a special investigation, Black had been exposed as a CEO who allegedly helped himself to millions of dollars without board approval.

Black's ardour for Southeastern's investment agreement had started to cool almost immediately after he announced the deal at the May annual meeting. In June, Black had told reporters at the annual meeting of Toronto parent Hollinger Inc. that Southeastern's proposed investment would have to be amended. Sometime later, Black phoned Cates and Hawkins to tell them that other parties, who had some interesting proposals for the company, had approached him. Would Southeastern mind if he pursued these overtures? The Memphis money managers were disappointed by Black's change of heart, but they held out hope that Hollinger International's CEO would revive the company's spiralling stock price by selling some of his stake or the company's assets to a new investor. And indeed, the company's stock price had been climbing for months on rumours of a pending sale. Nothing, however, prepared Cates for the shocking news he was reading on his computer screen that morning.

A few days later, Cates phoned Chris Browne in his New York office to concede that Southeastern had been mistaken about Black. "Not only were you right," Cates told Browne, "but thank you and congratulations. Thank you for doing the heavy lifting which we didn't think was going to work."

———

Black's exit from Hollinger International meant one thing to the stock market: the Black Factor, the dark cloud that had suppressed its stock price for so long, had vanished. The controversial CEO with his lavish corporate perks, penchant for self-enriching deals, and fractious shareholder relations, had been ejected. Immediately after the opening bell rang on the New York Stock Exchange at 9:30 A.M. on Monday, Hollinger International's stock catapulted madly up the price charts. By the end of trading that day, the company's stock price had leapt 15 percent to $15.59 with close to two million shares changing hands, nearly twenty times the stock's normal trading volume.

The latest corporate scandal to rock the markets had delivered a windfall to Hollinger International shareholders. In one day, Black's unseemly departure had increased the company's stock market value by

$165 million to $1.16 billion. In an ironic twist, the biggest winner that day was the disgraced Black. His personal Hollinger International stake had grown in value by nearly $50 million.

———

The many media adversaries Black had made over the course of his tumultuous twenty-five-year career came back to haunt him on the morning of November 18. The newspapers that had endured his papers' ferocious competition tactics, journalists who had been pushed out by cost-cutting purges, and reporters and editors who had been dragged through gruelling libel examinations—all were freed by Hollinger International's press release to go on the attack. From Vancouver, Canada, to Sydney, Australia, front pages were blanketed with the Hollinger International scandal, garnering the kind of coverage usually reserved for war declarations. The biggest news packages were printed in Toronto, where Black's formerly owned upstart, the *National Post,* had bruised the city's three dailies, and in Chicago, where Hollinger International's *Sun-Times* competed with the *Tribune.* "How a Peer Fell from Grace," thundered a huge, two-story package on the *Toronto Star*'s front page; "Black's Darkest Day," said a similarly sized page-one display in *The Globe and Mail;* "Black Cloud," said the *Toronto Sun.* The *Chicago Tribune* weighed in with a large front-page story, "Hollinger Brass Out in Payout Scandal."[4]

Readers of Hollinger International's *Telegraph* and *Sun-Times* had to hunt to find the story. After Radler's abrupt departure in Chicago, there had been little contact between the paper's staff and the preoccupied executives at Hollinger International's New York office. It was up to the *Sun-Times*'s shell-shocked editors to decide how to play the story, and reaching a consensus wasn't easy because many were convinced that Black and Radler would return. Black, after all, was the company's controlling shareholder and Radler had left explicit instructions that his office should remain untouched. If the paper printed a story that aggravated the ousted executives, their jobs might be at risk. The next day the *Sun-Times* printed a cautious story, deep inside on page fifty-one, about Black's departure, the unauthorized payments, and the potential sale of some of the newspapers. The tabloid plaintively observed that the announcement "begins a period of uncertainty for Hollinger International's newspapers." In London, the *Telegraph* published a story on page thirty-three that cast Black's ejection as a retirement. The story quoted *Telegraph* CEO Dan Colson, elevated a day earlier to chief operating officer of Hollinger International, playing down the significance of the unauthorized $32 million in payments: "There is no question of impropriety." And what did the future hold for his long-time boss and friend?

The great unknown is what Conrad decides to do, as he remains the controlling shareholder. Does he want to stay in control or would he prefer to write another book? I don't know.

———

A vintage blue Cadillac pulled up in front of an Indigo bookstore in Toronto's tony Yorkville shopping district shortly before noon on November 18. A scrum of two dozen reporters bearing large television microphones, cameras, and notepads edged towards the car until three large bodyguards stopped them. The largest of the trio reached down and opened the door. Wearing a dark blue pinstriped jacket, light blue shirt, and green tie, Conrad Black stepped out and calmly faced the waiting throng. If he had suffered any personal angst over his humiliating eviction, he was not showing it this morning.

"Do you have anything to say to your shareholders?" asked one reporter.

"I hope they're pleased, the stocks are rising like a rocket," he said.

"Were you forced to resign?" asked another.

"The board didn't force me to resign. We agreed upon a package of measures to help demonstrate how seriously we took this problem. These people hadn't documented otherwise unexceptional money transfers and you've got to deal with something like that, it's a serious matter."

Black's explanation that day was that "underlings" had erred by failing to properly document what he was describing as largely ordinary business transactions. It was an administrative mix-up, a glitch that would soon be corrected. As for the outpouring of negative stories in the newspapers that morning, Black lectured: "All you fellows who wrote today that I'm finished may not have it right. I am still the chairman … I'm still the controlling shareholder, I'm co-director of the strategic process and I'm chairman of the *Telegraph* and I made 50 million bucks yesterday. That's a flame-out I could get used to."

When one reporter asked, "Are you going to jail?" Black chuckled and said, "There is no suggestion of an impropriety."

"Was there an SEC investigation?"

His answer to this question was his most revealing public response to the question that many were asking that morning. Why had Black, the legendarily combative press baron, ever agreed to resign and sign an agreement that severely handicapped his clout as the company's controlling shareholder? The answer, Black seemed to imply, was Richard Breeden. Black had apparently convinced himself that by signing the agreement he had won the protection of the former regulator.

"My understanding is that Mr. Breeden, the former chairman [of the SEC] and special committee counsel, his view, quite clearly, is that it is a fully contained matter. The company was absolutely co-operative, responded very positively, didn't conceal anything. We have been completely forthcoming and are conscientiously making restitution … as soon as it came to light. He doesn't think it needs to go further."

Surprised by Black's seeming nonchalance about the scandal, reporters pushed him to explain his indifference.

"Have you no apologies?" asked one.

Rolling his eyes heavenward like a parent dealing with a truculent child, Black countered: "Ah, come on, you're being contentious. Fine. Yes, it's an indignity and I'll apologize. Yes, sure, I'll apologize."

When another reporter asked, "Are you above the law?" Black's cool veneer briefly cracked.

Bowing his head slightly, he replied hoarsely, "As I said yesterday, I am chastened, chastened by it."

Shortly after, he turned towards the bookstore and made his way down an escalator followed by the crush of reporters and cameramen who sent books and displays flying. Waiting for him was Indigo's CEO Heather Reisman, who was so flustered by the unruly mob of reporters that she yelped, "This can't happen, this is a bookstore," but to no avail. Reisman escorted Black to the centre of the bookstore, where more than a hundred seated customers were waiting to hear him speak about his book on Roosevelt. Many of them clapped when he appeared with the unwieldy caboose of reporters hitched to his backside. For the next hour he deftly fielded questions about everything from President Bush's controversial Iraq invasion to Roosevelt's talent for forging ties with international allies. His stories about the late president's life and times were compelling and his audience of book readers and reporters were riveted by the spectre of the besieged press baron talking about one of his heroes. When he reflected on Roosevelt's "abrasive" relations with his wife, Eleanor, Black could have been describing his own tortured relations with disgruntled shareholders. "She regarded him as frivolous and devious," Black said, while FDR regarded his wife as "a scold."

Black returned to his office at 10 Toronto Street later that afternoon to receive the worst possible news from New York. The SEC had issued subpoenas to him and a number of Hollinger International executives as part of a formal investigation into activities of company insiders. The frail hope that Black had held out to reporters only a few hours earlier was now shattered. He had horribly miscalculated his position. What did he have to show for signing a restructuring agreement that significantly weakened his grip on Hollinger International? The very investigation he thought he had headed off.

Shortly after 8 P.M. that evening Black took a step toward reclaiming his hold on his Hollinger empire. He faxed a handwritten, one-paragraph note to Aidan Barclay, son of the British magnate David Barclay.

If you want to buy all of Hollinger Inc. and therefore control of Hollinger International and the Telegraph *we can talk about it. If you want to look exclusively at the* Telegraph, *Lazard will be calling you.*[5]

The message was more like an ultimatum. The Barclays could join the long line of potential bidders at Hollinger International and talk to Lazard or they could deal directly with Black. If they talked to Black, he was effectively telling them, they would be circumventing the strategic process to gain control of the *Telegraph* by buying his shares in the controlling parent Hollinger Inc.[6] To move things along with the Barclays, Black's fax included a confidential memorandum that offered detailed financial and operating evaluations of Hollinger International's business. Hollinger Inc.'s Toronto adviser, Westwind, had prepared the document.[7] The "full support" Black had promised two days earlier for Hollinger International's new strategic process was evaporating.

The day after the SEC bombshell, Black added some heavy ammunition to his legal team, which had been remarkably small for a man faced with a boardroom investigation led by Breeden. He had thus far relied on very little outside advice to defend himself against the special committee investigation. In the fall he had hired Jesse Finkelstein, a Delaware lawyer, to counsel him about the committee's demands for confidential data and emails. But Black had done most of the legal footwork, including, on November 10, writing much of the lengthy reply to the committee's damning allegations. Two days before he signed the November restructuring agreement, he had retained David Boies's firm. But now that the SEC had jolted him with subpoenas, the battleground had changed. On November 19, he formally hired one of the United States' most respected litigators to join his team.

John Warden was a curious addition to Black's legal circle. The charming sixty-three-year-old from Indiana commanded huge respect as a tireless advocate for major U.S. companies and was a senior partner at New York's patrician law firm Sullivan & Cromwell. But Warden's expertise was anti-trust cases, the most recent of which had been his defence of Microsoft against U.S. Justice Department anti-competition charges. Warden's opponent in the Microsoft case, strangely enough, was Boies. For reasons of his own, Black wanted the former courtroom adversaries working together for him.

———

Just before 5 P.M. on November 19, the door in Paul Healy's New York office opened and Black poked his head in. Spying Paris, Hollinger International's CEO-in-waiting, Black said: "Ah, found you by deduction." He asked Paris to join him in the hallway, where he explained that he had been advised by his lawyers to resign two days ahead of schedule as Hollinger International's chief executive. The news was a big setback for Hollinger International. The company was just minutes away from filing to the SEC its quarterly financial statements, which were due before the close of business that day. Black's early resignation meant that he would not be certifying the financial statements as required by securities law. Paris would replace Black as CEO, but as a newcomer, he was in no position to certify the accuracy of the financial report. Hollinger International was going to miss the quarterly-filing deadline.

———

By the end of November, Black was leading a double life. Publicly, he was playing the role of a supportive advocate of Hollinger International's new strategic plan to sell assets. Privately, however, he was pursuing a rogue agenda to auction his newspapers through the sale of his Toronto company Hollinger Inc. Black was so consumed with his rebel plan that he was communicating almost daily through handwritten faxes, emails, and telephone conversations with his most fervent suitor, the Barclay family. His chief contacts were David

Barclay and his son Aidan, whom he was urging to quickly launch a takeover. Black proposed that the family acquire his Toronto holding company, Hollinger Inc., as an indirect route to buy the *Telegraph*. Playing to the Barclay's ardour for the *Telegraph*, Black indicated that a takeover could be consummated within weeks. As for the troubling matter of the board's investigation of the unauthorized payments, he explained, "The special committee process is largely concluded."[8] He also told the Barclays that he wanted a $10-million "redundancy payment" to compensate him for the loss of his executive income if the family succeeded with the takeover of Hollinger Inc.[9] Disgraced, pushed out of his core operating company, and under investigation by regulators, Black still had his hand out asking for millions of dollars.

When Black signed the November 17 restructuring agreement, he committed himself to supporting Hollinger International's new strategy to seek buyers for its assets under a process led by Lazard. Despite the promise, Black apparently told only one of Hollinger International's directors about his secret talks with the Barclays. That director was Colson, his long-time friend, former lawyer, and CEO of the *Telegraph*, who was now camped in Chicago filling the void left by David Radler. As Aidan Barclay would later observe, "I was very surprised that Dan Colson seemed to know a lot of what was going on, because Conrad Black obviously discussed a lot of things with him."[10]

———

On Friday, November 21, Black shifted his attention to a threat on his home turf in Toronto. Hollinger Inc.'s board of directors had called a special meeting that evening to consider an ultimatum that had been served earlier in the week by the company's audit committee. The committee's four independent directors had told Black that they would resign unless he gave up the CEO's title and Radler, Atkinson, and Boultbee also stepped down as executives.

The four people making the demand, Hollinger Inc.'s only independent directors, were not in the habit of saying no to Black. Fredrik

Eaton was a long-standing Hollinger Inc. director and childhood friend. Toronto businessman Douglas Bassett was godfather to Black's eldest son, Jonathan. Allan Gotlieb had been publisher of Black's former Toronto magazine, *Saturday Night,* and he had been the long-serving secretary of the Hollinger group's star-studded advisory boards. Maureen Sabia was a Toronto consultant.

Jonathan Rosenberg, a lawyer for Hollinger International's special committee, had contacted the Toronto audit committee's lawyer, Bill Ainley, the previous Saturday to alert the independent directors about the discovery of unauthorized payments to Black and his lieutenants. The warning left the Toronto directors with little alternative but to review the status of Black and his team at Hollinger Inc. Ainley had advised the independent directors that if they did not match Hollinger International's ejection of the disgraced executives, they could be vulnerable to shareholder lawsuits on the grounds that they were complicit in the alleged misdeeds.

The audit committee privately delivered a threat to Black during a meeting in his Toronto office on that Monday night. They would resign, the directors explained, if Black and his three executives did not step down. Even though Black had capitulated at Hollinger International, he angrily told the Toronto directors he was not prepared to retreat from Hollinger Inc. because it "would be an admission of guilt, which I am not prepared to do." As Black later explained, "I was very emphatic, I thought they were completely inappropriate suggestions."[11] Black asked the directors to withdraw the resignation demand for several weeks to give him time to prove his innocence. The audit committee gave him until the Friday board meeting to decide.

The problem with the audit committee's ultimatum was that its four members were outnumbered. The remaining directors included such Black loyalists as his wife Amiel; Colson; Charles Cowan, Hollinger Inc.'s corporate secretary; and Black's old friend Peter White. Unlike Hollinger International directors, the four Toronto directors did not have the support of a special committee or a heavyweight adviser like Breeden. It was no contest.

A group of reporters and photographers was camped outside Hollinger Inc.'s stately headquarters as the board deliberated the ultimatum that Friday night. When the independent directors emerged after the one-hour meeting, they would not speak to waiting reporters. The tense expressions on their faces, however, spoke volumes. As a Hollinger Inc. press release confirmed later that night, the four had resigned after Black and his top executives refused to step down.

Despite the startling revelations about the improper payments, at least one of the independent directors remained supportive of Black. In an interview with the *National Post*'s Barbara Shecter, departed director Bassett explained that he felt "love and admiration" for Black. "I have no embarrassment whatsoever of stating those feelings."[12]

CHAPTER THIRTEEN

End Run

INSIDE A SQUAT, gun-metal-grey building overlooking the Chicago River, managers at the *Sun-Times* were busy scouring the internet for information. They were looking for news, but not the kind that would be printed in the Chicago tabloid. That day, December 5, Hollinger International's chief operating officer Dan Colson had shown up at the *Sun-Times* with a man he introduced as Tom Hicks. With his burly, six-foot three-inch frame, monogrammed cowboy boots, fist-sized silver belt buckle, and Texan drawl, Hicks stood out like an oversized scarecrow in an Illinois cornfield. Marooned in Chicago, with no information from the New York office about the *Sun-Times*'s future, the paper's managers speculated that the visitor was on a shopping trip. Hicks was known to most of the paper's editors as the owner of the Texas Rangers baseball franchise, but they knew little about his business interests. When they punched his name into the internet search engine Google, their curiosity grew. The Texan headed one of the country's biggest corporate buyout firms, Hicks, Muse, Tate & Furst, in Dallas, and he had interests in a variety of radio, television, and movie theatre companies.

The mysterious visitor's intentions became clearer after 5 P.M. that day when Colson and Hicks sauntered into the office of *Sun-Times* publisher John Cruickshank, who was meeting with some of the paper's senior executives. Colson introduced Hicks to the group, and the financier answered questions about the big sports story of the day: his controversial negotiations to trade Texas Rangers' shortstop Alex Rodriguez, known universally as A-Rod, one of the world's highest-paid athletes. After several minutes, Hicks started to ask some questions of his own. Were there any synergies that hadn't been explored in the Hollinger's Chicago Group of newspapers, which included the *Sun-Times* and nearly a hundred suburban dailies and weeklies? How would the papers fit with his stable of radio stations?

Hicks's visit had put the *Sun-Times* executives in a very awkward position. Hollinger International's chief executive officer, Gordon Paris, had issued orders in employee-wide emails in November that no corporate information should be provided to any outsider without his permission. No one other than Lazard's bankers or Paris were to talk to interested buyers. When Hollinger International's Chicago-based counsel, Mark Kipnis, heard about Hicks's tour, he became concerned. Kipnis had been under extreme duress for months. Black had targeted the lawyer, who had received none of the unauthorized payments, in his letter to the special committee as a "negligent" lawyer whose administrative snafus were to blame for the fact that the board never approved the multi-million-dollar payments bestowed on the press baron and his three executives. Kipnis had been forced to resign along with Black and the others in November, but Hollinger International had rehired him as a consultant to complete negotiations with Donald Trump over a planned skyscraper on the *Sun-Times* riverfront property.

Kipnis's colleagues at Hollinger International believed that the affable father of four had taken more than his fair share of blame for the controversy. Radler had hired Kipnis from a Chicago law firm in the mid-1990s as Hollinger International's corporate counsel despite the fact he had no prior experience with media companies. From the beginning, Radler had placed a lot of demands on Kipnis. The lawyer often chauffeured his boss to work when he was staying in town.

When Radler called executives in for weekend meetings, which his subordinates dubbed "suck-up Saturdays," it was Kipnis who brought his boss his favourite bagels and smoked salmon. Kipnis often grumbled to his colleagues, "We're just the furniture around here." Having lost his full-time job, Kipnis did not want to have another problem on his hands. He phoned Paris immediately to alert him about the Hicks visit.

Paris was furious. Hicks's tour of the *Sun-Times* signalled that Black might be working outside Hollinger International's strategic process to sell the company's newspapers. The November agreement was supposed to bind Black to support the company and Lazard during the planned auction of its newspapers. Indeed, days after Black had signed the agreement, he had introduced Hicks to Paris and other Hollinger International executives as a possible strategic investor or buyer. But now Colson, Black's long-standing lawyer, was squiring the Texan around Hollinger International's second-largest newspaper without the knowledge of the company's board of directors or CEO.

Paris fired off an angry email to Colson on December 6, chastising him for the "completely inappropriate" tour with Hicks. By taking the financier on a shopping tour, he warned, Colson had violated Paris's November edict that no corporate information was to be provided without his approval.

The two men had been wary of each other since they were thrust together as the top executives at Hollinger International in November. Paris was a guarded investment banker who had never previously run a major public company, but the board tapped him as CEO because he had experience as a so-called "workout adviser" who helped troubled companies get back on their feet. Although Colson was closely allied to the ousted Black, he had not received any of the disputed payments and he had been promoted to chief operating officer to supplement Paris's lack of knowledge about the newspaper business.

Uneasy about Colson's ties to Black, Paris had been parsimonious with information about the progress of Lazard's talks with potential investors. For his part, Colson was so dismissive of Paris's lack of newspaper knowledge that he called the executive "Flash Gordon," to reflect what he anticipated would be a brief tenure by the executive at Hollinger International. When Colson got the angry email from Paris on December 6 and a subsequent telephone lecture, the London lawyer was so upset that he waited two days before he wrote an email reply.

Colson explained in the email that his meeting with Hicks was related to a possible investment by the Texan in the Toronto parent company Hollinger Inc.—which he said relieved him of his responsibility to alert Lazard or Hollinger International. Arguing that his actions were "above reproach," Colson warned Paris to

refrain in the future from sending me similar emails before you are in full possession of all the facts.... Meanwhile, I am not prepared to tolerate any suggestion by anyone that my integrity is being impugned, particularly given the events of the past few weeks.[1]

Hicks's Chicago tour was only the latest troubling sign that Black might be conducting his own auction of company assets. For weeks the company had heard rumours that Nelson Peltz's Triarc was in discussions with Black about a potential deal. If Black wasn't working with Lazard or Hollinger International, then he probably was seeking to cash in on Hollinger International's newspapers by selling his shares in the company' s parent, Hollinger Inc. Paris grew more alarmed the next day, December 9, when he received a snide letter from Tweedy's Chris Browne that began, "So Conrad is shopping Hollinger Inc." The money manager, which had interests in a number of other European newspaper companies, had heard rumours about Black's private auction. Did this mean, Browne sniped, that Hollinger International shareholders were paying Lazard to be Black's personal banker? If Black succeeded in selling Hollinger Inc., Browne warned, it would be "destabilizing" to Hollinger International shareholders. The letter didn't spell it out, but the implication was clear. If Black succeeded in selling Hollinger Inc., the new owner could gain control of Hollinger International's newspaper jewels without having to pay a cent to the U.S. company's shareholders.

———

Bruce Wasserstein and Louis Zachary tried to get some answers by phoning Black. The Lazard bankers had been building a relationship with the press mogul since Wasserstein visited Black at his London home in May to discuss a possible assignment at Hollinger International. Even though Black had resigned from Hollinger International, the bankers hoped their ties with the departed CEO would give them enough leverage to ask him about rumours that he was privately auctioning Hollinger Inc., the Toronto parent company. Wasserstein and Zachary arranged a conference call with Black, and when they asked him about the rumours, the press lord was guarded.

Black assured the pair that he was acting within the parameters of the agreement he had signed. If he was talking to anyone, he allowed, it was because Hollinger Inc. was under financial pressure to make some pending payments on its debt. This was an important technical point. As part of the November agreement, Black had reserved the right to sell his stake in Hollinger Inc. only if the company faced a mortal financial crisis such as insolvency. Even in that scenario, however, Black had promised to give Hollinger International's board "reasonable" advance notice about any sale of Hollinger Inc., the parent company. Black appeared to be telling the Lazard duo that he was free to sell Hollinger Inc. because it was in financial peril. He could use this loophole to sell the parent company and its indirect interests in the prized newspaper assets.

———

If there was one person who could get Black to talk it was Seitz. The former ambassador and *Telegraph* director had impressed everyone on

Hollinger's board of directors with his deft, diplomatic management of the mercurial Black. He had navigated a resolution to the thorny issue of cloning Black and Amiel's emails, and he had guided Kissinger, Black's long-standing ally, to appreciate the gravity of the allegations against the press baron. In recognition of Seitz's skills, he had been appointed chairman of the executive committee of Hollinger's board, which was overseeing the company's restructuring. A few days after the Lazard call, Seitz was on the phone to Black. He pointedly asked the departed executive if he was playing by the rules of the November agreement. Black assured Seitz that the pact was being honoured. Seitz pushed further, asking him if Hollinger Inc. was indeed under financial pressure as he had told Wasserstein and Zachary. Black cryptically replied that he had other resources and there was no reason to think Hollinger Inc. was about to go down the drain.[2] Furthermore, he told Seitz, he was looking forward to hearing what Lazard would be proposing for Hollinger International, because the restructuring could help him resolve the parent company's debts.[3]

Shortly after, Seitz summarized the conversation to Paris, Savage, and Breeden in an email. Black, he wrote, "... said [Hollinger] Inc. has other resources and people shouldn't think it would 'crater.'"[4] The email wasn't very reassuring. Black was sending some very mixed messages about his actions. What was he up to?

———

Behind the scenes, Black was busier than anyone on the special committee realized. By the middle of December he was quietly entertaining advances from some of the world's most powerful investors. On December 15, Tom Hicks's firm told Black that it was prepared to make a bid of $14.65 a share in a complex offer that would include Hollinger Inc. and Hollinger International. Black rejected the lowball bid and told the Texas firm to join the lineup of potential bidders talking to Lazard.

A few days later, Black opened the door of his Park Avenue co-op to another suitor. It was Dan Quayle, the former U.S. Republican vice-president who had shifted his career from Washington to Wall Street as chairman of Cerberus Global Investments. Named after the mythical three-headed dog that guarded Hades, Cerberus was a secretive private equity firm that had made a fortune snapping up distressed companies and squeezing out profits through aggressive cost-cutting. As Quayle and another Cerberus official explained to Black during the private meeting, Cerberus saw potential in Hollinger International's travails and it wanted to make an investment. After some hectic negotiations, Cerberus later tabled a plan to acquire a major stake in Hollinger Inc., the Toronto parent. Black dismissed the offer as inferior. Cerberus was asking for too much of Hollinger Inc.'s equity at too low a price.

A stream of potential buyers came and went during December. Black personally led most of the discussions with help from the small Toronto investment firm Westwind, which the press lord privately referred to as his "message bearer and receiver." Canadian media owner CanWest offered to buy Hollinger Inc. stock through a share swap, but Black lost interest in their offer when they demanded forty-five days to conduct their due diligence, or financial investigation, of the Hollinger group's business. At the same time Black juggled discussions with New York financier Nelson Peltz; New York private equity firm Apax Partners; Wall Street investment legend George Soros; Britain's Associated Newspapers Holdings Ltd., which owns the *Daily Mail;* and the German media group Axel Springer AG, publisher of the country's most widely read newspaper, *Bild.*

None of these talks, however, advanced very far. Either Black dismissed their offers as inadequate or suitors were turned off by the risks of buying Hollinger International's newspapers through a back-door acquisition of the Toronto parent. Their other fear was that the ongoing investigation by the special committee might reveal further alleged improprieties that could damage the company's worth. Even though he was under siege by an SEC investigation and the special committee probe, the embattled Black could afford to be hard-nosed with would-be buyers. He had a serious bidder in his back pocket that was willing to negotiate with him and, more importantly, pay top dollar.

While Black juggled potential investors, one of Hollinger International's major shareholders fumed. It had been more than two years since Tweedy had requested explanations from the company's board of directors about the self-indulgent executive payments, and no one but Black had bothered to respond. The six-month-old special committee investigation had triggered the departure of Black and his senior team, but Tweedy was dismayed that the company had yet to discover why the board had approved the spectacular annual management fees to Ravelston and the more than $70-million non-compete windfall from a variety of newspaper sales including the CanWest purchase. With the media so focused on the humiliating dethronement of the imperious Black, Browne and Jereski were not having much success attracting journalists' attention to what they believed was a bigger issue—the board's role in the scandal.

Browne found a platform to voice his concerns when he published a column in the *Financial Times* on December 11. Browne explained that Hollinger International's board of directors had given its blessing to more than $300 million in management services and non-compete fees over a seven-year period. These massive rewards were substantially larger that the $32 million in unauthorized payments targeted by the special committee in November and no one was offering any explanations for the excessive compensation. "How did the board justify these payments?" his column asked. "Which comparable companies did these board members examine in deciding these fees?" "Which compensation consultants did they seek out?" "Why did Lord Black, as the controlling shareholder, require such extravagant incentives?"

As far as Browne was concerned, Black and his crew had helped themselves to outrageous compensation over the years and the board had repeatedly approved the payouts.

Our focus is on the directors, who are the stewards of the interests of shareholders such as Tweedy Browne. It is the board—comprised over the years of such international movers and shakers as Lord Weidenfeld,

Richard Perle and Marie-Josée Kravis, the economist—that has had the ultimate responsibility for overseeing these disbursements.

Like Black, Hollinger International's board was now feeling the sharp bite of a demand from Tweedy. The firm was putting the directors on notice that they could be personally vulnerable if the special committee found that the $300 million in fees were inappropriate and the board had irresponsibly approved them. Browne wrote:

To the extent that Lord Black and his associates are unable or unwilling to repay those funds, any board member who served in this period could well be liable to the company. Resigning, as some have, does not get them off the hook. In this regard, the board and Lord Black may share an interest that is to the detriment of other shareholders.

Tweedy, the value investor that had told its managers to "act like owners," was reminding the directors who was in charge. "It is about time this board remembered for whom it works," Browne's column concluded.

———

Another shareholder jolted Hollinger International's board the same day when a handful of newspapers reported that a Delaware judge had granted Cardinal Capital the right to file a lawsuit against twenty former and current directors at the company. Details were scarce because Cardinal and Hollinger International officials would not comment, but the stories revealed that the Greenwich money manager had access to the company's board minutes, internal documents, and financial records.

The shareholders' attacks against Hollinger International's board couldn't have been more poorly timed for the special committee. The three independent directors and their adviser, Breeden, were grappling with growing signs in December that Black, the controlling shareholder, was reneging on the November agreement by auctioning Hollinger International's parent company. If this were true, the special committee's investigation and the board's efforts to muster a better deal for shareholders through a restructuring could be in peril. If Black wanted to play rough, the committee knew he could sell the Toronto parent, move to replace Hollinger International's board, and extinguish the investigation. The committee would need all the support it could get from Hollinger International's independent directors to thwart a potential end run by Black. Paris, Savage, and Seitz had worked hard to forge an alliance with such directors as Thompson, Burt, Perle, Meitar, and Kissinger, but if shareholders became hostile, the support of these directors could evaporate.

———

Two weeks after he signed the November agreement, Black was privately encouraging the Barclays in handwritten, faxed letters that they were getting very close to their desired acquisition of the *Telegraph*. The family's chief contact with Black was David Barclay, who faxed handwritten replies from his homes in Monte Carlo and the Channel Islands. Barclay was gracious and solicitous of Black's legal problems, he offered to send money to the press lord to assist with "liquidity" problems, and he sympathized about the outpouring of negative media stories, including a late-November article in the *Financial Times*. Black was grateful for their support, observing in a November 29 letter sent from his New York office that "This is a rough country, but the law will prevail and I will be vindicated."[5]

A day later Black was writing from his London office boasting to Barclay how he was "looking forward" to suing some of the newspapers that had printed negative stories about him. "It's time to turn this tide of vilification."[6]

In early December the Barclays started to get cold feet about buying the *Telegraph* through Hollinger Inc. The twins' lawyers at New York's Skadden, Arps had just received a copy of the terms of Black's

November agreement and they warned that it could limit Black's ability to sell Hollinger Inc. Compounding matters, Black's own lawyers were telling the Barclays' representatives that Black's plan for the twins to acquire Hollinger Inc. was unworkable. For example, Black's lawyers were warning they might have to make an expensive bid for all of Hollinger International. Black, it seemed to the Barclays, was not on the same page as his lawyers. On December 4, David Barclay raised the legal concerns in a letter to Black.

Your lawyer has informed [us] that Hollinger Inc. is unable to conclude a deal with us, because of an agreement you signed giving an undertaking to the Board of Hollinger International.[7]

Even though Black's own lawyers were waving red flags, the press baron reassured the Barclays that the legal issues were "exaggerated" and a "rectifiable misunderstanding."[8]

The Barclays continued to have misgivings and they pushed Black in emails and conversations to tell Hollinger International's board of their plan. The British twins' biggest concern was that Hollinger International didn't seem to require a vote of shareholder support, even from Black, to sell the *Telegraph*. This meant that the Barclays ran the risk of spending hundreds of millions of dollars to buy Hollinger Inc. only to see the subsidiary Hollinger International sell the *Telegraph* to another buyer. "We need their blessing," David urged.[9] Playing to the Barclays' enormous desire to own the *Telegraph*, Black brushed off their concerns and told them their best hope of buying the prestigious newspaper was to present Hollinger International's board with "a fait accompli" takeover of Hollinger Inc.[10] If the U.S. board objected and tried to sell the *Telegraph* to another suitor, he counselled them, "I assume you would move at once to assert your control over the board" as the new owner of Hollinger International's parent.[11]

The Barclays did take the step of telling Lazard that they wanted to be added to the list of interested buyers, but as a U.S. judge would later find, "They purposely remained silent and did not inform Lazard (or anyone at Hollinger International) that they were negotiating with Black."[12] By the end of December, desperate to buy the *Telegraph,* a newspaper they regarded as a "once in a lifetime opportunity," the Barclays appeared to have accepted Black's convoluted and risky takeover strategy as a "means to an end."[13] They would seek to gain control of the coveted paper by acquiring Hollinger Inc., the Toronto parent of Hollinger International. To help pave the way for the takeover, the Barclays were even prepared to finance the repurchase of Hollinger Inc.'s $120-million junk-bond issue, which had restricted Black's ability to sell his stake in his newspaper empire.

———

Black's double life as a private auctioneer of Hollinger Inc. and a supporter of the Hollinger International restructuring intersected on December 17 in New York, when he joined a board meeting for the U.S. company. During the session, Wasserstein confronted the ousted CEO about rumours that Black was quietly negotiating to sell the company's newspapers through an auction of Hollinger Inc.[14] Turning to the company's secretary, Black asked that his comments be recorded. The board minutes for the session state his reply:

—Neither Lord Black nor Hollinger Inc. have solicited any inquiries from potential acquirers or other sources of capital;

—Hicks, Muse, Tate & Furst (Hicks, Muse) initially made overtures to Hollinger Inc. regarding a potential offer for all of the shares of both Hollinger Inc. and the company; however, once Hicks Muse's offer changed to include only the interests of Hollinger Inc., Lord Black instructed Hicks Muse to join the queue of the strategic process run by Lazard;

—Lord Black has been faithful to the Lazard process and has done nothing to disturb the Lazard process.

—Lord Black acknowledged that Hollinger Inc. has liquidity issues and that he must be mindful of those; however, he will not favor Hollinger Inc. over Hollinger International Inc.[15]

What Black didn't tell the directors was that he had referred Hicks, Muse to Lazard only after he had rejected their offer as inferior. The Hollinger International directors would learn it was only one of several less-than-accurate comments by their former CEO.

———

One week after the Hollinger International scandal broke, Black could still count some prominent New Yorkers as friends. On November 24, Black and Amiel welcomed friends to Manhattan's power eatery, the Four Seasons Restaurant's Grill Room, for the launch of his FDR book. The event was hosted by Oscar de la Renta, his wife Annette, and New York society hostess Jayne Wrightsman. As waiting reporters and photographers lobbed questions to arriving guests, most, such as Kissinger, financier Ronald Perelman, ABC News journalist Barbara Walters, actresses Candice Bergen and Joan Collins, and *Vogue* editor Anna Wintour, rushed by mutely. Others such as talk-show host and columnist Tina Brown stopped to say they had come to support Black.

Inside, however, the celebration seemed more like a wake. Black was subdued and Amiel said little to their assembled friends. Fewer than half of the three hundred invited guests had shown up. Underlining the spotty attendance was an overflowing party next door for a new book by former U.S. treasury secretary Robert Rubin. A week later Tina Brown observed in a *Washington Post* column that "the meagre turnout was a bummer."[16]

———

By December, Black's large team of high-powered lawyers had proven to be unwieldy. In addition to the dozens of lawyers working on the case under Boies, Finkelstein, and Warden, the press baron had recruited one of Canada's most prominent criminal lawyers, Edward Greenspan, a close friend of Black's and Amiel's. Black was scheduled to meet with officials at the Securities and Exchange Commission on December 22 to be interviewed by the regulator's staff as part of its investigation into the alleged improper payments. Black's lawyers were divided over how to respond to the regulator's demand to question him.

Some of his New York lawyers insisted that co-operation was the proper course of action and recommended that Black answer the regulator's questions as best he could. Black himself, who was not in the habit of keeping quiet, was initially supportive. But other members of his legal team argued he should say nothing. Shortly before Black was scheduled to meet with the SEC, the *New York Post* had run a story that said the U.S. District Attorney's office in northern Illinois had launched a criminal probe into the activities of Black and Hollinger International, and that the Federal Bureau of Investigation was assisting in the investigation. Black's lawyers could not confirm the criminal probe, but the addition of Greenspan to the team indicated they were concerned about the threat. Anything Black told the SEC could potentially provide the criminal investigators with more ammunition to use against him.

As the legal team debated Black's SEC strategy, in mid-December his lawyers requested a postponement of the testimony, saying they needed more time to collect evidence for their client. When the SEC said no, Black offered to provide an informal briefing that would not be under oath, but that, too, was rejected. Three days before Christmas, Black met with the SEC's staff in Chicago. When an investigator began asking questions, Black replied that he was invoking his Fifth Amendment rights against self-incrimination. He would not be answering any questions.

"You'll have to excuse me," he told his questioners. "I'm usually more loquacious than this."

By the end of December, Black was backing away from other commitments he had made in the November agreement. He, Radler, and Atkinson had agreed to pay back 10 percent of the unauthorized $15.6 million they had personally received by December 31, and the remainder by June 1, 2004. Atkinson had been the first to repay the disputed rewards, writing a cheque for $350,000 in November. Radler sent his required 10 percent of $7.2 million he owed before the end of the month. Boultbee, who was suing Hollinger International for wrongful dismissal, had not agreed to pay the money back. Black had initially agreed to repay the $7.2 million he had pocketed, but by mid-December, he was telling the Barclays and Radler that new research was casting doubts on the special committee's claim that the non-compete payments were improper.[17]

Black had a big incentive to orchestrate his own exit from his newspaper empire. As long as the U.S. subsidiary controlled the auction of its newspapers, its board had the power to withhold the proceeds from any asset sale that Black was entitled to receive as a major shareholder. Hollinger International shareholders such as Tweedy were pressuring the board to examine more than $300 million in past management fees, and if the special committee agreed the payments were unjustified, they could freeze any money due to be paid to Black.

The special committee had no jurisdiction, however, to seize any funds Black generated by selling his stake in the Toronto parent. On December 31, the Barclays presented him with a document that gave him much hope for the new year. It was a draft agreement for a takeover of Black's Toronto holding company Hollinger Inc.

On New Year's Eve, David Barclay sent Black a short personal note with the good news that the draft agreement for a takeover of Hollinger Inc. would soon be rolling out of his fax machine. "All of the Barclay family," he concluded, "wish you and Barbara our very best wishes and good health and happiness for the New Year."

CHAPTER FOURTEEN

Et Tu, Brute?

FOR BLACK AND HIS ALLIES, the New Year arrived with ominous tidings. A recent lawsuit filed by Cardinal, one of Hollinger International's more vocal investors, was unsealed in Delaware's Chancery Court on January 2, 2004, and the allegations were incendiary. Relying on records of company board meetings that it had obtained after a lengthy legal battle, Cardinal depicted a "saga of greed and deliberate indifference to fiduciary duties"[1] within Hollinger International. It accused Black, Radler, and other executives of looting the company for hundreds of millions of dollars in a "stunning abuse of authority," and alleged that the two men "consistently look for opportunities to line their own pockets" at the expense of shareholders.

But that was only half the story. For the first time, Black's handpicked directors were being cast as enablers of the scandal. Cardinal assembled a devastating portrait of a "supine" board, one that routinely "rubber-stamped" suspicious deals in which Black and other executives were personally enriched and that rarely, if ever, raised questions about the tens of millions of dollars in management fees the company paid each year to Ravelston.

While the Hollinger Executives were treating Hollinger like their private piggy bank, Hollinger's board, including ostensibly blue ribbon independent directors and Hollinger's Audit Committee, were totally quiescent. Despite being presented with numerous self-dealing transactions, the Board without question or investigation repeatedly approved the actions of Hollinger Executives (often after the fact) and permitted their unfettered raid on Hollinger's finances.[2]

The list of defendants read like the invite list for a high-society charity ball: in addition to the executive directors—Black, Amiel, Radler, Colson, and Atkinson—Cardinal was suing Thompson, Burt, Kravis, Perle, Kissinger, and Meitar, the Israeli businessman. The suit also named former Hollinger International board members, including Dwayne Andreas of Archer Daniels Midland, Lord Weidenfeld, noted philanthropist Raymond Chambers, Alfred Taubman of Sotheby's, former U.S. ambassador to the Soviet Union Robert Strauss, and retailing czar Leslie Wexner. Although the allegations were now public, Cardinal and Hollinger International had agreed to suspend formal proceedings until the internal investigation was completed.

The suit detailed many of the same troubling deals that the special committee had already unearthed in its investigation. CanWest, being the largest deal, received extensive treatment. But some of the smaller deals looked even more disconcerting. In a handful of instances, Hollinger International had sold newspapers to Horizon Publications and Bradford Publishing, a pair of companies controlled by Black and Radler, for next to nothing. On May 11, 2000, the board had unanimously approved a swap of papers between Hollinger International and Horizon. The terms were baffling: the transaction called for Hollinger International to exchange profitable papers for less-profitable ones, according to a memo distributed to the board. "Incredibly, the memo states this is a good idea because it would leave Hollinger room to improve the performance of these less-profitable newspapers," Cardinal stated in its suit. Nevertheless, the board unanimously approved the sale, and there was no indication in records of the meeting that the directors even sought an independent fairness opinion.[3] In two other instances, Cardinal's suit claimed, Hollinger International sold newspapers to Horizon for just one dollar. Both times, the audit committee gave its approval, even though Horizon was owned by Black and Radler.

The suit also castigated the audit committee for taking a "carte blanche" approach to approving the lucrative management fees to Black's private holding company, Ravelston, apparently without any negotiation or independent review of these payments.[4] Black and Radler may have been the alleged beneficiaries, but these payments wouldn't have been possible without the board's consent, Cardinal insisted. The firm concluded its lawsuit with a scorching indictment of the company's directors.

Board members, when they chose to be present, without exception approved, without question, review, or basis, the self-dealing transactions involving management and the payment of fees to management.... The board never questioned why the Company would be advised to sell assets for $1.00 to the very people who were recommending the sale of these assets. The board never asked why the justification for the non-compete payments were always its own prior payments and never precedent from the market place. There was not ever a discussion outside the presence of the interested persons. The Board's actions with respect to these payments was [sic] so deficient that even when such payments were presented to them retroactively, and even when such payments had been modified by management without authorization, the Board ratified these actions without question.... In short, the Board never said no.[5]

The embattled board was also about to come under attack from Black, who felt betrayed that many of his hand-picked directors had seemingly turned against him. On Saturday, January 3, 2004, the day after Cardinal's suit was made public, Black sent a letter to the Barclays warning that Hollinger International was considering a so-called "poison pill," a complex instrument that is used to thwart unwelcome takeover bids. If the board adopted a pill at its scheduled meeting the next day, it would effectively sabotage Black's efforts to sell his controlling stake in Hollinger Inc., the parent company.[6]

The independent directors (some of them) are trying to insert a poison pill. But we believe we have a strategy to frustrate this, and our counsel will be discussing this Sunday morning. There have been slight delays from other causes. But there doesn't seem to be any reason at this point to vary our target date by more than a day or so. I will write you on your island as to the end of business on Sunday. Yours sincerely, Conrad.[7]

Black's strategy, as it turned out, was little more than brute intimidation. He contacted Kissinger, whom he believed to be one of his last remaining allies on the Hollinger International board, and threatened to begin firing directors and suing the members of the special committee and audit committee if the company tried to enact a poison pill.[8] Kissinger was aghast. It wasn't as though Black's dealings with the board over the past month and a half had been excessively cordial, but to this point both sides had managed to avert a full-fledged fight. Now the gloves were off. Kissinger's lawyer, Paul Saunders, immediately contacted Breeden and informed him of Black's salvo.[9] He said he feared that Black's attempts to remove the board could lead to another "Saturday Night Massacre," a reference to October 1973, when former president Richard Nixon ordered the firing of Archibald Cox, a special prosecutor appointed by the U.S. Congress to lead the Watergate investigation.

Hollinger International wasn't exactly Watergate, but there were enough parallels between the two situations that Kissinger, formerly Nixon's secretary of state, was feeling queasy. Saunders told Breeden that Henry "already lived through one of those [and] he didn't want to live through a second."[10] There was only one solution. Kissinger, revisiting his salad days as a shuttle diplomat, called Black to broker a cease-fire between him and the directors. Black agreed, and his representatives met with Breeden on Sunday, the day the board was supposed to hold its meeting, to hammer out a deal. At 4.27 P.M., John Warden, one of Black's lawyers from Sullivan & Cromwell, emailed Breeden with the skeletal outline of a two-week "standstill" agreement.

We have mutually agreed to extend the time for payment of the amount specified to be paid by Lord Black to Hollinger International in December until January 18. Between now and then we will discuss a global resolution of all issues involving Hollinger International, Hollinger Inc., and Ravelston. Prior to January 18, there will be no transaction, direct or indirect, in shares of Hollinger Inc. or Hollinger International by Lord Black or Ravelston or any of their affiliates. This is without prejudice to the position of any party on any issue.[11]

The idea was that both sides would temporarily drop their cudgels—the poison pill, in the case of the special committee, and the possible sale of Hollinger International or its parent company, in the case of Black—and try to reach a compromise. But privately, Black hardly appeared willing to make concessions, much less drive a spike into his secret sale deliberations with the Barclays.

After Breeden agreed to the two-week truce, Black wrote another letter to the Barclay brothers gloating over his victory.

We have just secured a deferral of the proposed [board] meeting, having frightened them with our threats of litigation and alteration of the composition of the board. We can finish our negotiations and tailor them to different contingencies. The standstill is extended two weeks. We will be ready for anything at the end of that time and are having substantive negotiations with them in the meantime.[12]

The standstill may have temporarily defused tension and prevented a brawl, but the special committee wasn't in the mood to take chances. In recent weeks, Black had dropped even the pretense of civility with Hollinger International's board and was adopting a posture of brazen confrontation. It was the culmination of a gradual but steady evolution of his attitude, which had migrated from conciliation, to defiance, to outright hostility. The members of the committee had seen enough and instructed their legal team to begin readying a lawsuit against Black, in the event the two sides could not resolve their bitter feud in the next two weeks. As added insurance, lawyers for the committee had also relayed to the SEC Black's threats to fire the board, the stock market equivalent of calling in the cops.[13] As a Delaware judge would later conclude, the company's independent directors had "whiffed the strong smell of Black's betrayal and began to try to rein him back in."[14]

———

The special committee members suspected that Black was scheming to sell his controlling stake in the parent company, Hollinger Inc., but they didn't know who the buyer would be. Although the media had widely rumoured the Barclays to be suitors, the directors were more concerned at this point that Black might be on the cusp of an agreement with Triarc, the holding company controlled by Arby's mogul Nelson Peltz, or with Tom Hicks,[15] the Texan buyout specialist who had toured the *Chicago Sun-Times* building with Colson in December.

Their concerns were not completely unfounded. Black continued to negotiate with Triarc, and even forwarded Peltz a confidential email on the proposed poison pill, while at the same time providing daily words of reassurance to the eager Barclay brothers.[16] It was as though the standstill agreement did not exist. Black had agreed to hold good-faith talks with Breeden and Paris, yet his private communications with David Barclay suggested he intended to sell Hollinger Inc., regardless.

I am confident we can deal with the [Hollinger] International board one way or another and design our deal around the poison pill threat which we can defeat. Let's let counsel proceed and perhaps speak directly in mid-week. We can suspend the standstill and consummate about Monday.[17]

The Barclays were heartened by Black's confidence but decided to store his reply in an internal memo, away from the eyes of their lawyers at Skadden, Arps, Slate, Meagher & Flom LLP. "This information is for your eyes only," one of the brothers wrote. "I do not think it is necessary to repeat to Skadden, Arps."[18]

————

Richard Breeden wanted to storm out of the room. He and Paris were sitting at Sullivan & Cromwell's midtown Manhattan offices on Wednesday, January 7, only a few days after the standstill agreement had been put in place. The four men had gathered to discuss ways of reconciling their differences and averting what could otherwise become a nasty confrontation. But Black, who was accompanied by one of his lawyers, John Warden, wasn't in the mood for peace treaties. As Breeden later recalled, Black began the meeting with a belligerent screed, immediately threatening the special committee with defamation suits in Canada or the United Kingdom, countries where it is typically easier to win a libel judgment. But Black was not content merely to sue these directors: he wanted them to pay. He said that he knew where Seitz had property in Britain, and where Savage's home was in Toronto, and he would attempt to take their belongings away from them. Breeden was furious and had to fight the urge to get up and walk out the door.[19] This meeting was supposed to be geared towards compromise, but instead it had degenerated into personal intimidation and threats. Black wasn't finished, either. He told Paris and Breeden that the restructuring agreement he had signed in November was no longer valid because he had uncovered new evidence showing that the audit committee had in fact authorized the non-compete payments he received.

There were several ways they could deal with the situation, an emboldened Black continued. His $7.2-million payment, due on June 1, could be reduced or deferred. Better yet, Breeden and the special committee could rectify his public embarrassment by issuing a statement claiming they had found no evidence of wrongdoing by Black. Paris and Breeden refused to capitulate.[20] The group concluded its meeting without any agreements, but the four men promised to consider their options and meet again the following week to see if they could reach some sort of middle ground. It was early in the game, but judging by Black's outburst, there wasn't much reason for optimism.

Black, meanwhile, was fighting another sort of battle within the parent company: trying to staunch the rapid exodus of allies and advisers. Torys and KPMG had each resigned from Hollinger Inc. in late 2003, and the board was becoming increasingly emaciated: long-serving director Charles Cowan and Black's close friend Dan Colson had both stepped down that month, not long after Sabia, Eaton, Bassett, and Gotlieb quit en masse.

Now, Black learned he was losing another staunch loyalist. Peter Atkinson, who had been providing the Hollinger group with legal advice for nearly twenty-five years, had relinquished his executive post and resigned as a director of the company for "personal reasons."[21] Regarded in Toronto legal circles as a bright and ruthless litigator, Atkinson had become a shell of himself in recent months. Physically, he looked pale and haggard, and those who were in contact with him described him as a ghost. He seemed distracted, as though he were having difficulty focusing, and when asked questions he would often gaze into space absently without replying. His departure meant that over half of Hollinger Inc.'s twelve directors had disappeared in six weeks, leaving the board with only the close-knit coterie of Black, Amiel, Radler, Boultbee, and Peter White.

Black's outer circles were shrinking as well. He had decided not to stand for re-election to the board of the Canadian Imperial Bank of Commerce, where he had spent twenty-six years as a director, follow-ing in the footsteps of his father. Black's group insisted his departure had nothing whatsoever to do with his current problems, but given the timing, and the public scrutiny on his directorships, that seemed a bit of a stretch. In the next three months, he would step down from the boards of CanWest Global Communications (in unison with Radler), Sotheby's, and Brascan, a Canadian conglomerate. The taint was spreading.

Time was running out. Breeden and Warden had agreed to have a final meeting on Friday, January 16, just two days before the standstill agreement was set to expire, in a last-ditch effort to break the current impasse and reach a compromise. But there was a problem. The night before the meeting was scheduled to take place, Paris was informed that the SEC planned to take imminent action against the company and had provided Hollinger International with an ultimatum. The board could sign a so-called "consent decree," agreeing that the company had published misleading financial statements and promising not to commit any future violations of securities laws. Or, it could refuse, in which case it would be charged with securities fraud. There was really no choice but to co-operate.[22]

Shortly before noon on Friday, Breeden notified Warden that he was cancelling their meeting because the company was in discussions with the SEC. Warden was planning to fly to Florida to visit his parents and asked Breeden whether the matter was serious enough that he should call off his trip and remain in New York for the weekend. Breeden refused to elaborate on the matter but promised to contact Warden by 1:30 P.M. if he had something useful to add.[23] Warden waited, but the call never came, so he drove to the airport that afternoon and boarded a flight to Florida. Shortly after taking off, while he was thousands of feet above the Eastern Seaboard, his client got hammered with a devastating one-two punch: the SEC filed an injunction against Hollinger International in Chicago, and the company itself launched a $200-million lawsuit against Black and Radler, as well as Ravelston, and Hollinger Inc.

The truce was officially over.

The SEC struck first. Shortly after 6 P.M. on Friday, the regulator announced that it had obtained a court order against Hollinger International, with the company's consent, that would allow the special committee's work to continue, regardless of what changes Black wanted

217

to make to the board. If Black attempted to remove the special committee, limit its progress, or oust other directors before their terms were up, Breeden would automatically be appointed a "Special Monitor" of the company with wide-ranging investigative powers. Hollinger International would have to pay $750,000 to fund the special monitor's probe, and its executives would be ordered to co-operate fully with his requests.

The suit, filed in Chicago at the U.S. District Court in the Northern District of Illinois, alleged that "corporate insiders" had benefited from $32 million in unauthorized non-compete payments, and warned there were "growing indications that some of the very same Hollinger International corporate insiders and related entities who improperly received corporate assets are attempting to thwart and obstruct the efforts of the Special Committee."[24] In a strongly worded statement, the SEC said it was continuing its investigation and promised to "bring to justice" those individuals responsible for the alleged transgressions. Wrote Stephen Cutler, the regulator's director of enforcement:

> *We are taking these immediate steps to protect the interests of Hollinger International shareholders and to ensure that the ongoing work to recover and protect corporate assets may continue unimpeded. Our work, however, is not finished.*[25]

Black's attempt to bully the board into submission had backfired in spectacular fashion. By threatening to fire the independent directors, he had essentially given the SEC no choice but to take legal action. From a man widely regarded for his skill in corporate warfare, it was yet another strategic blunder.

———

Earlier that day, Paris held separate meetings with the special committee and audit committee and asked them to authorize a $200-million lawsuit against Black, Radler, Ravelston, and Hollinger Inc., the

Toronto parent. Both committees gave their assent, and the suit was filed late that afternoon, shortly after the SEC action in Chicago.

It was a blistering attack on Black and his long-time lieutenant, Radler, painting them as avaricious executives who "diverted and usurped" the company's assets and freely dipped into the corporate coffers to fund their "extravagant" lifestyles. There were numerous email excerpts cited as evidence of Black's "proprietor's entitlement" and "contempt for the public shareholders." For the first time, the suit also publicized the preliminary results of the special committee's investigation, detailing the various deals in which Black, Radler, and other executives allegedly arranged for themselves to collect non-compete fees without telling the board.[26] The suit accused Black and Radler of signing "sham" agreements, attempting to "window-dress" payments to themselves, and fabricating records of the money they received.

Hollinger International was seeking to recover more than $200 million, plus fees and interest, including "improper" non-compete payments to Black, Radler, and others that had now swelled to $90.2 million. The remainder of the claim centred on the company's management services agreement with Ravelston. Hollinger International claimed that Black used his voting control to force it to pay "tens or hundreds of millions of dollars in excessive, unreasonable, and unjustifiable"[27] fees to Ravelston and Hollinger Inc., rather than allow it to simply hire its own management and advisory team. The suit argued that Black and other controlling shareholders had breached their fiduciary duties by imposing roughly $224 million in management fees on Hollinger International since 1995.

Although the suit was filed late Friday, its sordid laundry list of accusations would remain buried until the following morning, when Hollinger International announced the move publicly.

———

Unbeknownst to the special committee, however, Black was in the final stages of selling the company. Press Holdings International Ltd., the holding company controlled by the Barclays, had quietly entered into a confidentiality agreement with Black a few days earlier that would enable them to conduct a due diligence review of Hollinger Inc.'s financial position.[28] The idea was for the Barclays to buy Black's voting stake in the Toronto parent and then make a follow-up bid for the remainder of the company, effectively giving them control of Hollinger International and its trophy title, the London *Daily Telegraph*. At one point, David Barclay even appeared to be encouraging Black to take an adversarial position with the board. "Sometimes the best defence is to attack," he advised the press baron in a letter. "I am sure you have thoughts about it, particularly with the board at Hollinger International."[29]

But the Barclays were also growing anxious. They had heard that Lazard, the investment banker, was beginning to contact bidders for Hollinger International, and they feared their chance to lay claim to the *Telegraph* was slipping away. David Barclay wanted to complete his deal with Black on Friday, before the situation got any more complicated. "If possible," he urged Black in a letter, "I would like to sign by the close of play today. I hope you agree."[30]

Black counselled that there was no need to rush the matter. "Lazard is only sending out books next week," he replied. "I think our existing timetable is fine."[31] Later that day, however, after learning of the SEC suit, he wrote to David Barclay once more and suggested they deal with the proposed sale of Hollinger Inc. the following day, just before a scheduled meeting of Hollinger International directors.

The action of the SEC today, with the connivance of some of Hollinger's management and the special committee, has been thoroughly examined by counsel for both of us and does not seem to me, to any of us, to affect what we are planning. An executive committee meeting has been called for 7.00 tomorrow (Saturday) evening, with a very unspecific agenda. In the circumstances, and given who we are dealing with, I suggest we aim at a 6 P.M. closing. Much of the recent antics of these people is legally assailable, and we shall act, but we should make our proposed transaction bullet-proof.[32]

Black's directors had sued him, and his hands had essentially been tied by the SEC action. Yet there was still one more indignity awaiting him. On Saturday evening, he dialled into the executive committee teleconference. Seitz, who was overseas, chaired the meeting by telephone and was joined by Paris, Breeden, Savage, Thompson, and Burt. Beforehand, the group had agreed there was one additional thing they had to do: having already forced Black to step down as CEO, they were now going to strip him of his chairman's title. Given the events of the past twenty-four hours, one might have expected the meeting to be a heated affair, full of insults and threats, yet it proved to be anticlimactic. When the committee passed a motion to turf him as chairman, Black remained remarkably composed, almost as though he had been expecting it. But there was another reason for his reticence: earlier that day he had put the finishing touches on his deal with the Barclays. He didn't mention this to the other directors that evening. He wanted the element of surprise.

At 8:28 that evening, after the meeting disbanded, a fax machine in Gordon Paris's empty office at Hollinger International whirred to life and began inching out a sheet of paper.[33] It was a letter from Black, but its extraordinary contents would remain undiscovered until the next morning.

I am writing to inform Hollinger International Inc. that the Ravelston Corporation Limited and the undersigned intend tomorrow to enter into an agreement with Press Holdings International Limited, an English company, that will provide for Press Holdings to make an offer in Canada to purchase any and all of the outstanding common shares and preference shares of Hollinger Inc. and for Ravelston the undersigned to tender all such common and preference shares held directly or indirectly by us into the Offer, all on the terms and conditions to be set forth in the agreement.[34]

Black had agreed to sell his majority stake in Hollinger Inc. out from under the noses of the independent directors. If the deal went through, the Barclays would indirectly win control of Hollinger International and its prized publication, the *Telegraph,* which in turn could have grave consequences for the special committee. The members feared a successful Barclays bid could essentially kill any chance of auctioning off the company's assets to the highest bidder, in addition to complicating their attempts to seek financial damages from Black.

Following the filing of the lawsuits, there was a blur of activity. On Sunday morning, each member of Hollinger International's board received a letter from Black that outlined his deal with the Barclays and staked out his new position: he no longer believed the November restructuring agreement was valid, because his lawyers had uncovered evidence that the unauthorized payments had in fact been properly approved. Black had no intention of repaying the money. "The entire sequence of events based on the premise that these were 'unauthorized payments' has been invalid," he contended. "I am of the view that this Board was misled."

Black accused the special committee of making misrepresentations to him and insisted the lawsuit was a "spurious complaint" and a "desperate attempt" to prevent him from striking a deal for Hollinger Inc.

Further, I do not accept the validity of the Executive Committee's purported removal of me as Chairman of the Board, nor most of its other recent initiatives, which clearly were undertaken because the authors of these steps lack confidence in their ability to win a vote of the whole Board.[35]

Like the other members of the special committee, Seitz was incredulous. As far as he could tell, Black had violated the November restructuring agreement by agreeing to sell Hollinger Inc. The agreement stipulated that Black could only sell ownership of the parent company if it was facing a "material default or insolvency," which didn't seem to be the case. Even if the parent company was on the brink of financial collapse, he was required to give Hollinger International "as much advance notice as reasonably possible" before selling his shares. Faxing a letter to a deserted office just a few hours before the standstill agreement ran out did not strike the committee as sufficient warning.

Seitz was equally baffled by Black's contention that the non-compete payments had been approved. The "new" evidence he cited didn't seem new at all; rather, it seemed remarkably similar to information Black had highlighted in his letter to the special committee the previous November. "I had the feeling," Seitz would later recall, "that … this was a bit like the invasion of Czechoslovakia, and that I was in the unhappy role of Neville Chamberlain, because we had a perfectly good faith agreement in November, and I had expected that would be adhered to. But in the course of December, and in January, it became clear that, in my view, Mr. Black was reneging on several parts of that. And then when this letter came, I was confirmed in my suspicions."[36]

The directors also received a letter from the Barclay brothers, who had just announced their deal with Black and Ravelston. The Barclays had agreed to buy Ravelston's 78-percent stake in Hollinger Inc. for about C$424 million and also promised to assume about C$182 million in company debt. That worked out to C$8.44 for every common share of the company, more than double the stock's last trading price of C$3.90.[37] Still, it was a pretty inexpensive way to seize control of the *Telegraph*, which in itself was worth around US$1 billion, not to mention the *Chicago Sun-Times* and *The Jerusalem Post*.

The Barclays requested a meeting with Hollinger International's board as early as possible, so they could explain how the deal would benefit the company's shareholders. They insisted their planned acquisition of Hollinger Inc. was the "only viable alternative" to resolve the current impasse and pledged not to interfere with the special committee investigation. Their letter stated,

We believe this continued media controversy is significantly harming the public image and stock price of Hollinger International and undermining its credibility in the financial markets. As part of the acquisition, the negative media attention should cease.[38]

Black himself echoed these sentiments in a brief statement to the public. "[It] will be distressing to part from the *Telegraph* newspapers, the *Spectator,* the Chicago newspapers and *The Jerusalem Post,*" he said, but "these fine titles must not be hobbled any longer by the current controversies and financial uncertainty. They will be in good and caring hands, and we will be able to focus exclusively on resolving current legal and public-relations concerns."[39]

But in a handwritten fax that same day to David Barclay, Black indicated he was not content merely to strike a deal and move on. He planned to fight the SEC injunction and take legal action against his enemies.

My lawsuits will begin tomorrow. The most important early test will be our challenge of the outrage with the SEC in Chicago. Counsel say our prospects are good. In any case, we will prevail eventually, and indications are that the opposition is very flustered and befuddled about what to do. They have called a directors' meeting for Tuesday morning and I will do some canvassing beforehand and keep you abreast of events.[40]

David Barclay's reply was sympathetic. "It is a conspiracy to defraud you out of your rights to sell and get maximum value for your shares," he wrote, referring to the executive committee's removal of Black as chairman and its attempts to thwart a sale of Hollinger Inc. "It is vindictive and malicious."

———

Once again, the special committee members had been saddled with an added set of responsibilities. Their investigation had essentially stalled for the past several weeks as they attempted to reach a compromise that would prevent Black from trying to sell Hollinger Inc. Now, however, they found themselves locked in a vicious takeover battle, a consuming challenge that could delay their probe indefinitely. The diversion came at the worst possible time, in that both the SEC and the FBI were quietly ramping up their investigations of the company. Indeed, the FBI, which functions as the investigative unit of the U.S. Justice Department, had invited some of the special committee's lawyers to attend meetings in which the FBI was questioning witnesses.

For now, however, the special committee's most pressing task was protecting Hollinger International's shareholders and getting the highest price for the company's assets. The committee feared that Black's deal with the Barclays could kill Lazard's efforts to find a buyer for Hollinger International, since prospective bidders would think the "game [was] already over" and not bother to submit offers.[41] Faced with these difficulties, the board called another meeting to discuss their options.

Almost from the beginning, there was trouble. Paris, who had been appointed as the interim chairman over the objections of Black and Amiel, proposed the creation of a "corporate review committee" to examine Black's proposed deal with the Barclays and consider the company's alternatives. The committee would consist of all of Hollinger International's directors, with the exception of Black, Amiel, and Colson, all of whom had ties to Black's private holding company, Ravelston. Amiel immediately took issue with being excluded from the committee and snapped that "it was an interesting legal theory that by virtue of marriage one could be deemed to have a conflicting interest."

Black, meanwhile, had worked himself into a fury over the lawsuit the company had filed against him. He described the allegations as "frivolous and fictitious" and insisted that the directors knew he had never resorted to bullying tactics. Yet in the same breath, he warned that "anyone supporting this defamation will feel part of the response to this."

When Thompson asked the board to formally approve the suit, Black and Amiel objected. Colson abstained from the voting, while Paris,

Seitz, Savage, Burt, and Thompson each voted in favour. That left Kissinger, who was clearly ill at ease. Of all the directors, the former secretary of state appeared to be the most pained by the recent feuding. He still counted Black as a close friend and had tried to avoid this sort of unpleasant scene by brokering the ceasefire agreement in early January, yet his personal reputation was also at stake in this mess. When Thompson finally called upon him and asked how he planned to vote, Kissinger answered in the affirmative: he was supporting the suit. For a moment, it was as though all of the air had been sucked out of the meeting. Black, dumbstruck at the possibility that a comrade had betrayed him, thought there must have been some kind of mistake and asked Kissinger whether he had heard his reply properly. Kissinger awkwardly confirmed that yes, he was voting to ratify the lawsuit. There was a brief pause before Black growled a Shakespearean parting shot: "Et tu, Brute?"

After sniping at Kissinger, Black clashed briefly with Breeden. The former SEC chief had outlined the gist of the special committee's investigation and insisted that contrary to Black's claims, there was "no new evidence here" indicating that the board had approved the payments he received. "There were no minutes, no resolution, no evidence of any corporate action justifying the payments," Breeden told the other directors.

"It may not be new to you but it is new to me," Black barked in response. He maintained that there had been an "endless campaign to defame" him and that the special committee was releasing damaging information, "endlessly harping about backdated documents." There was not "one single shred of evidence that [he] knew" the non-compete payments were unauthorized, Black went on, even though he admitted that "obviously [he] could have done things better."

He finished his speech by saying he did not know whether history would judge him to have committed an honest error or some kind of negligence, but he did know this much: the lawsuit was a "mendacious" manoeuvre meant to destroy his reputation and ruin his financial stability. He accused the special committee of launching a "series of Pearl

Harbor attacks" and said they had violated the November restructuring agreement in myriad ways. "It is all very interesting to insist on implementing an agreement you've reduced to Swiss cheese," he said.

At the conclusion of the hour-long meeting, Kissinger asked to say a few words. He began by acknowledging that he had been a friend of Black's for decades and that he had taken major pains to help reconcile the current dispute. He wanted to go on record as saying that while he was not supporting every allegation in the lawsuit against Black and Radler, he did support the right of the special committee to defend Hollinger International's shareholders with legal action, once all other avenues of compromise had been exhausted.

Kissinger's attempts at appeasement, and even his expressions of friendship, proved to be little comfort. Black's league of high-profile allies on the company's board, once a source of such pride and enjoyment, had steadily turned against him, leaving him increasingly alone. In response to Kissinger's monologue, Black angrily insisted: "The shareholders do not need protection from me."

After the meeting, Black dashed off another handwritten note to the Barclays to provide them with an update.

It was an unpleasant meeting this morning. They have high-jacked the company and set up a corporate review committee from which Barbara and Dan Colson and I are excluded, to consider our deal. The only method of blocking our deal we can see is to try to sell the Telegraph *separately, which would have disastrous tax consequences.*[42]

Black may have been excluded from the corporate review committee, but that didn't mean he was about to stop fighting. Although the SEC action deterred him from firing the entire board, Black believed he had found a new way to neutralize the directors: through what is known as a "written consent," he had made the parent company change the corporate bylaws of Hollinger International. The effect, in general terms, was to disband the corporate review committee and give Black veto power over pretty much any significant board decision. From now on, the unanimous consent of every director would be required for any "special board matter." The implication was clear: if Black didn't agree with the majority of the board on an important issue, like a poison pill, he could shoot them down with a single vote. Shortly after changing the bylaws, he sent the Barclays a letter boasting of how he had once again outfoxed the independent directors.

> *The enemy's pathetic press release, as well as our second release, is enclosed. We caught them with their pants down, preparing more skullduggery. We will throw an injunction at them in London Monday morning re the* Telegraph, *and they may have abandoned the Lazard's fire-sale nonsense. The New York press is finally on their backs. Counsel think we can already stop a poison pill with what we did today. They were going to do another Saturday night special. If we need to do more, we will. Obviously, the SEC won't bail them out this time. We think we can hold the fort and will be suing them in three countries next week.*[43]

Black's rhetorical flourishes against the special committee were even more heated the next day. In yet another letter to the Barclays, he told them he looked forward to a "glorious victory over truly wicked people."[44]

———

The corporate review committee had no intention of heeding Black's bylaw amendments. Although the Barclay brothers promised not to interfere in the strategic process, Hollinger International's directors knew how much the British twins coveted the *Telegraph* and were unconvinced the brothers would agree to sell the storied newspaper if Lazard found a willing buyer at the right price. The committee wanted the flexibility to get the best deal for all shareholders, not just for Black and other Ravelston owners. The directors were also worried that the Barclays deal could hurt their chances of recovering the allegedly improper payments to executives.

Faced with these problems, the group met on the last Sunday in January—almost three weeks after Black had initially threatened to sue the directors—and swiftly took action. First, they adopted the poison pill, otherwise known as a "shareholders rights plan," to make it impractical for the Barclays to complete their bid. Second, they agreed to file a lawsuit the following day in the Delaware Chancery Court asking a judge to block the proposed transaction with the Barclays. The lawsuit also sought an injunction against Black to prevent him from breaching the November restructuring agreement, and a ruling that he could not nullify the poison pill by dismantling the review committee. The first line of the lawsuit, filed the next day, encapsulated the acid nature of the rift between the two sides. "This is an action to prevent a disloyal director and controlling shareholder of the Company from manipulating the Company's corporate machinery for his own selfish financial purposes."[45]

Black, however, insisted he was relishing the fight and once again vowed to emerge the victor. From Toronto, he wrote the following in a letter to David and Frederick Barclay:

We are now organizing the pre-trial and trial in Delaware, and much looking forward to it. There was almost violence between some of our lawyers over who would have the pleasure of questioning Breeden, Paris, and Thompson. They have been so sleazy and dishonest throughout this process, we will give them a real sleigh-ride. I only have to tell the truth, and have a reasonable grasp of the facts. I am looking forward to finally getting my story out. If they go to trial, they are making a serious mistake.[46]

CHAPTER FIFTEEN

Delaware

IT IS DIFFICULT to think of a more unlikely home for some of the world's most powerful companies than the diminutive state of Delaware. Measuring just thirty-five miles from tip to tip, and a scant nine miles across at its narrowest point, the triangular sliver of land on the Atlantic coast is the second-smallest U.S. state after Rhode Island. Its entire population, estimated at about 820,000, wouldn't even rank among the top ten cities in the country. Yet what Delaware lacks in size, it makes up for in bragging rights: roughly 58 percent of all Fortune 500 companies are incorporated here, as are more than half of the publicly traded companies in the United States.[1]

There are several reasons why big companies call the Diamond State home. It's one of the cheapest and easiest places to incorporate. There are favourable tax advantages. And, most importantly, it is the only state that maintains a separate court system specializing in corporate law. The centuries-old Delaware Court of Chancery is one of the world's most respected arbiters of corporate disputes, with an unparalleled reputation for making fast and concise rulings on highly complex financial matters. Its decisions, which routinely set precedents for other U.S. courts, have long been regarded as fairly predictable, since there are no juries: instead, the chancery has five judges—one chancellor, and four vice-chancellors—each with extensive expertise in the area.

Historically, many of the court's decisions have been regarded as business-friendly, adding to the state's appeal. But in the post-Enron world, where investor confidence had been sapped by an unrelenting string of major corporate scandals, the court was beginning to hold controlling shareholders and boards of directors to a much tougher standard. The judge presiding over the fight between Black and his adversaries was no exception.

Vice-Chancellor Leo E. Strine, Jr., had been named to the chancery bench in 1998 at the precocious age of thirty-four, but only by a relatively slim twelve-to-eight margin (many of the previous appointments had been unanimous). Some of Strine's detractors felt he was too young, too inexperienced, and too cheeky to assume the post. He had worked for a few years at the legal firm Skadden, Arps, which was now representing the Barclay brothers, and before taking the bench had served as counsel to Delaware governor Thomas Carper. His opponents feared he could scare away one of the state's biggest cash cows: tax dollars from incorporated companies. "It would be hard for me to believe a corporation would pull out of Delaware on that basis,"[2] Strine responded, shortly after his nomination.

By 2004, Strine's six years on the bench had earned him a reputation as a highly capable judge who was not afraid to make unpopular decisions and who did not shy away from sharply worded rebukes in his voluminous written opinions. In 2001, he ordered Tyson Foods, Inc. and IBP, Inc. to consummate their $3-billion merger, after Tyson attempted to back out because of financial troubles at IBP. And just recently, in late 2003, he had ordered the former head of HealthSouth Corporation, Richard Scrushy, to repay a $25-million loan he had borrowed to buy shares in the company.

This was clearly not the same Chancery Court of a decade earlier.

On the morning of Wednesday, February 18, 2004, a throng of British, American, and Canadian media shuffled in a lineup outside the New Castle County Courthouse, a gleaming new building in the decaying downtown core of Wilmington. They had come to this small town, about a thirty-minute drive southwest of Philadelphia, to witness a much-anticipated three-day legal showdown between Black and his adversaries at Hollinger International. Black's outsized persona and bombastic repartee had always magnetized reporters, but now the media were salivating at a much more tantalizing spectacle: the prospect of seeing the embattled press baron humbled in a courtroom.

Just a week earlier, Black had slapped Breeden, Paris, Seitz, Savage, Thompson, and Burt with a colourfully worded C$850-million libel suit, accusing them of turning him into a "loathsome laughingstock" and "social leper" by setting out to destroy his reputation with "vicious vaporings and a vile tissue of lies."[3] But the libel suit paled in comparison with what was at stake in Wilmington, Delaware, where lawyers on both sides had deposited a thicket of legal briefs.

Hollinger International wanted Judge Strine to block the Barclays deal, scrap Black's attempts at rewriting the company's bylaws, and force him to abide by the November restructuring agreement while the special committee completed its investigation. Black, through Hollinger Inc., had filed a countersuit that sought to disband the review committee, scrap the restructuring agreement, and nullify the poison pill, which was characterized as "blatant thievery" of the parent company's voting rights. It was a devilishly complex set of arguments, exacerbated by the Hollinger group's convoluted corporate structure. But Judge Strine intended to issue a prompt ruling. The fate of Hollinger International, and of Black's deal with the Barclays, would be decided in just over a week.

Gordon Paris was the first to take the stand on Wednesday. Black, who was not testifying until Friday, the last day of the trial, had arrived in Wilmington earlier that week but did not show up for Paris's appearance. The twelfth-floor courtroom was buzzing with reporters, governance experts, shareholders—including Tweedy and Cardinal—and enough lawyers to start a respectable-sized firm. Dozens more observers who were unable to get a seat in the actual court were crammed into an overflow room, where they had to settle for watching the proceedings on a closed-circuit monitor.

Paris, dressed in a dark suit and a bright red tie, took the court through the formation of the special committee and repeatedly explained how its investigation could find no authorization for tens of millions of dollars in non-compete payments to Black and other executives. For the first time, he offered a behind-the-scenes glimpse of the committee's dealings with Black in the feverish week leading up to the November agreement when Black agreed to step down as CEO and repay $7.2 million in fees. Paris discussed his meetings with Black in general terms, including the dinner discussion at Le Cirque. "This was a matter of utmost importance," he said of the special committee's need to act following the discovery of the allegedly improper non-compete payments. "In our judgment, there was inaccurate disclosure in the marketplace, and there needed to be corrected disclosure as quickly as possible."

He also told Judge Strine that Black had been negotiating with the Barclays for much longer than anyone had known, and indeed had passed along confidential information to the British twins—including Hollinger International's consideration of the poison pill defence—in the early days of January. He maintained that the sale of Hollinger Inc. to the Barclay brothers would have a "chilling effect" on Lazard's auction process and undermine the company's ability to find the best deal for shareholders.[4] Paris testified that Black, meanwhile, had threatened to kick independent directors off the Hollinger International board when he discovered their contemplation of a poison pill and had threatened some of them with legal action.

Paris, who appeared confident and very much in command of the complicated nuances of the case, was at times combative when answering questions in cross-examination from Black's lawyers, who tried to cast doubt on the special committee's allegations that Black had collected money improperly. But throughout his five-hour testimony, he repeatedly stuck to the same assertion. "The fact is—and I will go back to the statement—that these are unauthorized payments and they are inappropriate and we found no evidence of authorization," he insisted in one testy exchange. Later he maintained that the basis for some of these non-compete payments to Black was utterly "fictitious."[5]

He was followed in the stand by Seitz, who also said that after a thorough investigation, the special committee could find no sign that the payments to Black and others had been approved. The initial payments, he explained, were diverted to Hollinger Inc., the parent company, ostensibly without authorization. In later deals, however, they flowed directly to the executives, and in one instance the executives actually received money not to compete against American Publishing, a Hollinger International subsidiary. "Obviously, it's odd ... to agree not to compete with yourself," said Seitz, who described the trajectory of these payments as moving "from the peculiar to the bizarre."[6] Like Paris, he stated that the committee had no choice but to confront Black about the payments, demand an explanation, and then take action to correct Hollinger International's previous financial statements to the public. "It was very clear to us that there was a lot of misinformation in the marketplace, that the disclosure about these transactions was flawed at best, and false at worst."[7]

Seitz cited a conversation in December when Black told him that Hollinger Inc. had "other resources" and would not "crater" by March 1, when it was scheduled to make a $7.4-million interest payment on its junk bonds. It was a key point, since it cast doubt on Black's argument that he needed to sell his controlling stake in the parent company to help it avoid financial collapse. Indeed, a calamity of this sort was the one loophole Black could use to negotiate a sale of his shares in the parent company under the November restructuring agreement.

"My belief," Seitz told Judge Strine, in reference to the proposed sale to the Barclays, "is that this transaction is an effort by a controlling shareholder of International to satisfy his self-interest without any regard to the independent directors or to the shareholders."[8] Black's lawyers showed Seitz copies of resolutions by the executive committee—consisting of Black, Radler, and Perle—apparently approving some non-compete payments to both Hollinger Inc. and specific individuals. But Seitz fired back that two of the three committee members were "self interested," and the committee merely "approved payments to itself."[9]

It was Breeden's turn on Thursday. The former SEC chief painted Black as a bumptious bully who had gone back on his word to co-operate with the special committee. "Mr. Black begins many conversations by threatening everybody, or at least many of the conversations I've been involved with."[10] He recounted how a January meeting with Black and his lawyer began by the press baron

> ... glaring at us and telling us that he had every intention of bringing the actions against the members of the special committee, that he didn't care what defamation law in the United States was, that the law in the United Kingdom and the law in Canada was very different.

He also told Judge Strine of Black's threats to seize property from Seitz and Savage and "fix their wagon good."[11]

Breeden testified that shortly before signing the two-week standstill agreement in early January, Black had told him that he had "no intention whatsoever of doing a transaction at Hollinger Inc." and that he was going to support Lazard's strategic auction process. The Barclays' deal, Breeden said, was a threat to Hollinger International in any number of ways, including the possibility that Black could abscond with the proceeds from the sale and limit Hollinger International's ability to recover money for its shareholders.

If it is completed and Mr. Black can liquefy its holdings, indirect hold-ings, in Hollinger Inc., and take the cash and get out of Dodge ... before a judgment is reached and anyone could seek to enforce the judgment, that inherently poses a risk of interfering with the process.[12]

That Thursday night, Black was having dinner with a few lawyers at a corner table in the Green Room, a French restaurant located on the ground floor of the four-star Hotel du Pont. Across the room, an ornately decorated space with flowing red drapery and carved oak panelling, Breeden and Paris were tucking into their food with some colleagues. Close by, at yet another table, was Bert Denton, the share-holder activist who had worked on the Hollinger file with Tweedy and Cardinal, and his dining companion Charles Elson, the noted corporate governance expert and University of Delaware professor.

Midway through the meal, one of Breeden's associates sauntered over to a nearby group of reporters and public relations officials. "Watch this," he said. The group looked on as the lawyer walked over to Black's table and, in an act of grand showmanship, served him with the papers for Hollinger International's $200-million lawsuit, launched more than a month earlier.

Warden, who was sitting with Black, quickly grabbed the papers. After a cursory glance, he emphatically threw the documents on the floor. It was entertaining theatre for the reporters fortunate enough to have snagged a table at the posh eatery, and a fitting prelude to Black's testimony the following day.[13]

On Friday morning, Black's hulking figure loomed into view atop the crest of a street that sloped gently down to the entrance of the New Castle County Courthouse. His entourage consisted of about eight people, including lawyers and a public relations executive who was attempting to shield him from the media. A gaggle of photographers and television reporters, who had been lurking expectantly a short distance from the court, surrounded the beleaguered press baron as he attempted to make his way to the building. This was clearly not the same Conrad Black who had defiantly jousted with a swarm of reporters at the Indigo book signing in late November. Recent events had taken a visible toll on his physical bearing: he appeared ashen with exhaustion, and the pendulous bags under his creased eyes seemed to have billowed overnight, aging him in the process. The bluster was gone, and he was in little mood to spar. A reporter for the British Broadcasting Corporation pestered him as to why the Delaware proceedings were so important.

"Who do you work for?" Black asked.

"The BBC, sir," the reporter answered. "Could you tell us why you're here?"

"Not to talk to the BBC."

Just before Black entered the building, another reporter hollered, "Are you bullying the members of the board, Lord Black?" Black stopped momentarily, stole a quick look at his inquisitor, and countered, "Circumstances would suggest not."

———

Before the media could watch Black on the stand, they had to witness the conclusion of Peter White's testimony. White, a Ravelston shareholder and the chief operating officer of Hollinger Inc., had been a colleague of Black's for forty years. A week earlier, he had written a comment piece in *The Globe and Mail* titled "Don't Let Lilliputians Win," in which he accused Tweedy Browne of creating a media "frenzy" in order to pressure the board into launching an internal investigation and drawing the attention of securities regulators. He coined the term "Browne-mail" to describe Tweedy's use of legal and media pressure tactics.

There is probably no public company against which the Tweedy Brownes of this world could not assert some accusation of malfeasance, and self-righteously demand corrective action, in the hope of forcing a sale of the company's assets.[14]

He also singled out Black as an "undeniably great leader" who had done nothing illegal, and warned that

Overzealous attempts to circumscribe our leaders' actions risks immobilizing them, like Gulliver among the Lilliputians, defeating the point of great leadership.[15]

The focus of White's testimony was the financial situation of Hollinger Inc., which he characterized as precarious. He told the court that with the looming debt repayments, he had asked his advisers to investigate the company's options for seeking protection from its creditors.[16] "We don't have the money," Mr. White insisted. "We're broke."[17]

Lawyers for Hollinger International, in a tense cross-examination, disputed his testimony and pointed out that the company could easily repay its debt by calling in one of Black's loans from Ravelston or simply by selling shares in the company.

———

Black was the final witness in the three-day hearing, and as the onlookers well knew, the outcome could hinge on his testimony. Dressed in a dark suit, with a pale grey shirt and tie, Black explained how he learned from the special committee that some of the non-compete payments he had received were not approved by the board and told of how Paris had threatened him with "draconian measures"[18] if he was uncooperative with the committee's requests. Black then proceeded to outline the evidence his legal team had collected since the restructuring agreement was put in place in November, evidence he claimed suggested the non-competes had been given the board's blessing.

He cited three main items as proof, echoing the letter he had sent to the special committee in late January: minutes of an audit committee meeting at Hollinger International in February 2002, indicating unanimous approval of financial statements that listed various non-compete payments as having been approved;[19] minutes of a Hollinger Inc. meeting in March 2002, in which auditors KPMG confirmed that the non-compete payments at Hollinger International had been approved by the audit committee; and notes of a conference call in which Thompson, the head of Hollinger International's audit committee, allegedly told an outside law firm that his committee had approved some of these payments in question (an allegation that Thompson denied). Said Black:

> *While I'm open-minded about this, I do not think any reasonable person in my position at this time would conclude that it's necessarily clear that I have a legal or moral duty to repay this money.*[20]

It was not long, however, before Black asked the court if he could say a few words about this scandal that had besmirched his name.

> *In consequence of the controversy that's arisen over these payments I have been horribly defamed. In fact, I've been characterized and stigmatized as an embezzler. And I had been assured many times by people whom I trusted—and indeed it's come to light in depositions prior to these proceedings—that these particular authorizations, approvals, references, however they may be described and whatever credence you may wish to attach to them, sir, did not exist. Nothing like them existed. I am trying, apart from the direct legal proceedings, to retrieve my reputation as an honest man....*[21]

At one point in the day, during a break, Black was accosted in the bathroom by a process server representing yet another shareholder who was suing him. The server found him in a stall and then proceeded to serve him with papers.[22]

Later that afternoon, upon cross-examination, Black appeared far less certain of himself. When asked whether he entered into a personal non-compete agreement as part of a newspaper sale to Community Newspaper Holdings, he answered, "I'm not sure if I did."[23] Similarly, he was "not sure"[24] whether documents he signed in 2002, disclosing his non-compete agreement with a Hollinger International subsidiary, were false. He was "not sure"[25] about the non-compete agreement with Forum Communications Inc., another newspaper purchaser. When Hollinger International's lawyer, Martin Flumenbaum, asked if a company financial report in March 2003 was "false," partly because Black and others had received backdated payments, Black shrugged and said, "I don't know."[26]

The relentless questioning continued throughout the afternoon, as Flumenbaum attempted to depict Black as an underhanded CEO who diverted improper payments to himself, violated his agreement with the company by secretly negotiating a transaction with the Barclay brothers, and then threatened various members of the board.

The six-hour testimony ended in dramatic fashion. Responding to a contention that he had referred to critics as "a bunch of self-righteous hypocrites and ingrates," Black replied, "Only certain of [the critics]. The stock has risen 140 percent since then, Mr. Flumenbaum."

"Does that give you the right to steal other people's money?" Flumenbaum shot back.

"Objection," shouted David Braff, one of Black's lawyers.

"Overruled," snapped Judge Strine.

Black was forced to respond. "The answer," he said, "is no."[27]

Gordon Paris was sitting in his Fifth Avenue office at Hollinger International when he received the news. It was a little before 6 P.M. on Thursday, February 26, less than a week since Black's testimony, and

Judge Strine had just released his opinion. Paris only had to scan the first page to realize that Hollinger International had scored a decisive victory—and that Black, who had been fairly bursting with confidence before the trial, had been dealt a crippling and humiliating blow. Judge Strine's opinion began,

> *[The] most interesting corporate law cases involve the color gray, with contending parties dueling over close questions of law, in circumstances where it is possible for each of the contestants to claim she was acting in good faith. Regrettably, this case is not one of them. Rather, in this case, defendant Conrad M. Black, the controlling stockholder of Hollinger International, Inc.... a Delaware public company, has repeatedly behaved in a manner inconsistent with the duty of loyalty he owed the company.*[28]

Judge Strine issued an injunction that killed Black's deal with the Barclays and that prevented him from further violations of the November restructuring agreement. The ruling also struck down Black's attempts to single-handedly alter Hollinger International's bylaws and upheld the board's efforts to protect the company with a poison pill. "At worst, the [Hollinger] International board was purposely duped and there was fraud on the board," Judge Strine stated. "At best, they were entirely uninformed. In either instance, the [Hollinger] International independent directors did not properly approve the non-compete payments under Delaware law."[29]

It was bad enough for Black to lose such a one-sided decision. But however painful that might have been, it paled beside the damage inflicted upon his reputation. Although Judge Strine was known for his pointed commentary, nobody had foreseen the extent to which he would assail Black's character and question his integrity. Judge Strine concluded,

> *As to Black himself, it became impossible for me to credit his word, after considering the trial testimony in light of the overwhelming*

evidence of his less-than-candid conduct towards his fellow directors
... I found Black evasive and unreliable. His explanations of key
events and of his own motivations do not have the ring of truth. I find
it regrettable to say so but it is the inescapable, and highly relevant,
conclusion I reach.[30]

For instance, Judge Strine concluded that Black breached the November restructuring agreement in a "cunning and calculated" way, by diverting a potential buyer—the Barclays—away from Lazard's efforts to sell Hollinger International's assets. "Stated bluntly, Black steered the Barclays toward doing an end run around the Strategic Process,"[31] he wrote. The ruling also found that Black broke his contractual duties "persistently and seriously."

During the course of his dealings, Black misrepresented facts to the
[Hollinger] International board, used confidential company informa-
tion for his own purposes without permission, and made threats, as he
would put it, of "multifaceted" dimensions toward Hollinger
International's independent directors.[32]

The Barclays were also singled out for knowingly concealing important information from Lazard and the company's independent directors. "[They] purposely remained silent and did not inform Lazard (or anyone at [Hollinger] International) that they were negotiating with Black."[33]

These opinions contrasted sharply with Judge Strine's impression of Hollinger International's three primary witnesses. He described Paris, Seitz, and Breeden as "entirely credible" and said he could "discern no improper motive they may have had at any time to testify other than truthfully."[34] For the entire Black team, the ruling was nothing less than a scathing indictment. For Hollinger International, it was pure vindication.

When Paris read the decision, he exchanged high-fives with a handful of other executives at Hollinger International's New York offices. Someone was sent down the street to fetch a few bottles of champagne, and the group had a celebratory toast. Shortly afterward, Paris and his associates strolled to the Carnegie Club, a bar near Carnegie Hall, for drinks with the legal team at Paul, Weiss.

The Black camp, meanwhile, was devastated. In the days following the trial, both he and his lawyers had been feeling confident and upbeat. They believed the case had gone rather well and that, at the very least, they would be able to limit the duration of the poison pill. But the Strine decision had been delivered with the force of a sledgehammer.

That evening, after the ruling was published, Black's legal representatives at Sullivan & Cromwell arranged a conference call with his cadre of lawyers. Everyone was incredulous. There had always been the possibility that Black might lose the case, but no one could have foreseen just how bloodied he would become in the aftermath. Warden began the call, and as each new lawyer came on the line they expressed their outrage at the decision.

When Black responded he sounded subdued, but not utterly distraught. "What are we going to do?" he asked gravely. "I have been excoriated by the court."

CHAPTER SIXTEEN

RICO Offensive

WITH THE THRASHING he had suffered at the pen of Judge Strine, almost everyone agreed that Black's ability to finagle a sale of his controlling stake in Hollinger Inc. had been all but extinguished. Everyone, that is, except for Black himself. While the ruling barred him from interfering with Lazard's efforts to auction off the company and prevented him from meddling with the special committee investigation, and while publicly, Black appeared chastened and promised to abide by the verdict, privately, he was carrying out a different agenda. Only days after the devastating Delaware judgment had been handed down, the hobbled press baron was at it again, holding covert financing talks that he hoped would neutralize his adversaries on the special committee.

In late February, he sent a letter to Joe Steinberg, the president of New York buyout firm Leucadia National, pitching an investment in his private holding company, Ravelston. Black claimed that an investment would enable him to "repossess the company, restore order, [and] see off the Special Committee." He also described "Breeden and his fascists" as "truly evil people, who are a menace to capitalism as any sane and civilized person would define it."[1] With each setback, Black seemed to become more embittered and desperate. Clearly, he was not about to sit idle while Lazard sold the company.

——

Hollinger International, meanwhile, had little time to revel in its decisive triumph in Delaware. The Strine ruling had enabled Lazard to attract a number of additional bidders, some of which had been frightened away by the proposed Barclays deal. Just as important, the special committee was now able to return to its investigation, which had fallen into neglect since the late fall. On March 8, the committee members converged in Greenwich at the restored barn that served as Breeden's office. Just days earlier, the board had stripped Black of yet another title, removing him as chairman of the Telegraph Group Ltd., the subsidiary that housed his crown jewel, the *Telegraph*. Today, however, they were huddled around a conference table discussing how to wind up their probe. In front of each of them was a recently prepared report on Hollinger International's transactions with Horizon and Bradford, the private newspaper companies controlled by Black and Radler. The document was brimming with examples of apparent self-dealing by the two men for their own financial benefit. There were also reports on other problematic items, including a bizarre bonus plan at investment subsidiary Hollinger Digital and Amiel's seemingly inexplicable annual salary.

It was clear that the special committee would have to file at least one more lawsuit, or possibly an amended version of its January complaint, to enumerate these findings and complete its work. What had yet to be resolved, however, was whether the group would pursue legal action against the board of directors. This was a delicate subject, since many of the directors, particularly those on the audit committee, had been an instrumental part of the investigation and important allies in the battle against Black. By the same token, the special committee members agreed that the audit committee had been less than thorough at the best of times and seriously ineffective in general.

After debating these issues for the better part of an hour, Savage turned to Breeden and asked, "Have you ever thought of having this place swept for bugs?" It was an attempt at gallows humour, but it also underlined the increasing stakes of the investigation. Black was always the primary target, yet now their focus was widening to include some high-profile directors, including Richard Perle, the supremely well-connected policy hawk.

Breeden, who appeared momentarily startled by the question, replied, "No. Why would I do that?"

Savage shrugged and said, "A lot of people would like to know what goes on here."

In the face of adverse rulings and public humiliation, Black pressed on. The same day the special committee held its meeting in Connecticut, Black's private holding company, Ravelston, filed a $170-million lawsuit against Hollinger International in an Ontario court. Ravelston claimed that Hollinger International wrongfully terminated its management services agreement, which had been such a lucrative income stream for the past several years. The suit was demanding $150 million in damages, plus other amounts Ravelston said it was still owed.

Days later, Black filed an appeal of Strine's judgment. Hollinger Inc. said it "respectfully" disagreed with the judge's view of the facts but would continue to support the Lazard auction.[2] The appeal, which would prove unsuccessful, was one of a number of smaller legal skirmishes Black engaged in with Hollinger International over the ensuing months, some of which, surmised Judge Strine in a subsequent ruling, looked suspiciously like stall tactics.[3]

The first round of informal bids poured into the Lazard office on March 23, the day after Black lost his appeal of the Delaware ruling.

At first glance, the offers appeared exceedingly promising. Of the 116 parties that signed confidentiality agreements, almost half submitted bids by the deadline. Five or six suitors had expressed interest in buying all of Hollinger International at a wide range of prices. Ten offers were submitted for the Chicago Group, with a high bid of nearly $1.2 billion, and nine offers were made for the Telegraph Group, also with a high bid of $1.2 billion. Rounding out the offers were more than twenty letters of interest in the Canadian newspapers, the highest being $117 million, and another nine for the Jerusalem Group, running up to $25 million.[4]

After reviewing the expressions of interest, Lazard invited nine bidders to participate in the second round. One of them was the Barclay brothers, who were still smarting from Strine's opinion. Sir David, in a rare public statement, accused Strine of making "damaging, unwarranted and uncalled-for allegations" against him and his brother that were "grossly unfair" and violated "the basic principles of natural justice." Despite the scolding in Delaware, however, the Barclays were not about to give up their quest for the *Telegraph*.

Although Lazard had received bids for the overall company, the firm was beginning to doubt whether it could sell the entire thing in one chunk. Any such deal would be complicated by a range of tax issues. There was also the ongoing battle between Black and Hollinger International, which had prevented the company from filing audited financial statements. Obviously, most buyers were worried they might get caught in the legal crossfire between Black and his adversaries and wanted to be assured they would not face major legal liabilities. The more Lazard examined the situation, the more it looked like Hollinger International would be bundled off in pieces.

Around the time the bids were being collected, Black was losing yet more allies within the company. On March 15, his wife stepped down from her position as vice-president of editorial at Hollinger International after the special committee wrote to her seeking an explanation of her salary. In essence, the committee was giving her an opportunity to justify her compensation before the next lawsuit was filed. Amiel had received $276,000 from the *Chicago Sun-Times* in 2002, even though the newspaper's senior managers had not seen her on the premises since 1999. She also was paid a smaller sum, $29,297, by the *Telegraph* for penning columns.[5] Amiel replied with a curt note informing them she was giving up her post. "To whom it may concern," she wrote on personal letterhead emblazoned with her title, Lady Barbara Amiel Black. "Effective immediately, I hereby resign as an officer (but not as a director) of Hollinger International Inc. Sincerely, Barbara Amiel Black."

She wasn't the only Black loyalist in the special committee's crosshairs. For weeks, the committee members had been discussing what to do about Colson, the CEO of the *Telegraph* Group and chief operating officer of Hollinger International. He had known Black for many years and had helped negotiate the purchase of the *Telegraph* in 1985 when he was still a lawyer with the Toronto firm Stikeman Elliott. Once the Delaware ruling was issued, it was clear to the special committee that Colson had to go. Judge Strine concluded that Colson, on Black's instruction, had provided the Barclay brothers with some key information about one of the *Telegraph*'s assets but never informed the board or Lazard what he had done.[6] Colson had also given Tom Hicks of Hicks, Muse a tour of the Chicago operations in December without telling Paris.[7] Shareholders immediately began to clamour for Colson's ouster. Jereski fanned the flames by sending an email to the board after the Delaware proceedings, demanding that Colson go. She said she was "completely perplexed as to why an executive and director that shows that degree of duplicity draws a salary at a public company."

In truth, Colson's position with the company had been the subject of debate within the special committee since the previous fall. Although he was good friends with Black, Colson had not been dismissed from his executive position for a simple reason: unlike Radler, Atkinson, or Boultbee, he had not received any of the allegedly improper non-compete payments. As the internal investigation progressed, however, the committee began to grow concerned. They discovered that Colson appeared to have received suspicious-looking bonus payments from the company after the CanWest deal.

The committee members decided to act. In early December, when Seitz was in London, he invited Jeremy Deedes to a meeting. Deedes, who was good-naturedly nicknamed "Custard Socks" for his colourful footwear and Savile Row suits, had retired as managing director of the *Telegraph* the previous month after nearly twenty years at the paper. Popular among his staff and within the industry, the sixty-year-old Deedes viewed the *Telegraph* as an extension of his family. His legendary father, Bill Deedes, had started at the paper in 1931, eventually climbing his way to the editor's job. Now age ninety, he was still contributing regular columns. Deedes's twenty-six-year-old son, Henry, had recently joined the *Telegraph* as a reporter.

Seitz, who had known Deedes from his days on the *Telegraph* board, quickly outlined the situation over a cup of coffee. There was a possibility that Colson could be leaving in the near future, and the flagship newspaper needed a temporary replacement. For Deedes, the timing of the proposal was inconvenient, since he was planning a lengthy retirement vacation in South Africa with his wife. Yet at the same time, he was worried about morale at the *Telegraph,* which had continued to sink under the weight of the Black imbroglio. It really wasn't a difficult decision: if Colson departed, Deedes said he would step into the breach. As it turned out, his retirement would last just three months. Shortly after the Strine decision was released, Seitz phoned Colson and explained that the special committee no longer wanted him running the *Telegraph*. Colson agreed it would be best if he stepped down once the bids were received on March 23. Seitz then called Deedes. On March 24, barely a week after he had returned to London from Africa, "Custard Socks" sprang out of retirement.

———

Running the *Telegraph* was no ordinary assignment. In addition to battling it out with rival papers in one of the world's most cutthroat media markets, Deedes spent much of his time reassuring employees about the *Telegraph*'s future and desperately trying to buoy morale. It was not easy. In addition to the pervasive anxiety over who their new owners might be, staff at the venerable London broadsheet, like their colleagues at other Hollinger International papers, had been subject to a general wage freeze for the past few years. The litany of Black's alleged excesses, unearthed by the special committee and detailed gleefully in rival publications, was a cruel juxtaposition to the financial belt-tightening at his flagship paper. The cutbacks had become particularly demoralizing in the summer of 2002, long before the scandal broke, when Amiel famously declared in a *Vogue* profile that she had "an extravagance that knows no bounds." To punctuate the point, she gave her interviewer a tour of her closets in London, revealing approximately one hundred pairs of Manolo Blahnik designer shoes and dozens of jewel-encrusted handbags.

As the controversy swirled around Black, some of the *Telegraph*'s competitors tried to take advantage of the turmoil. This reached a level of absurdity at 8:40 on the morning of April 22, when Deedes and a handful of associates gathered at West Ferry Printers on the Isle of Dogs in East London. The group had arrived five minutes early for one of its monthly conferences with Richard Desmond, who co-owned the printing plant with the Telegraph Group. Words like "colourful" and "eccentric" would not even begin to describe Desmond, a self-made man who had amassed a personal fortune in the pornography business before branching out into less coarse media fare as head of the Express Newspapers chain. He had only recently pulled out of the race to buy the *Telegraph* after he was told he would have to increase his bid. So intent was he on obtaining the coveted paper that he sold off the bulk of his adult magazines, including *Asian Babes, Horny Housewives,* and *Big Ones International,* to garner an added measure of respectability.

When Deedes arrived to discuss the finances of the West Ferry operations, Desmond greeted him with a bad German accent. *"Guten Morgen, mein Herr,"* he said, welcoming him into the room. Deedes was momentarily puzzled, but then he realized it was probably a jibe about Axel Springer, the German newspaper operator that was one of the leading contenders to purchase the *Telegraph*. When Deedes replied that he was fine, Desmond chimed in with a *"sehr gut"*: German for "very good." It was all rather peculiar, but Deedes paid little heed. Desmond was a singular character, a man whose butler punctually served him bananas twice daily on a silver tray,[8] and Deedes figured this was just a rehearsed routine to have a little fun at the *Telegraph*'s expense. But when Desmond did not get a response, he suddenly became confrontational.

"Well, what do you think it's going to be like being owned by fucking Nazis?" he asked.

Deedes and his associates were taken aback. "Richard," said Deedes, "that is completely out of order to refer to them in that way." Deedes went on to explain that one of the founding principles of Axel Springer's newspapers was an acknowledgment of the "vital rights" of Israel.

But Desmond was unmoved. "They're all fucking Nazis," he insisted. Exasperated, Deedes beckoned him to sit down and begin the meeting. Desmond, who had recently kicked his cigar habit and was chewing gum furiously, exploded. "Don't you tell me to sit down, you fucking miserable piece of shit!" Then, in a grotesque parody of Basil Fawlty's Hitler impersonation, he began goose-stepping around the room, holding two fingers under his nose in place of a moustache. All the while, he unleashed a two-minute tirade of profanity, railing against "fucking wankers" and "fucking cunts," and telling Deedes he must be a crook "if he works for a fucking crook like Conrad."[9]

When Deedes tried to gently intercede, Desmond told him to take off his coat and settle the matter outside. That was enough. At 8:55 A.M., just fifteen minutes into the meeting, Deedes motioned to his colleagues to leave. Desmond then ordered his subordinates to rise from the table, provide a *"Sieg Heil"* Nazi salute, and serenaded the departing *Telegraph* staffers with a rendition of *"Deutschland über Alles,"* the German national anthem under Hitler. They obediently stood up and began to sing.

After the meeting dissolved, Deedes and his colleagues scrambled back to the *Telegraph's* headquarters in nearby Canary Wharf and assembled in his office. Deedes sat down and, with everyone's input, typed a summary of what had happened. He then rushed to a lunch at the Lazard offices, where he was scheduled to attend a presentation by Apax, another bidder for the newspaper. Apax was one of about six buyers that had been shortlisted for the *Telegraph,* a group that included the Barclays, 3i, the Daily Mail group, Kohlberg Kravis Roberts, and, of course, Axel Springer, the German publisher.

By the time the Lazard meeting had wrapped up, news of Desmond's antics was everywhere. *The Guardian* had posted a detailed version of events on its website, prompting a flood of interview requests—a list two pages long—for Deedes. Knowing the kind of media bombardment that would ensue in the following day's papers, he quickly phoned the head of Axel Springer and apologized in advance for any embarrassment the company might suffer. The Germans were disappointed with Desmond's comments, but given the circumstances, they were remarkably understanding.

With the Lazard process gathering steam, and bidders targeting a mid-May deadline, the special committee was under pressure to complete its investigation and file an amended version of its earlier lawsuit. By late April, the committee members and their legal team had agreed upon a bold strategy: they weren't merely going to sue Black and his allies, they were going to bludgeon them with a RICO claim and allegations of racketeering. The RICO Act, short for the Racketeer Influenced and Corrupt Organizations Act, has been synonymous with mobsters ever since the early 1970s, when the U.S. government introduced the legislation in an effort to wipe out organized crime and dismantle the illicit drug trade. A decade later, lawyers began to file suits under the act for just about any fraud case, viewing RICO as a gold mine: if a civil claim is successful, RICO obliges the defendant to pay up to three times the damages, plus costs and legal fees.

The special committee's move would be a headline-grabber, and could very well recover a substantial amount of money for Hollinger International's shareholders, but it was not without its risks. In recent years, the U.S. government had cracked down on indiscriminate use of the racketeering act, making it much more difficult to win a RICO claim. The case would have to be almost airtight to withstand Black's inevitable legal challenge.

———

At 5:30 P.M. on May 7, a Friday afternoon, newsrooms across Canada, the United States, and Britain erupted in chaos. Hollinger International had filed its amended lawsuit in a Chicago court, and it was monumental in scope. The company was suing Black and a handful of associates for $1.25 billion under the RICO Act, accusing them of committing "unlawful acts" through a "pattern of racketeering activity." Broken down, Hollinger International was aiming to recover $380.6 million in damages—a figure that could be trebled under RICO—along with $103.9 million in prejudgment interest. It was a spectacular move in the legal one-upmanship between Black and the special committee, one punctuated by bluntly worded allegations. "During a prolonged period, the Black Group used Hollinger as a cash cow to be milked of every possible drop of cash, often in a manner evidencing complete disregard for the rights of all Hollinger [International] shareholders."[10] The suit also contended that Black, Radler, Amiel, Colson, and Boultbee "freely plundered the company's coffers to subsidize their own lifestyles."[11]

Whereas the earlier lawsuit in January had focused almost exclusively on larger items like the non-compete payments and management fees, the amended version expanded its scope to include smaller, but more colourful, instances of alleged abuse and extravagances—the kind that reporters would quicky seize upon to illustrate their stories. For example, the lawsuit claimed Amiel charged Hollinger International when she tipped the doorman at Bergdorf Goodman, a posh clothing store in Manhattan. The company was billed about $90,000 in 2002 and 2003 for repairs on Ravelston's limousine, a 1958 Rolls-Royce Silver Wraith, so that "Black and Amiel-Black could travel London in classic style without paying for the ride."[12] The company also footed the bill for Black's personal staff, including chefs, security personnel, footmen, and an impressive hierarchy of liveried servants: senior butlers, butlers, and under-butlers. Hollinger's two corporate jets, which had been grounded since the previous November and had cost the company nearly $24 million to operate since 1997, were used "indiscriminately" for personal trips.[13] Black and his wife used one of the planes to fly to the tropical island of Bora Bora in the South Pacific and to go back and forth between their homes in London, Palm Beach, New York, and Toronto. Radler, meanwhile, allegedly used the Challenger jet to visit his vacation home in Palm Springs, California. A year earlier, at Hollinger International's annual meeting in New York, a shareholder had asked Black how much flight time was devoted to non-corporate purposes. "None for personal use," he answered.[14]

When one added together the salary, bonuses, management fees, non-compete payments, aircraft and personal staff costs, and other assorted compensation, Hollinger International calculated that Black and his associates had paid themselves nearly $391 million over the past seven years, equivalent to a staggering 72 percent of the entire company's profit. By contrast, the suit stated that the top five officers of the New York Times Company collected only 4.4 percent of that company's overall earnings, while the brass at the Washington Post Company got even less: just 1.8 percent. The conclusion of Hollinger International, simply put, was that Black, Radler, Colson, and Boultbee, along with their affiliated companies, "looted" the company.[15] The majority of these payments—citing a by now familiar set of allegations—consisted of management fees paid to Ravelston over the past several years, which Hollinger International insisted were "unjustifiable and unreasonable by any measure."[16] But the real revelations in the amended suit centred on two different issues: Hollinger International's dealings with Horizon and Bradford, a pair of private newspaper companies controlled by Black and Radler; and bonus payments to executives from Hollinger Digital, the internet investment subsidiary formerly run by company director Richard Perle.

In six different transactions with Horizon and Bradford, some of which had been revealed in Cardinal's lawsuit, Black and Radler had been cutting favourable deals for themselves at the expense of Hollinger International and its shareholders, the suit claimed. "In each of these transactions, they avoided independent director scrutiny of their self-dealing through deception," including the manipulation of financial information and the concealment of rival offers for Hollinger International's newspapers.[17] One deal stood out in particular. In May 2000, Hollinger International's board approved the sale to Horizon of two small publications—the *Skagit Valley Argus* and *The Journal of the San Juan Islands*—for just $1, "plus or minus a working capital adjustment." As the lawsuit would reveal, this "adjustment" required Hollinger International to pay Horizon $150,000 to take the two newspapers off its hands. Making matters worse, Radler had allegedly received a $750,000 bid for one of these papers but neglected to tell the Hollinger International board. Instead, the audit committee approved the giveaway after it was told that both papers were likely to lose money that year. Although the papers had been portrayed as worthless—to the point where Hollinger International was actually paying money to get rid of them—Horizon turned around and sold them eighteen months later for a combined $700,000. According to the lawsuit, there was no indication that Black or Radler ever told the board how they had flipped the two papers for such a handsome profit.[18]

Hollinger Digital, run by Perle, was another focus of the special committee's investigation. The subsidiary had been formed in 1996 to invest money in nascent technology companies, and in early 2000 it had introduced a "management incentive plan" in which 22 percent of the unit's profit would be awarded to Hollinger Digital executives.

Essentially, it was a bonus system, but with one crucial twist: investment losses were not taken into account when Hollinger Digital calculated its payout to employees.

Most investment companies base their bonuses on net profit: the total amount of investment gains, minus the total amount of investment losses. Even KPMG, the company's auditors, reinforced this view in a letter to Boultbee.[19] Yet when it came time for the audit committee members to approve this unusual arrangement, they were told that this plan was "typical" of those used by other investment banking and venture capital firms.[20]

The effect of this management incentive scheme was to reward executives for a money-losing operation. By the end of 2003, Hollinger Digital had gained $95 million on some investments but lost a whopping $160 million on the rest. That translated into a total loss of $65 million. Even with this horrible record, it managed to pay out $15.5 million in bonuses, since it only based its rewards on the winning investments. More than $5 million of this sum went directly to a close-knit group of senior executives—Black, Radler, Boultbee, and Colson—along with Perle. When the special committee members stumbled upon this highly irregular scheme, they were mystified. As the suit explained, "This is an approach analogous to computing a baseball player's batting average by considering only hits, and disregarding outs."[21]

There were a few other nuggets on compensation. Amiel, who unlike the other four executives was not accused of racketeering, nevertheless received $1.14 million in salary and bonus from the company between 1999 and 2003, despite having done "little if any work" to justify her title as vice-president of editorial for Hollinger International, the suit alleged. It also claimed that the only reason Amiel received this money was that she was married to the controlling owner. It labelled the payments as "excessive" and "wasteful." The suit also pointed out that she had already been handsomely compensated in this period through other means: $167,000 for being a director; $94,000 for writing columns, $1 million in dividends from a private holding company she owned with Black, and three hundred thousand stock options worth "millions" of dollars. The company had even donated $250,000 to charities on her behalf.[22]

The suit also alleged that Black arranged for Hollinger International to pay $1.1 million to Colson after he apparently requested a share of the lucrative non-compete payments from CanWest to Black, Radler, and others. Even though such payments were supposed to require board approval, the lawsuit claimed that neither Black nor Colson ever cleared it with the company's directors. Colson later filed a motion to dismiss the charges against him in the RICO claim. His motion stated he had "no involvement whatsoever" with "self-dealing" or other allegations. The list of supposed transgressions went on and on, but by now each of the new allegations reflected a familiar pattern of abuse.

———

Black, predictably, was incensed. His private holding company, Ravelston, issued a press release on behalf of all the defendants, slamming the lawsuit as "tabloid journalism masquerading as law" and adopting a cynical view of the RICO accusations. "Overreaching use of the Racketeer Influenced and Corrupt Organizations Act has been frowned upon in virtually every circuit court in the United States," the statement maintained. "When this complaint is heard in a court of law, the poverty of this case will be plainly demonstrated."

Black and his associates also insisted, as they had done previously, that the company's board had approved a "vast majority" of items in Hollinger International's suit, including sales of newspapers, management fees, and non-competes. "Hollinger International's directors, audit committee members and advisers were all extremely sophisticated professionals," they said, pointing out that Thompson, the audit committee chairman, is a former governor and U.S. attorney who now presides over a major corporate law firm.

Black's hasty rebuttal raised a touchy point. One of the most striking things about Hollinger International's suit was not what it alleged but what it so clearly lacked: a comprehensive discussion of the role of the board. Whereas Cardinal had opted to sue the company's past and present directors, Hollinger International was eerily quiet on the subject. If the board did sign off on $1 newspaper sales and $220 million worth of management fees—regardless of whether they were misled in some instances—didn't that suggest they bore some of the responsibility for what had unfolded?

There were a few veiled suggestions on this point scattered throughout the suit, but no substantial allegations. For example, the audit committee routinely approved the management fees to Ravelston each year "based on what appears to be the most cursory 'negotiations' imaginable."[23] Hollinger International also claimed that Black and Radler knew how to "manipulate and dominate" this committee: not a flattering reflection on the independence of these directors.

For its part, the audit committee did not retain its own experts or financial advisers to provide independent data and analysis regarding the management fee, and thus it did not put itself in a position where it could negotiate with Black and Radler in a meaningful way. Even assuming for purposes of argument that the audit committee was seriously deficient in its review of the fees to the Black Group, and irrespective of whether or not the independent board members satisfied their own fiduciary duties of care, any failings by the audit committee would not immunize the Black Group from liability to Hollinger [International].[24]

It was hardly an endorsement of the board's performance, but it wasn't exactly a public flogging either. The directors had been given a pass, at least for the moment.

CHAPTER SEVENTEEN

The Hollinger Chronicles

HOLLINGER INTERNATIONAL'S LAWSUIT held few surprises for Tweedy's partners. Yes, the RICO charges were an aggressive move, and yes, the details about Black's holiday expenses and Amiel's shopping habits were sensational. Not surprisingly, the media had concentrated most of their attention on the Bora Bora trip and the Bergdorf Goodman tips as further evidence of an imperious CEO who wantonly dipped into the company's coffers. Tweedy's partners had expected this. They knew that the directors would once again be insulated from blame.

Paris and Breeden had paid a visit to the money manager on May 6, the day before the lawsuit was filed, to provide an update on the special committee's progress. Paris explained that they had found new evidence that suggested a much more systemic pattern of improper activities by Black and his team. But Browne and Jereski had grown increasingly impatient. While Black continued to be the target of the internal investigation, there were as yet no signs the special committee was willing to hold the directors accountable for their role in the spreading scandal. When Jereski demanded to know why the lawsuit would not address the board's apparent lack of vigilance at Hollinger International—a subject Tweedy had first raised nearly two years earlier—Paris responded that he and the other members of the committee had more immediate priorities. Their primary mandate was to ensure that the company and its shareholders reaped the largest possible gain from a sale of Hollinger International's assets, specifically the *Telegraph*. Black had almost sabotaged this process once with his attempts to sell to the Barclays, and if Hollinger International wanted to shield itself from further rear-guard actions, Paris said, he was going to need the full support of the board. He described the directors as his allies and said they had worked very hard since October to support the special committee's investigation and the ongoing auction of the company. Jereski was not persuaded and insisted that the directors should be held liable for their repeated failure to protect investors over the years.

"Laura," Paris replied with exasperation, "you live in the theoretical world."

Four days after the meeting, Browne sent a very non-theoretical letter to Paris, Seitz, Savage, and Breeden. Tweedy's managing director was writing to express his dismay at the special committee's decision not to target the company's directors or auditors, KPMG, in the RICO action. Many of the allegations against Black and other executives, he claimed, reflected the "inadequacies, derelictions and fundamental failures" of the board. It was time that all of Hollinger International's directors, not just Black and his deputies, be held accountable for "corporate malfeasance."

The special committee members were irritated by Browne's comments. Privately, they agreed that there had been numerous serious lapses by Hollinger's directors. It was clear from their investigation that the board had frequently failed to follow the most basic boardroom practices, such as seeking independent reviews of Hollinger International's numerous newspaper sales, extravagant executive payments, and lucrative self-dealing. But as Paris and Breeden had painstakingly explained to Tweedy, now was not the time to target the directors. The special committee needed the board's help if it was going to be able to sell the *Telegraph* and fend off another challenge from

Black. As far as Paris, Seitz, Savage, and Breeden were concerned, Tweedy just didn't get it. The men made their decision: they would not respond to Browne's letter.

———

Snubbed by the special committee, Tweedy resorted to tougher pressure tactics. It publicly called on Hollinger International to sue its directors in a formal demand letter, written by its lawyer Curry and filed with the SEC.[1]

> *Your failure to respond to Mr. Browne's letter, coupled with your inaction and your comments in recent months, has led us to conclude, reluctantly and tentatively, that the special committee is not committed to pursuing all responsible parties, and is not committed to recovering the full amount wrongfully diverted from the company....*
>
> *We wish to provide you a final opportunity to demonstrate that your paramount objective is the welfare of the company and its stockholders, and not the welfare of your colleagues on the Board of Directors.*

The letter accused the committee of telling only part of the story in its most recent lawsuit. The "looting" of Hollinger International by Black and his inner circle could never have happened without the approval of the company's board and audit committee, Tweedy claimed. Furthermore, the firm doubted that Black and Radler had enough money to reimburse shareholders, assuming the special committee's lawsuit was successful. A more fruitful course of action, the letter asserted, would be for the company to sue former directors like Taubman and Wexner, each of whom "have sufficient resources to satisfy the entire amount that was looted during their term of service on the board." Tweedy was delivering an ultimatum: if the company didn't launch proceedings against its directors, then the money manager would take matters into its own hands. Although not spelled out in the letter, the message was clear: Tweedy was prepared to sue all the directors, including the members of the special committee.

The special committee's members were not about to let Hollinger International's outspoken shareholder push them around. While Tweedy had legitimate issues that deserved to be addressed, the money manager seemed unwilling to appreciate that the committee was engaged in a delicate balancing act that was being thrown off by Tweedy's assaults. Paris, Savage, and Seitz were obligated as directors to act in the best interests of shareholders, and to them that meant trying to get the highest price for Hollinger International's newspaper titles. They recognized that their mandate included an examination of the board's performance, but they were not going to cave to Tweedy's demands immediately. By May, the committee had decided how to juggle its conflicting responsibilities to restructure the company and investigate the board. It would issue a final report on the deficiencies of the directors, but not until Lazard had wrapped up its auction of the company.

Tweedy would have to wait.

———

Louis Zachary, Lazard's managing director, brought mixed news when he arrived at Hollinger International's New York boardroom on May 27 to present the corporate review committee—all directors except Black, Amiel, Radler, and Colson—with a list of offers. The bad break, he told them, was that there had not been a single formal bid for the entire company. A few bidders had made verbal offers to buy all of Hollinger International, but they refused to pay an adequate price because of persistent concerns over tax issues and legal liabilities. The good news, however, was that Zachary had received a number of written offers for the *Telegraph* and the *Sun-Times*. And they were generous.

Bidders were willing to pay between $1.04 billion and $1.18 billion for the flagship *Telegraph* and its affiliated papers, including the *Spectator*. Three of the contenders—the Barclay brothers, Axel Springer, and Britain's Daily Mail and General Trust PLC, were newspaper operators, while the rest consisted of investment companies, including the British venture capital firm 3i Group PLC, New York investment fund KKR, and Bain Capital. The *Chicago Sun-Times* had attracted bids that were marginally less lucrative, ranging from $900 million to $950 million. New York investment fund Blackstone Group, *USA Today* publisher Gannett Co., and Yusef Jackson, the son of Reverend Jesse Jackson, numbered among the suitors. But the *Sun-Times* situation was not so simple. If Hollinger International sold the Chicago tabloid it would, thanks to aggressive accounting practices, face a crippling tax bill that would virtually wipe out any gains on the sale. Compounding matters, newly installed management at the *Sun-Times* had uncovered unethical circulation practices that had depressed the paper's resale value to potential investors. After weighing its options, Hollinger International's review committee quickly agreed they could not sell the entire company. The *Sun-Times* would be pulled from the auction block until the tax and circulation issues had been sorted out. In the meantime, the committee would devote its attention to finding a buyer for Black's beloved *Telegraph*.

Black, meanwhile, soldiered on. Undeterred by his humiliating legal defeats, he continued to talk with potential investors in a bid to regain control of his newspaper empire. Shortly after Hollinger International announced that it was pursuing a sale of the *Telegraph*, Black was negotiating what he called a "New Investor" proposal with two New York companies, Cerberus and Nelson Peltz's Triarc.[2] The plan was for Black and investors to buy all of the publicly traded shares of Hollinger Inc. and Hollinger International, an expensive move that would be funded by a quick sale of the *Sun-Times* and the auction of a 50-percent stake in the *Telegraph*. Throughout the course of these dealings, Black peppered his communications with insults about the special committee and the Delaware court decision, which he referred to as the "Strine disaster."

After a few weeks of discussions, however, Cerberus and Triarc appeared to lose interest. As time began to run out, Black was almost pleading with investors. In one letter to Cerberus near the end of June, Black implored: "Could I please hear from somebody reasonably promptly."[3]

––––––

By mid-June, the bidding for the *Telegraph* had narrowed to two suitors: the Barclays and 3i. The Daily Mail and General Trust had been a close third in the negotiations, but the newspaper publisher pulled out after its finance director, Peter Williams, explained that the bidding, which had surpassed the $1-billion mark, had reached "silly territory."[4] The Barclays' desire to obtain the *Telegraph* at almost any cost had helped Lazard fuel a rich bidding war.

Although the talks to acquire the *Telegraph* were confidential, it was almost impossible to contain leaks about the newspaper's future. Media in London, New York, and Toronto were remarkably well informed about the progress of negotiations and published stories almost daily about the paper's fate, sparking concern among the *Telegraph*'s managers. They feared that 3i, which knew little of the newspaper business, would be motivated to squeeze costs and jobs to boost their investment gains, a galling prospect considering Black had allegedly drained so much of the company's resources for his own benefit while his employees were shackled with wage freezes.

The *Telegraph*'s fate was decided in Hollinger International's New York boardroom at a noon meeting on Tuesday, June 22. Assembled in the room or listening by phone were all of Hollinger International's directors, with the exception of Black, Amiel, Radler, and Colson. The company's old-guard directors, having been embarrassed in the media, sued by Cardinal, and criticized by Tweedy, suddenly appeared to have found corporate governance religion. Kissinger, who had missed 75 percent of board meetings in previous years, not only showed up in person, but asked a number of insightful questions about currency exchange rates and inquired about the finer details of the competing bids. Zachary led the board through a lengthy presentation explaining the offers.

When the investment banker finished his analysis, Paris called the *Telegraph*'s Deedes, who was waiting in London. The British publisher knew that the two bids were close, and he wanted to make a personal plea to tip the scales in favour of the Barclay brothers. In a brief but impassioned speech, Deedes, the beloved "Custard Socks" of the newsroom, told the board that it would take more than the smart financial people at 3i to help the paper realize its long-term potential. What the *Telegraph* needed, he insisted, were patient, long-term proprietors such as the Barclays, who were experienced stewards in the newspaper business and who would be more warmly received by employees.

What Deedes didn't know was that Hollinger International's board of directors had all but agreed that the Barclays' bid was the best on the table. In dollar terms, the family was offering $1.21 billion, or $18 million more than 3i. Just as importantly, the Barclays had fewer conditions. When the final vote was cast after 6 P.M., and the sale to the Barclays was approved, Paris walked over to Healy, slapped him on the back, and suggested that he call Deedes with the good news. Healy was thrilled. He had lobbied the board to hear Deedes's speech, and now, after months of legal turmoil, bidding theatrics, and uncertainty, he finally had some good news for the *Telegraph*. Healy called Deedes on his cell phone and the British executive answered after one ring. It was just after 11 P.M. in London, and he had been waiting at home in nervous anticipation.

"Well, Jeremy, it's an honour and a privilege for me to tell you that the Barclays are your new proprietors," Healy said.

He heard a sharp intake of breath at the other end.

"That's fucking fantastic."

———

Black retaliated immediately. A few hours after the sale of the *Telegraph* was announced, Black's Toronto-based Hollinger Inc. issued a statement demanding that the sale be put to a vote by all shareholders of Hollinger

International. One week later, Hollinger Inc. bolstered the demand by filing a complaint in Delaware's Chancery Court, the same court that had eviscerated Black for his secret negotiation of a "fait accompli" sale of the *Telegraph* to the Barclays.

Black's legal challenge was a long shot, but few were surprised by his move. After all, it was the *Telegraph* that was at stake. To strengthen his case, Black sought to cast himself as a disinterested bystander, and supported a board resolution at Hollinger Inc. that said he would not personally vote on any sale. That job would be handed to the parent company's only two independent directors, Richard Rohmer and William Walker. By taking this step, Black was appealing to a bedrock principle of the Delaware courts that protected the rights of majority shareholders, such as Hollinger Inc., to exercise voting rights over their subsidiaries. But Strine didn't buy it. He quickly concluded that the eighty-year-old Rohmer, who had previously been on the boards of four Black-owned companies, and Walker, a Conservative Party stalwart and friend of Hollinger Inc. chief operating officer Peter White, were little more than well-paid recruits doing Black's bidding. According to a legal brief submitted by Hollinger International, the two directors had never voted against Black in board meetings, had approved changes to minutes of a Hollinger Inc. meeting they did not attend, and had rubber-stamped bylaw amendments without reviewing materials or seeking independent advice. And, in a breathtaking display of corporate largesse, Hollinger Inc. had doubled their annual directors' fees, the day after the *Telegraph* sale was announced in June, to C$100,000 each, four times that of any other company director.[5]

Black was only likely to win his Delaware challenge if his lawyers could prove that the *Telegraph* purchase by the Barclays involved substantially all of Hollinger International's business. Under Delaware law, shareholders have the right to vote on any transaction that involves the vast majority of a company's assets. But there was a troubling irony in Black's challenge. Four years earlier, he had sold $2 billion worth of newspapers to CanWest—more than 50 percent of Hollinger Interntational's value at that time—without seeking shareholder approval. Extensive economic analysis filed in the Delaware court showed that the *Telegraph* amounted to only half of Hollinger International's worth. Further undermining Black's case was an email he had sent to the Barclays in November in which he acknowledged that a sale of the *Telegraph* would probably *not* trigger a shareholder vote.[6]

On July 29, Black received his second major blow from Delaware. Judge Strine ruled that the sale could proceed without a vote, agreeing with Hollinger International's board that the *Telegraph* did not represent substantially all of the company's assets. In his decision, Strine wrote that the embattled owner's latest legal skirmish smacked of a delaying tactic and described Hollinger Inc.'s challenge of the *Telegraph* sale as an attempt to "forestall any major transaction" until the court injunction protecting the special committee expired in October.[7] Hollinger Inc. tried to appeal Strine's decision that day, but it was immediately denied.

The next day, nearly twenty years after Black had acquired his first stake in the *Telegraph*, the storied British newspaper passed into the waiting arms of the Barclays. Black vowed to continue fighting, but he had lost his crown jewel, the paper that transformed him from a provincial press baron dabbling in nondescript publications to an international media celebrity. His cunning acquisition of the *Telegraph* in 1985, and his rejuvenation of its operations and editorial content, had undoubtedly been the shrewdest move of his career, both financially and socially. The Tory broadsheet was Black's entrée into London's most exalted circles, a passport that bought him entry to the House of Lords, 10 Downing Street, and even Buckingham Palace, where he had enjoyed private audiences with the Queen and the Queen Mum. It was the *Telegraph* that had enabled him to recruit such an impressive roster of high-powered political and corporate allies for Hollinger International's board of directors and advisory group. Black's admission into this rarefied club was just as important as the prospect of growing rich, and now he was losing his membership privileges.

As he insisted in his libel suit in February, the actions of the special committee had resulted in his being "spurned and shunned by persons who had personally accepted his hospitality in London, New York, and Palm Beach," and turned him into a "social leper."[8] Black may not have been about to give up, but one thing was clear: with the *Telegraph* gone, he had lost the primary source of his power and influence. Black had also been forced to repay the non-compete payments he allegedly received without board approval. A Delaware court had ordered him and Hollinger Inc. to pay Hollinger International $30 million: $7.2 million for Black, $16.55 million for the parent company, plus over $6 million in interest. The money was repaid in July, but Black and Hollinger Inc. filed an appeal of the ruling.

————

After more than a year of gruelling work, including the Delaware show-down and an exhausting takeover battle, the special committee was finally able to return to its investigation. By now, the spadework had been done, and most of the allegations against Hollinger International's executives had been richly detailed in the amended lawsuit in May. Yet the sale deliberations with the Barclay brothers had prevented the special committee from concluding one key task: addressing the role of the company's board of directors in the scandal.

The committee members, who were under public pressure from Tweedy Browne to sue their fellow directors, were divided over how to proceed. Savage, the Toronto fund manager, was the most outspoken critic, urging that many of the directors be held accountable for neglecting to question the lucrative payments to Black and his cronies and for consistently failing to seek independent advice—things that are basic responsibilities of direc-tors. Paris disagreed. He argued that the directors had washed away many of their previous sins by providing so much support in the battle against Black and in the tortuous efforts to sell the *Telegraph*. Sandwiched between Paris and Savage, former ambassador Seitz was diplomatically neutral.

Breeden, along with Jonathan Rosenberg, one of the committee's lawyers, explained that it was exceedingly difficult to bring successful lawsuits against company directors. The committee would have to demon-strate to the court that the directors had personally benefited from their involvement with Black and his team, and only one board member— Richard Perle—appeared to fall into this category. Furthermore, they would have to prove that the directors' sloppiness was premeditated. Confronted with such imposing hurdles, the committee decided against legal action and resolved instead to help negotiate a settlement between most of the independent directors and the shareholders who had sued the company and its board. Cardinal's suit, which had been stayed since January, was a derivative action, meaning any money it recovered would go straight back to Hollinger International. In a derivative suit, shareholders sue directors or management on behalf of the company itself, rather than on behalf of themselves directly. Three other shareholders—the Teachers' Retirement System of Louisiana, the Washington Area Carpenters Pension and Retirement Fund, and Kenneth Mozingo—had filed class-action lawsuits, which, if successful, would disperse their proceeds among all investors. The bulk of the money gained in any settlement would most likely be paid by a syndicate of insurance companies led by American International Group, Inc., which provided the company's management and board with directors' and officers' liability insurance.

For almost four weeks following the *Telegraph* sale, Breeden and his team, with regular input from Paris, Seitz, Savage, and the lawyers at O'Melveny & Myers, painstakingly crafted the special committee's final report. It was to be the last chapter in their investigation, a mammoth and exhaustive account that would catalogue every instance of abuse, every sordid detail that they had uncovered in the past fourteen months. Shareholders and the media had been anticipating this report for several weeks, yet they were not the only ones desperate for closure. The members of the committee had grown fatigued by the demands and pressures of the assignment. It had involved forty meetings, interviews with more than sixty witnesses, and a review of more than 750,000 pages of documents. By August the committee members were impatient to move on.

Paris, who had been unexpectedly parachuted into the CEO's chair, and later the chairman's post, had devoted far more time to Hollinger International than he had bargained for and was eager to return to his family and his investment banking career. With the report mostly finished in August, he took his daughter, a high school senior, on a scouting tour of prospective East Coast universities for the following academic year. Seitz, meanwhile, had retreated to northern Europe to work on a travel-writing feature and put together some ideas for a pair of books he was contemplating. An accomplished author, Seitz had already written a well-regarded book about his experiences as an ambassador living in London, and only a few months earlier he had been named specialist writer of the year by Britain's Periodical Publishing Association Awards for travel pieces he had contributed to *Condé Nast*.

Savage was also keen to close the book on Hollinger International, but his reasons were much more pressing. In April, while Lazard was in the middle of sale discussions with the Barclays and a small number of other suitors, the Toronto money manager suffered a mini-stroke and underwent surgery to clear an artery in his neck that was 85 percent blocked. The news quickly became more serious when tests revealed that he had a brain aneurysm that had to be removed. Savage had asked his doctors to delay the operation until October so that he could help the special committee finish its work.

If there was one person who didn't appear worn by the battles with Black and the demands of the investigation, it was Richard Breeden. The former SEC chairman, the principal author of the report, also faced an important medical date. August marked the one-year anniversary of his chemotherapy treatments for colon cancer and his first test to determine if the disease had returned. When his doctor confirmed mid-month that the cancer was in remission, Breeden threw himself into the final stages of the report. Breeden became so engrossed in editing and rewriting the massive document that it was filed only minutes before an August 30 deadline in a U.S. District Court in Chicago. The report was submitted so late in the afternoon that media were unable to obtain a copy until the following morning. As one of Breeden's advisers said, explaining the delay, "We just couldn't get the pencil out of Richard's hands."

The summer months had brought Black something of a reprieve from the incessant media scrutiny he had attracted since the scandal broke the previous November. There were still stories about the beleaguered press baron, but they tended to emerge sporadically, and they typically dealt with his fight to hold a shareholder vote on the *Telegraph* sale. All that changed, however, on the morning of September 1. Once again, Black would awake to find his image and tales of his alleged misdeeds plastered on the front page of newspapers and frozen on television screens from New York to Toronto to London.

The flashpoint was the special committee's 513-page report, informally titled the "Hollinger Chronicles." The report described Hollinger International as a "corporate kleptocracy" and offered up salacious new details of how Black and Amiel had allegedly plundered the company's coffers to finance their sybaritic lifestyles. The lavish birthday that Black had thrown for Amiel at Le Grenouille, the one with lobster ceviche, beluga caviar, and sixty-nine bottles of wine, had in fact been financed with $42,870 worth of company money, the report claimed. The committee had dug up Black's personal expense reports, which revealed the company had shelled out $2,463 for handbags for Amiel, $140 for her "jogging attire," $2,785 for opera tickets, $2,083 in exercise equipment, $3,530 to buy silverware for Black's corporate jets, and the brow-furrowing sum of $24,950 for "summer drinks." This miscellany of expenses, spanning food, cell phones, car repairs, and even perfume, was simply further evidence, the committee contended, that "In Hollinger's world, everything belonged to the Blacks."[9]

Not even charitable contributions were sacred. The report said Hollinger International often footed the bills for donations while executives like Black and Radler took the credit and had their names memorialized on hospital wings and universities. The litany of seemingly underhanded behaviour was mind-boggling in its breadth: in one instance, Black, Radler, and Colson had received $5.3 million in "incentive compensation" from Hollinger Digital, money which was then wired to an offshore Barbados company called Argent News. *L'argent* is French for "money." Meanwhile the FDR memorabilia, which Black had purchased for $8 million, turned out to be a poor investment. Hollinger International sold the collection, but only received $2.4 million.

Aside from these arresting allegations, much of what was contained in the report had already been made public previously in the lawsuits filed by the special committee and Cardinal. What was different, however, was the severe, in some cases sarcastic, tone of the special committee's language, and the all-encompassing, narrative structure in which the allegations had been assembled. It was perhaps as harsh an assessment of an executive team as has ever been presented. Black and Radler were motivated by a "ravenous appetite for cash,"[10] the report concluded, and Hollinger International, under their reign, "lost any sense of corporate purpose, competitive drive or internal ethical concerns" as the two executives looked for ways to "suck cash" out of the company.[11] So overwhelming was this abuse, the special committee stated, that Black, Radler, and their associates received approximately $400 million in unjustified compensation, fees, perks, and other payments between 1997 and 2003. Putting the figure into stark relief, the committee concluded the amount represented more than 95 percent of Hollinger International's entire adjusted net income during that period.[12]

In a sense, the report could be viewed as a road map to guide the SEC and the Department of Justice investigators through the maze of self-dealing and complex executive payments at Hollinger International. It was a thinly veiled plea for regulators to get involved before a key October 31 court injunction evaporated. On that date, a U.S. District court in Illinois was set to drop an SEC injunction that restricted Black from interfering with Hollinger International's board and the special committee investigation. Without an extension of this deadline, or action by regulators to ban Black from serving as an officer of a public company, he could theoretically reinstall himself as chairman and CEO and then fire the entire board. Such an outcome would be intolerable, the report said.

[The] special committee believes that judicial proceedings should permanently foreclose the ability of any of the defendants in the Illinois Action to act as an officer or director at Hollinger, or participate in the conduct of its business. We leave to appropriate governmental and judicial authorities whether similar restrictions should be imposed

relating to any other U.S. public corporations as a remedy for any violations of the federal securities laws and Delaware law that are ultimately found to have occurred.[13]

Black issued a venomous response through his private holding company, Ravelston, on the day the report was released. Despite the breadth of the allegations, he was defiant, painting the investigation as a smear campaign.

The Special Committee's report is recycling the same exaggerated claims laced with outright lies that have been peddled in leaks to the media and over-reaching lawsuits since Richard Breeden first began his campaign against the founders of Hollinger International....

Mr. Breeden and the Special Committee have squandered more than $25 million of shareholders' money in a futile 14-month investigation that paralyzed Hollinger International, eroded the value of its assets, and persecuted and defamed the men and women who created the value they are now vandalizing.

Once again, Black claimed that the company's audit committee, a group of "renowned and sophisticated directors," had explicitly approved the supposed improper payments collected by him, Radler, and others.

Radler was equally dismissive of the report, arguing that the audit company and the company's auditors, KPMG, had approved the disputed payments. In his statement, he said,

It is a highly inaccurate and defamatory diatribe written more like a novel than a serious report.... Far from objectively reporting facts gleaned from an investigation that has already cost International tens of millions of dollars, it twists the substantial evidence in its possession to reach pre-ordained conclusions.

As far as the special committee was concerned, the board's support for some of the controversial deals was no justification for Black and

Radler to siphon off virtually all of the company's profits. On a number of occasions, the report concluded, Black and his team had misled the board when they sought approval for some of their deals. In other cases, the audit committee failed to do its job properly and simply acceded to their demands without much, if any, fuss.

This was a watershed moment. Since its investigation had begun, the special committee had been virtually mute on the performance of Hollinger International's independent directors, despite the fierce criticism of the board by shareholders. But with the *Telegraph* sale successfully completed, the special committee was free to provide a devastating portrait of the directors, a group that allegedly "functioned more like a social club or policy association than as the board of a major corporation, enjoying extremely short meetings followed by a good lunch and discussion of world affairs."[14] It was particularly critical of the audit committee directors Thompson, Kravis, and Burt. They were chastised as "ineffective," "careless," and "inert" when they approved more than $225 million in management fees paid to Ravelston each year and nearly $60 million in non-compete payments to Black, Radler, and other executives

In one eighteen-month period between January 2001 and June 2002, the committee approved nearly $114 million in payments to Black, his private holding company Ravelston, Radler, and other executives; sold publications to a company controlled by Black and Radler for less than what they were worth; and signed off on an annual report that contained serious errors.[15] Rather than negotiate the lucrative management fees to Ravelston, and hire outside financial experts for a fairness opinion on the large payments, Thompson and Radler would agree on a figure—sometimes as much as $40 million in a single year—in the time it took to "consume a tuna sandwich."[16] Thompson, Burt, and Kravis never even asked about Ravelston's annual costs or why it required such a massive payout from Hollinger International.[17]

The Audit Committee simply did not make the effort to put itself in a sufficient position to recognize untruthful or misleading information, or even to make informed decisions on the issues before it.[18]

The report devoted nearly twenty-five pages to the conduct of the audit committee and other directors, outlining an unmistakable pattern: the board pretty much allowed Black and Radler to take what they wanted, without subjecting their requests to tough scrutiny or independent review by compensation consultants. Two of the independent directors, Meitar and Kissinger, escaped virtually unscathed from the criticism, since the special committee concluded that the two had good reason to rely on the recommendations of the audit committee when making decisions on board matters. But in general, the findings were stinging: "At some point a director's failure to question even the most basic elements of a significant related-party transaction calls into question whether any decision made by that director was a decision at all but rather only a rubber stamping of a non-arm's-length transaction."

Thompson, who was busy in the summer of 2004 serving as a member of the National Commission on Terrorist Attacks Upon the United States, informally dubbed the "9-11 Commission," defended himself against the allegations of the report. "I agree with most of the conclusions of the report, [but] I do not agree with all the criticism of the audit committee and I'll simply note that there was no finding of any violation of the fiduciary duty," he said in an interview with the authors. "The report credits the independent directors, including me, with working very hard and very ably to clean up this mess." Thompson, one of the few members of the board who had been willing to step out of the shadows and speak publicly with the media throughout the siege at Hollinger International, was reluctant to discuss his specific objections, since he and other directors were still facing litigation from Cardinal and other major shareholders. He defended his actions as those of a trusting director who had no reason to think ill of Black's motives. "You don't start with the presumption that your CEO is a crook."

Although the report was harshly critical of Hollinger International's directors, it stopped short of demanding that they be held personally liable for their carelessness. All of them, that is, except for Richard Perle. The special committee was unsparing in its criticism of Perle, who served on the executive committee of the board with Black and Radler. The committee enjoyed unusual powers to make major decisions on behalf of the company, subject to later ratification by the full board. At the same time he was collecting director fees to represent shareholders, Perle was receiving a substantial paycheque and bonuses from Hollinger Digital. The special committee said the former chairman of the Defense Policy Board admitted to them that he would typically sign off on executive committee resolutions without even reading them, much less discussing their contents. These resolutions included a generous reworking of the interest rates on a loan Hollinger International made to its parent company, numerous deals that included non-compete payments to Toronto parent Hollinger Inc., and the consent to purchase the infamous FDR memorabilia. The report concluded,

> [Perle's] Executive Committee performance falls squarely into the "head-in-the-sand" behaviour that breaches a director's duty of good faith and renders him liable for damages under Delaware law ... It is difficult to imagine a more flagrant abdication of duty than a director rubber-stamping transactions that directly benefit a controlling shareholder without any thought, comprehension or analysis.[19]

In essence, this was virtually the same allegation that had been directed against members of the audit committee. But the report considered Perle's behaviour to be especially egregious, since he had pocketed more than $5.4 million from the company and its subsidiary, Hollinger Digital, in the past seven years.

Perle had been enriched not only by Hollinger Digital's unusually generous incentive plan, but by Hollinger International's $2.5-million investment in Trireme, the venture capital fund he had helped to create. Perle was evidently so slick in his attempts to secure this investment that even Black was forced to admit a grudging admiration for his tactics. Without any apparent irony, Black described Perle in an email to Atkinson and Boultbee as a "sharper" who engaged in "nest-feathering." Perle and his colleague Gerald Hillman "were trying to smoke one past us," with the Trireme investment, Black wrote. "I think they have done a really good job rummaging all this together, but they should treat us as insiders with our hands cupped as the money flows down, and not as outsiders pouring in the money."[20]

Faced with this web of related-party dealings involving Perle, the special committee decided to play hardball. In its report, it described Perle as a "faithless fiduciary" and said it would attempt to recover all of the money he received—incentive payments, salary, and directors' fees—through either a settlement or legal action. Perle, who was vacationing at his home in France when the report came out, denied any wrongdoing and said he was dumbstruck that the special committee had pursued him so much more vigorously than the other directors.

"There was no quid pro quo. My actions as a director were in no way related to my executive responsibilities [at Hollinger Digital]," he insisted in an interview with the authors shortly after the report was published. "My compensation was the same as others who worked for Hollinger Digital, and it was unrelated to any other behaviour on my part, completely unrelated." Perle promised to fight the charges after consulting with his lawyers, yet he seemed more startled than defiant. Asked how things were allowed to careen so wildly out of control, he had a simple answer. "We trusted Conrad," he said. "We had no reason not to trust him."

It took Gene Fox two days to wade through the Hollinger Chronicles. It was a riveting and encyclopedic account of virtually every problem the special committee had uncovered and a gratifying vindication of the allegations that Fox and his partners at Cardinal Capital had raised in their lawsuit a year earlier. The report, however, had a serious shortcoming. By failing to insist that Hollinger International's audit committee members be held personally liable for their inaction, Fox feared the special committee might have weakened Cardinal's legal claims against the board. His reaction was not dissimilar from that of Hollinger

International's most outspoken and tenacious critic. Laura Jereski, the analyst who had relentlessly hounded Black for nearly three years, and who more than any other person was responsible for his fall from grace, offered a rare bit of praise for the special committee's work. "It is a good first step," she told the authors in an interview. "I wonder if a bunch of adults ever got together to do less than this board?"

But she was still far from declaring the report a victory. Success, she insisted, would only be measured by how much of the $400 million pocketed by Black and his lieutenants was returned to the company's shareholders.

The proof of the pudding will be in whether we actually get meaningful money. The special committee is far short of the final mark here. They've produced a document. They have done a lot of work. They have come to some conclusions, but they have not fully exercised all of their powers. Until they do and we see money coming back, we don't know whether this exercise will have been futile or productive.

The proof, as Jereski suspected, would take some time in coming. Although Hollinger International was engaged in the final stages of settlement talks with its insurers and directors, even the most optimistic observers understood this process would contribute little more than $100 million of the disputed $400 million in fees, non-compete payments, perks, and various other forms of compensation. Clearly, the company and its shareholders were hoping to extract the lion's share of the remaining $300 million from Black and Radler, but by the fall of 2004 there was little hope of a quick resolution. Black had hunkered down for a series of prolonged legal skirmishes. He was challenging the RICO lawsuit, pursuing libel claims against Breeden, some of Hollinger International's directors, and a variety of media outlets. Despite his humiliating setback in Delaware, despite the regulatory investigations and the outpouring of harsh media stories, Conrad was determined to soldier on. The press-baron famous for his daring blitzkrieg corporate assaults was not about to admit defeat.

Epilogue

IT WOULD BE EASY to dismiss Conrad Black as one in a series of imperious chief executive officers who have been dethroned in a scandalous era of corporate greed. By the time Black was toppled in November 2003, more than a dozen other executive gluttons had been cast out. Gone were Tyco's Dennis Kozlowski, WorldCom's Bernie Ebbers, Adelphia's John Rigas, and Enron's Kenneth Lay, Andrew Fastow, and Jeffrey Skilling, each charged with fraudulently pocketing tens of millions of dollars from their public companies.[1] They lived like kings on shareholder money while their businesses crashed. These tabloid tales have defined this period as a disturbing age of corporate profligacy, a dark time that has made us deeply cynical about public companies and the men and women who lead them. But unchecked avarice is only part of the Conrad Black story.

What makes his fall so extraordinary is that shareholders rose up against a belligerent corporate titan and seized control of Hollinger International's destiny, despite the overwhelming fact that Black controlled the majority of the company's votes. By contrast, investors who were victims of other corporate scandals had watched helplessly as their investments at Enron, WorldCom, Adelphia, and Tyco all but evaporated. Each of these one-time stock market darlings, except Tyco, was forced into bankruptcy proceedings, wiping out thousands of jobs and billions of dollars of pension savings and stock market value. But by the time Hollinger International's shareholders were growing troubled by the multi-million-dollar executive payments in 2002, they had become so incensed by tales of fraud and deception at Enron and other companies that they were no longer willing to stand idle. Fuelling their resistance were tough new boardroom rules, such as the U.S. Sarbanes–Oxley Act, which were holding corporate officers and directors to higher standards of governance. When Black and his lieutenants refused to give up their self-indulgent practices, the shareholders went on the offensive.

Both Tweedy Browne and Cardinal Capital had two things going for them when they began to rebel against Hollinger International. The Delaware courts, which suddenly realized the need to police boardrooms more strictly in order to ward off further corporate debacles like Enron, responded to the crisis at Hollinger International with unprecedented alacrity and severity. Black, meanwhile, seemed incapable or unwilling to appreciate the powerful forces that were being marshalled to fight badly governed companies, and as a result, he completely underestimated his adversaries.

One of the most remarkable things about this story is that Black probably could have defused Hollinger International's shareholder uprising and averted his fall from grace. Instead, he chose to ignore, mislead, or sidestep his shareholders, a strategy that only hardened their resolve. It was as if Black believed he was still operating in the boardroom of his mentor Bud McDougald, a rapacious ghost from an era when securities regulation was in its infancy and shareholder activism had yet to be born. Another explanation may be that Black had engaged, according to the special committee, in "self-dealing, misrepresentation and other abusive and unethical practices" for so long that to him they had become "indistinguishable from normal everyday practice."[2]

Black's indifference to investors was a fatal mistake. Had he responded to Tweedy's letter of complaint in October 2001 by curtailing Hollinger International's excessive executive payouts, he might have written a different ending to the Hollinger Chronicles. With all his business and political contacts he should have understood Tweedy's clout and tenacity, which had successfully challenged so many laggard public companies, and bowed to the firm's demands. Some believe that Black refused to exercise restraint because Hollinger International's management fees to Ravelston were a lifeline to the heavily indebted Toronto parent Hollinger Inc. Even if that were so, Black had other options he could have chosen to solve his financial troubles. Numerous suitors were eager to buy some or all of his Hollinger International shares. Such a step would have been drastic, but surely more preferable to the humiliating ouster and investigations he subsequently endured. Never one for compromise, Black seemed convinced that he could outfox his mutinous shareholders. Contributing to his apparent sense of invincibility was the remarkable influence he exerted over his board of directors, a loyal group who seldom questioned his controversial indulgences. His directors supported him through more than a year of shareholder complaints, their fealty dissolving only when their own reputations were threatened.

Overplaying his hand, Black privately dismissed complaining shareholders as idiots while publicly promising reforms that did not materialize. Following Tweedy's demand for a special committee to investigate his activities, Black virtually rolled out the red carpet for his executioners, approving the appointments of Paris, Savage, and Seitz, and their enforcer Breeden. Presented with a damning list of alleged misdeeds, Black did not immediately call in a SWAT team of high-powered lawyers, but rather penned his own rambling reply to the accusations. Ultimately he signed his death warrant in November 2003 when he approved the restructuring agreement and resigned as CEO in the misguided belief that Breeden, the former chairman of the SEC, would protect him from a regulatory investigation. That hope quickly proved fanciful.

When the SEC did pounce with subpoenas, Black tried to outsmart his opponents by entering into secret takeover negotiations with the Barclay brothers that culminated in the January takeover announcement. But Black's end run was anything but the artful exit he was seeking. Instead of delivering hundreds of millions of dollars into his hands and freeing him from the reaches of the special committee, the secret deliberations with the Barclay brothers resulted in a nasty takeover battle that landed the two sides in a Delaware courtroom.

In Delaware, Black found himself defending a controversial deal in a court that had grown increasingly impatient with corporate chicanery.

Six weeks after the Barclays' deal was announced, Judge Strine not only squelched the transaction but eviscerated Black's conduct in an unusually caustic opinion. Four months after that, Black lost again in Delaware when Judge Strine dismissed his objections to the *Telegraph* sale. The speed and harshness of Black's defeats in Delaware will be remembered as a turning point in shareholder battles. Rarely had the court ever responded with such urgency against an alleged corporate delinquent. By comparison, it had taken Disney shareholders more than seven years merely to win the right to contest a $140-million severance payment to ousted president Michael Ovitz. The formerly slug-like pace of corporate justice appeared to have a strong new wind at its back.

Other forces are holding corporations to a higher level of accountability, and one of the most telling examples of shareholders' increased muscle is Richard Breeden. The former SEC chairman and corporate lawyer left a lucrative post at a leading New York audit firm to hire himself out as a corporate cop to troubled businesses. His small Connecticut firm has reaped millions of dollars from one of North America's hottest growth industries: the corporate governance movement. Breeden's actions at Hollinger International are a wake-up call to executives, directors, and advisers of public companies that they may suffer serious reputational and financial reversals if they fail to properly safeguard shareholder money. The report produced by the special committee under his direction will endure as a cautionary tale of how a public company failed its shareholders.

Time and again Hollinger International's board, auditors, KPMG, and law firm, Torys, failed to sound the alarm when Black and his team structured irregular payments, a failing which, in the words of the special committee, enabled the executives to "loot" the company. Their inaction is inexplicable. Why, for instance, did KPMG, who presumably had known of Amiel's salary since she started collecting it in 1999, wait until March 2003 to tell Hollinger International's audit committee that she had been paid a total of $1.1 million in salary and bonus, a windfall that was never revealed to shareholders? Why didn't Torys push Hollinger International to reveal to shareholders the exorbitant $53 million in non-compete payments to Black and his three lieutenants after the CanWest sale in 2000? Why didn't the audit committee or other directors question the extravagant management fees, the suspicious payments of non-compete fees, and the highly irregular $8-million investment in the Roosevelt memorabilia? These are all difficult questions to answer, since neither Torys nor KPMG have been willing to discuss their role at Hollinger International.

Part of the explanation for the inaction, according to the special committee, is that a "duplicitous" and "parasitic" executive group had snookered the directors and the company's advisers. More than $32 million worth of personal payments to Hollinger Inc. and the Big Four—Black, Radler, Boultbee, and Atkinson—were allegedly never brought to the board. Management had allegedly misled the board on other payments too. Even if this were true, it does not explain why directors blessed more than $200 million in management fees to Black's Ravelston.

The best answer may be that Hollinger International's boardroom operated more as a political salon or club than as a corporate cabinet whose duty was to protect shareholders. In the presence of so many political heavyweights, directors spent more time discussing world events than their company's business. They seldom asked questions, almost never sought independent advice, and rarely bothered to read Hollinger International's public financial reports. One of the blindest directors was Richard Perle, whose defence in a September statement was that critical information was omitted or obscured by senior managers when he made decisions as a director. He also vigorously disputed that he placed his interests ahead of shareholders.

When other directors were asked to explain their lack of vigilance, their excuses were appalling. Hollinger director Robert Strauss told the committee he would have "raised hell" had he been aware of the total management fees paid to Black's Ravelston. Yet, as the special committee pointed out, Strauss had attended three of the meetings at which the annual fees were approved. Furthermore, the fees were outlined in the company's annual proxy statements for anyone to see. Raymond Chambers, a successful and admired New Jersey business-man, offered the amazing explanation that he was unaware the management fees had increased. Lord Weidenfeld, Alfred Taubman, and Leslie Wexner, three very experienced businessmen, could not recall any discussion of the Ravelston management fees. Shmuel Meitar was aware of the fees and told the committee he felt they were justified in light of management's skills and standing in the commu-nity. Tweedy Browne sent each of these directors letters in October 2001, so it is difficult to understand why they did not grasp that shareholders felt they were being gouged.

Explanations offered by the three members of Hollinger International's audit committee were even more disturbing. Thompson, the committee's chairman, said the annual fee was usually proposed verbally by Radler over lunch or coffee; he evidently never asked for a shred of analysis to support the massive fees. Burt and Kravis said they deferred to Thomson's annual recommendation to approve the fees. Kravis, a veteran of blue-chip corporate boards, said she believed another board committee was responsible for approving the Ravelston fees. While the special committee's report concludes that Black and Radler were "the truly 'bad actors'" at Hollinger International, "the consistent inaction of the Hollinger board also resulted in squandering."

The final chapter of the Hollinger Chronicles has yet to be written. As of September 2004, shareholders were still waiting to learn what the consequences would be for Black, his executives, the board, and the company's advisers. One of their primary concerns was whether the company's board would succeed in its quest to claw back the missing $400 million. The money was being pursued on a number of fronts. In August, former U.S. District Judge Nicholas Politan was quietly appointed to mediate a settlement among the directors, their insurance company, and shareholders who had sued the company and its board. At stake was a $130-million insurance policy, which had already covered more than $20 million in legal fees for all of the directors, including Black. The company was negotiating to pay as much as possible of the remaining $110 million into a special pool to settle these investor lawsuits. Perle, meanwhile, was being asked to repay the $5.4 million in compensation he had received from Hollinger International, or face legal action.

Also under pressure to reach into their pockets were the three members of the audit committee, Thompson, Burt, and Kravis, whom the report chastised for their "nearly complete lack of initiative, diligence or independent thought." Corporate directors have rarely been forced to compensate shareholders in the past. The degree to which Hollinger International succeeds at recovering money from its directors could prove to raise the bar for future board accountability.

The bigger question was what would happen to Black, Radler, Boultbee, and Atkinson, the four executives who profited from the treasure chest of management fees and non-compete fees. Of all of these men, only Atkinson has expressed contrition: Black's long-time legal adviser has co-operated with the special committee's investigation and agreed to repay $2.8 million in non-compete payments and Hollinger Digital incentive bonuses as part of a settlement with the company, which dropped him from the list of defendants in its amended lawsuit. He already paid $350,000 to Hollinger International in 2003, and cashed out stock options valued at more than $4 million, the proceeds of which are being held by the company until the settlement is approved by the court. Hollinger International will keep just over $2.4 million of this sum, and return the rest to Atkinson. However, Cardinal and the other investors are still suing him.

Boultbee, meanwhile, has been defiant since the scandal first erupted last fall, maintaining he has done nothing wrong. He was fired by the board after he refused to resign his positions with the company in November 2003, and responded with a wrongful dismissal suit that is not expected to be heard in court until sometime next year.

Radler, Black's right-hand man, dismissed the special committee's final report as a "defamatory diatribe" and insisted his repeated offers to settle the dispute have been utterly rejected. He argued that he has co-operated with the probe and even given back some of the money the special committee said he improperly collected. Nevertheless, the special committee concluded, he and Black were "by far the most culpable people in causing damage" to the company and were the "truly bad actors"[3] in this squalid tale.

But in the public's mind, at least, Conrad Black is the unmistakable star of the Hollinger Chronicles. He basked in the headlines as Hollinger International made its ascent and he was trapped in the media's harsh glare when things went terribly wrong. This is partly due to his role as CEO and controlling shareholder. But more than this, it was because he was Conrad Black: a man who unabashedly used his newspapers as pulpits to promote his own right-wing agenda; who deserted his country when it refused to grant him entry to the British House of Lords; whose extravagant tastes transformed him at times into a caricature of press barons past and whose bilious insults and aggressive corporate manoeuvres earned him legions of detractors.

Some of Black's closest associates at Hollinger International believe that his greatest failure was his inability to adhere to the increasingly rigorous standards of governance expected of CEOs of publicly traded enterprises. A throwback to another era of executive entitlement, he should have bought out minority shareholders years ago and taken his companies private. As the scandal progressed, even Black could see the wisdom of this view. By September associates say he was privately acknowledging that he had failed in his role as CEO to appreciate modern management standards or to ensure that proper practices were followed inside the company. He continued to insist, however, that he had never misled people in order to line his own pockets. He had repaid $30 million to the company in late June—an amount representing the money both he and Hollinger Inc. had allegedly received in improper non-compete payments, plus interest—but his financial resources were clearly strained. The man many in Canada had mistakenly viewed as one of the country's richest people was forced to borrow C$32.3 million from Quest Capital Corp., a Vancouver merchant banking firm, at the usurious rate of nearly 13-percent interest. His palatial homes in London and Toronto were pledged as collateral.

By the time the special committee released its final report in September 2004, Black was resigned to the drubbing he would take in the press. He had agreed, against his natural inclinations, to remain quiet while his name was sullied by countless accusations of thievery. As painful and humiliating as it was to endure, Black's view, according to his advisers, was that he had merely lost a public relations battle, and he remained optimistic that he would prevail in the courts, where the allegations had yet to be proven.

Some of the legal skirmishes were already fairly well defined. There was the amended RICO suit filed by the company against Black, his private holding company Ravelston, Radler, and various executives, along with the lawsuits by Cardinal and other shareholders. Lurking in the background, however, were the more sinister possibilities of regulatory and criminal actions. In late August, just before the special committee's report was released, enforcement staff of the SEC informed Hollinger Inc. and some of its officers, including Black, that it planned to recommend civil proceedings against them for allegedly violating securities laws. If the SEC does charge Black, he could choose to contest these charges in court, or he could agree to a settlement, which legal experts say could result in a lifetime ban from his serving as an officer or director of a public company in the United States.

But what everyone would like to know is whether Black will suffer the same fate as such fallen business stars as Martha Stewart, Enron's Fastow, and Adelphia's Rigas and be sentenced to jail. The U.S. Justice Department has been quietly pursuing a criminal investigation of Hollinger International for nearly a year, but there has been no indication yet as to whether it plans to bring criminal charges against Black or any of the other executives. If it does, the process could drag on for years. Criminal cases involving corporate malfeasance tend to be lengthy affairs that are notoriously difficult to prosecute. Black isn't taking any chances. He recently hired Washington criminal lawyer

Brendan Sullivan, who is currently defending former New York Stock Exchange chairman Richard Grasso over his controversial $187.5-million severance package, and who previously represented retired Lieutenant-Colonel Oliver North in the Iran-Contra Affair.

By the fall of 2004, most observers were predicting that the SEC would not allow Black to regain a senior executive role at Hollinger International. In light of the special committee's final report, most legal experts believe the SEC will take some kind of action to block Black from making such a last stand. Even if he does manage to win some of his legal battles, any victory would have to be weighed against what he has already lost. Black has been toppled from his perch, his empire has been broken up, his name has been horribly tarnished, and his network of high-powered friends has dissolved. Few believe Black will run a public company again. It's difficult to imagine many investors would be willing to back another one of his ventures.

How is Black coping with his many defeats? His autobiography, *A Life in Progress,* published over ten years ago, offers some clues. In the book, Black recalled a conversation he once had with former Montreal mayor Jean Drapeau, who imparted some advice on dealing with the vicissitudes of life in the public eye. "It's like baseball," Drapeau told the young Black. "They cheer a player one night and boo him the next. They cheered me in 1954, booed me in 1957, and are cheering me now. It doesn't mean anything. The only popularity that counts is to be popular with oneself."[4]

Stripped of his corporate offices, spurned by directors he had called friends, pilloried in the media, and targeted by regulators, Black has become a social outcast. He has been soundly booed, and this kernel of wisdom from Drapeau may be one of the few things Black has left.

Black didn't merely study history, he occupied it. He was an anachronism, a man who had modelled his corporate conduct on a lost generation of freewheeling business moguls who fashioned empires on their own terms, unfettered by the modern nuisances of shareholder activism and regulatory oversight. Blindness, perhaps as much as hubris, was the source of Black's downfall: he was unable either to recognize or to acknowledge that the rules had changed, that the dreams nurtured by the likes of Bud McDougald were fit for another era, but not for his. Conrad couldn't or wouldn't read the signs, and he clung to the old way, the wrong way.

Acknowledgments

WE COULD NEVER have written this book without the remarkable generosity of a large number of people who shared our interest in having this story told. Despite an intimidating thicket of lawsuits, libel actions, and court battles, dozens of former and current associates of Conrad Black and Hollinger International agreed to be interviewed, in many cases against their better judgment and contrary to their lawyers' advice. Most would not appreciate being named, but they know who they are, and we are enormously thankful for their assistance.

We are indebted to our editors and colleagues at *The Globe and Mail* for their support. *The Globe's* publisher Phillip Crawley, editor-in-chief Edward Greenspon, and our Report on Business editors—Giles Gherson, Michael Babad, and Cathryn Motherwell—granted us leaves of absence and patiently endured our preoccupations. Their backing and understanding were instrumental. We would also like to thank *Globe* reporters Richard Blackwell and Paul Waldie for graciously sharing their time and extensive knowledge about Hollinger. Other key assists came from Report on Business reporters Richard Bloom and Derek DeCloet, *The Globe's* librarian extraordinaire Celia Donnelly, researcher Jane Young, photo editor Paula Wilson, and photographer Tibor Kolley.

Books are truly collaborative efforts, and they require the vision, dedication, and care of an energetic editor. Diane Turbide, Penguin Canada's editorial director, was that person for us. She overcame enormous obstacles to make this book possible, and her incisive feedback helped us immeasurably. The keen eyes of Helen Conford, our London editor, and Allyson Latta, our impressively thorough copy editor, provided valuable advice and suggestions. Tracy Bordian somehow managed to make an insane publishing schedule seem sane, and our lawyer Bert Bruser helped us navigate a project fraught with legal minefields. Our agent Dean Cooke was always there to lend a steady hand during the inevitable bumps in our writing journey.

It is not possible to write a book without the love and tolerance of friends and family. In our travels to research this book, many friends gave us shelter and valuable insights. We would like to thank Kathy Hughes, Jeff Honea, Susan and Michael Furman, Larry Black, Andrew Bary, John Lute, and Susanne Craig.

Jacquie McNish would like to thank her parents, James and Diana McNish, sisters Michelle Haizman, Rachael Pierce, and Catherine McNish, and Heather and Bill Riedl, who helped in more ways than can ever be measured. She also thanks her husband Stephen Cole, who in addition to writing his own book was an exacting editor of this work and a devoted parent to our sons Harry and Lewis.

Sinclair Stewart would like to thank his mother, Donna Warner, and brother, Jay Stewart, for their constancy. Andy Hoffman, as a reporter with Report on Business Television, shared valuable footage of interviews with Conrad Black in Toronto and Delaware, and as a friend, provided words of encouragement and sage advice. Chris Donaldson imparted numerous bits of wisdom and helped in myriad ways. Most of all, Sinclair Stewart would like to thank his partner, Lianne George, whose unswerving support, patience, and remarkable selflessness allowed him to take on such a daunting project and see it through to completion.

Notes

Chapter 1 **Uprising**

1. Independent directors are defined as those with no meaningful economic ties to the corporation on whose board they sit.

Chapter 2 **Holy Mackerel**

1. Carrington was a director of Hollinger Inc. from 1988 to 1990. Subsequent to that he was an adviser on the company's advisory board.

2. Peter Newman, *The Establishment Man,* McClelland and Stewart, 1982, p. 138.

3. Conrad Black, *A Life in Progress,* Key Porter Books, 1993, p. 143; *The Establishment Man,* p. 71.

4. Ibid., p. 147.

5. Newman, pp. 98–99.

6. Black, p. 279.

7. *A Life in Progress,* p. 328.

8. John Heinzl, *The Globe and Mail,* Sept. 22, 1993.

9. A warrant for Drabinsky's arrest was issued in the United States after he failed to appear in court to hear the charges, which were still pending in the fall of 2004. In 2002, Drabinsky and an associate were charged by the Royal Canadian Mounted Police with nineteen counts of fraud related to their involvement in Livent. Drabinsky denies any wrongdoing.

10. Ravelston shareholders and Argus directors who were bought out by Black included Ralph Barford, Fred Eaton, Douglas Bassett, and John Finlay; Black, p. 328.

11. Black, p. 328.

12. Ibid., p. 402.

13. Newman, p. 191.

Chapter 3 **Black Factor**

1. Conrad Black, *A Life in Progress,* p. 15.

2. Ibid., p. 11.

3. Ibid., p. 15.

4. Ibid., p. 25.

5. Ibid., p. 142.

6. Peter C. Newman, *The Establishment Man,* p. 130.

7. Canadian Broadcasting Corporation, *The Canadian Establishment,* July 25, 1980.

8. Black, p. 201.

9. Ibid., p. 266.

10. Ibid., p. 314.

11. Ibid., p. 143; Newman, *The Establishment Man,* p. 71.

12. Hollinger Mines Ltd. paid $87.7 million in cash and stock to Ravelston, three days after the mining subsidiary generated $80 million from the sale of an investment. In exchange for the transfer to Ravelston, Hollinger Mines received preferred and common shares of Argus. Hollinger Argus Ltd. annual report 1979, p. 5.

13. Argus and affiliates paid C$139 million in dividends to Ravelston in 1998 to extinguish "notes receivable." No details are provided about the notes receivable, nor is an independent valuation offered on the related party transaction. Argus Corp. Ltd. 1998 annual report, p. 21. In 1997 Ravelston borrowed C$137 million from Argus. The loan was made in the form of unsecured notes that did not require interest payments. Argus annual reports 1997 and 1998.

14. Paul Goldstein, *The Globe and Mail,* Feb. 2, 1983.

15. Black, p. 232.

16. *Toronto Sun,* Oct. 14, 1980.

17. Regina Hickl-Szabo, *The Globe and Mail,* Jan. 29, 1986.

18. Paul Waldie and Casey Mahood, *The Globe and Mail,* May 28, 1996.

19. *The Globe and Mail,* Aug. 7, 1981

20. Jack Willoughby, *The Globe and Mail,* Aug. 7, 1981.

21. Lawrence Ingrassia and Suzanne McGee, *The Wall Street Journal,* Nov. 8, 1994.

22. Black, p. 388.

23. *Hollinger International Inc. v. Conrad Black et al.,* first amended complaint, May 7, 2004, p. 67.

24. In 2000, Hollinger International bought a 12-percent stake in a money-losing internet venture called Bidhit.com Inc. and regulatory filings show that Ravelston Holdings Inc. received $350,000 of the online auction company's stock that year to pay for advisory services. Bidhit.com, Inc. SEC form 10-QSB, June 30, 2000, p. 9.

25. *Hollinger v. Black et al.,* first amended complaint, May 7, 2004, p. 81.

26. Report of the Special Committee, Aug., 2004, p. 388.

27. Ibid.

28. Bob Colacello, *Vanity Fair,* February 2004, p. 136.

29. Elizabeth Lambert, "A Classically English Attitude," *Architectural Digest,* March 2000, p. 152.

30. Report of the Special Committee, p. 25.

31. Black repaid Hollinger International $90,000 in May 2004 for the Rolls-Royce repairs. Report of the Special Committee, p. 392.

32. Ibid., p. 24.

33. Ibid., p. 409.

34. Ibid., pp. 414–420.

Chapter 4 A Canterbury Tale

1. The quote is excerpted from a story in *Maclean's* magazine, published Aug. 14, 2000, by Robert Sheppard with Cheryl Hawkes and John Geddes. Black's presence in Bayreuth at the time of the conference call with directors has been confirmed by the book's authors.

2. See p. 3 of Hollinger International's 2000 annual report to shareholders.

3. Ibid.

4. Ibid., p. 4.

5. According to the terms of the original transaction agreement, dated July 30, 2000, Hollinger would receive approximately $2.35 billion (C$3.5 billion) in cash and CanWest stock. However, when the deal closed in November, the price was reduced to roughly $2 billion (C$3.1 billion) after CanWest experienced difficulty with a financing and chose to exclude certain publications it had intended to buy. The proceeds to Hollinger consisted of $1.1 billion in cash (C$1.7 billion), $440 million in CanWest non-voting shares (C$685 million, valued at C$25 a share), and $483 million ($750 million) in subordinated non-convertible debentures of a CanWest holding company. Some published reports valued the overall deal at $2.1 billion. A lawsuit filed against Black, Radler, Ravelston, and others on May 7, 2004, calculates the price to be $2.33 billion. For the purpose of avoiding confusion, we have chosen to use the figure of $2 billion appearing in Hollinger International's public filings. Obviously, the final number fluctuated significantly because of a change in the underlying values of CanWest securities.

6. Thompson's briefing on the CanWest deal, and the attendance records for the July 26, 2000, board meeting, are discussed in *Cardinal Value Equity Partners L.P. v. Conrad M. Black, Barbara Amiel Black, Richard Burt, Daniel W. Colson, Henry A. Kissinger, Shmuel Meitar, Gordon A. Paris, Richard N. Perle, F. David Radler, Graham W. Savage, Raymond G.H. Seitz, James R. Thompson, Marie-Josée Kravis, Dwayne O. Andreas, Lord Weidenfeld, Raymond G. Chambers, Leslie H. Wexner, Peter Y. Atkinson, A. Alfred Taubman, Robert S. Strauss, Bradford Publishing Company, and Horizon Publications Inc.,* filed in the Court of Chancery for the State of Delaware on Jan. 4, 2004, p. 20 (the Cardinal suit).

7. Cardinal suit, p. 21, and Hollinger suit, p. 54. According to the Hollinger suit, Black referred to a $39-million deduction, representing ten times the amount Ravelston would collect annually from a management services agreement with CanWest.

8. *Hollinger International Inc. v. Hollinger Inc., The Ravelston Corporation Ltd., Ravelston Management Inc., Conrad M. Black, F. David Radler, John A. Boultbee,*

Daniel W. Colson, Barbara Amiel-Black, Horizon Publications Inc., Horizon Illinois Publications Inc, Horizon Hawaii Publications Inc., Horizon Publications U.S.A. Inc., Horizon California Publishing Inc., and Bradford Publishing Company. Filed in the U.S. District Court for the Northern District of Illinois, p. 55, May 7, 2004.

9. The minutes, obtained by Cardinal, are discussed in Cardinal's lawsuit. The specific discussion of this meeting is found on p. 21.

10. According to allegations in the Cardinal suit, the board did not condition its approval on receiving an audit committee report. It adds that there is no evidence in records of the meeting that any director asked questions about the propriety of these payments to management, or the fact it negotiated fees on its own behalf. The suit also contends the board did not receive a fairness opinion.

11. Hollinger's total debt load was roughly $1.8 billion before the CanWest deal was completed (see p. 193 of the Report of the Special Committee, Aug. 30, 2004). The company paid $142.7 million in interest expense in 2000, according to financial records, but used US$972 million of the CanWest proceeds to pay off virtually all of its bank debt on Nov. 16, 2000. Total debt at the end of 2000 stood at $807 million, a reduction of more than 50 percent. The following year, in 2001, the interest expense dropped to just $78.6 million.

12. Conrad Black, *A Life in Progress,* p. 74.

13. According to Hollinger's financial statements, the *National Post* had US$13.1 million of launch costs in 1998, along with a US$7.9-million loss that year. In 1999, the loss was US$48.7 million. In the first six months of 2000, the *Post*'s loss before interest, taxes, depreciation, and amortization was US$14.7 million. In total, by June 2000, when Black met with Asper, the *Post* had cost Hollinger US$84.4million, or roughly C$100 million.

14. Report of the Special Committee, Aug. 30, 2004, pp. 194–195.

15. Illinois Periodicals Online, Oct. 1975, Illinois Issues/297.

16. According to the Hollinger suit, Ravelston, which charged Hollinger millions of dollars each year to manage and advise the company's newspaper titles, claimed it would reduce its fee in 2000 because of the CanWest sale. This was presented as justification for the $30 million in termination fees it sought. Furthermore, Ravelston said this move would increase Hollinger's profitability figure, thereby allowing it to receive more money from CanWest in the newspaper deal. By the end of 2000, however, Ravelston had not reduced the fees it charged Hollinger.

17. The two deals named in the memo were Community Newspapers Holding Inc. (CNHI) in 1999, and American Trucker, in 1998.

18. *Hollinger International v. Hollinger Inc. et al.,* amended complaint, p. 55, May 7, 2004.

19. Cardinal suit, p. 23.

20. Ibid.

21. Cardinal suit, pp. 24–25.

22. Hollinger International proxy circular, March 27, 2001.

23. Report of the Special Committee. Aug. 30, 2004, p. 233.

24. The $24.6 million figure contained in the Kipnis memo was inaccurate. Ravelston actually collected $26.4 million. The original amount allocated to Ravelston was $20 million.

25. Report of the Special Committee, Aug. 30, 2004, pp. 207–212.

26. Cardinal suit, p. 30. The suit, relying on board minutes, claims there is no indication that any board member tried to verify the contents of the memo.

Chapter 5 Act Like Owners

1. Raymond D. Smith, Jr., "Tweedy Browne Company: Recollections from the First Seventy-five Years," privately published, p. 13.

2. Arthur Levitt, Testimony before the Committee on Banking, Finance and Urban Affairs, U.S. House of Representatives, April 13, 1994. Jereski shared the Loeb Award with *Wall Street Journal* reporter Michael Siconolfi for their coverage of the collapse of Kidder, Peabody & Co.

3. Susan Beck, *The American Lawyer,* June 1997, p. 42.

4. Smith, p. 29.

5. Calvin Trillin, *The New Yorker,* Dec. 17, 2001.

6. Barbara Amiel, *Maclean's,* Aug. 30, 1999.

7. Conrad Black, "I Dreamt of Canada," *National Post,* Nov. 16, 2001.

8. Linda Frum, *National Post,* Nov. 10, 2001.

Chapter 6 Epidemic of Shareholder Idiocy

1. Peter Newman, *The Establishment Man,* p. 202.

2. Bob Colacello, *Vanity Fair,* March 2004, p. 136.

3. Sally Armstrong, *Homemakers,* Jan./Feb. 1999, p. 30. In the article, Barbara Amiel discusses her illness.

4. *Hollinger International Inc. v. Hollinger Inc., the Ravelston Corp. Ltd. et al.,* District Court for the Southern District of New York, Complaint, p. 10.

5. Report of the Special Committee, Aug. 30, 2004, p. 401.

6. Ibid., p. 9.

7. Ibid., p. 10.

Chapter 7 We Can Get Around That

1. Report of the Special Committee, Aug. 30, 2004, p. 405.

2. Kimberly Seals McDonald, "He Scares CEOs," *New York Post,* June 29, 1997.

3. Keith Damsell, "Black Takes Aim at Hollinger Critics," *The Globe and Mail,* April 23, 2003.

4. Jeremy Mullman, "Paper's Money, Lord Black's Loot," *Crain's Chicago Business,* April 26, 2003; Robert Lenzner, "Press Lord Pressed," *Forbes,* May 26, 2003.

5. The case against Kozlowski ended in a mistrial in 2004 and prosecutors have moved for a new trial.

Chapter 9 **The Executioners**

1. Kevin G. Salwen and Laurie P. Cohen, *The Wall Street Journal,* May 10, 1990.

2. Kathleen Day, *The Washington Post,* Oct. 14, 1990.

3. *The Independent,* Jan. 30, 1993.

4. Company documents and amended lawsuit, *Hollinger International v. Hollinger Inc., Black et al.,* May 7, 2004. The lawsuit contends Ravelston received more than $224 million between 1996 and 2003. The precise number is difficult to pinpoint, given that Ravelston received some payments in Canadian currency and others in U.S. dollars. The $220-million figure will be used for the sake of consistency, even though this might modulate slightly because of exchange rate fluctuations.

5. The special committee would eventually conclude that Hollinger Inc. and Ravelston, and Black and Radler had received $90.2 million in non-competes (see *Hollinger International v. Hollinger Inc., Black et al.,* Jan. 16, 2004, p. 3). The breakdown of the non-compete payments is as follows: Black and Radler each received $21.4 million; Boultbee and Atkinson each received $2.2 million; Hollinger Inc., the parent company, received $16.55 million; and Ravelston received $26.5 million.

6. *Hollinger International v. Hollinger Inc., Black et al.,* May 7, 2004. After completing its probe, the special committee estimated that Black and his allies received $391 million in various compensations since 1997: $218 million in management fees to Ravelston (a number that includes an estimate for 2003 fees), $90.2 million in non-competes, $12.1 million in salary and bonuses, $218 million in management fees to Ravelston since 1997, $39 million in bonuses, $3.2 million in directors' fees, $1.4 million for personal staff, $23.7 million for corporate aircraft expenses, $1.9 million for corporate apartments, and $352,860 for company cars.

Chapter 10 **Follow the Cash**

1. *Hollinger International Inc. v. Hollinger Inc., Ravelston Corp., Ravelston Management Inc., Conrad Black, and F. David Radler,* Jan. 16, 2004, p. 10. According to the suit, the email was dated Aug. 3, 2002.

2. Black's observation is drawn from a foreword he wrote for *The Chief: The Life of William Randolph Hearst,* by David Nasaw, Houghton Mifflin, 2000.

3. In a statement to the authors, Radler said that if he made such a comment, it was not in relation to the Horizon deal.

4. *Hollinger International v. Hollinger Inc., Black et al.* May 7, 2004, p. 56. The special committee lawsuit alleges CanWest did not insist that non-competes go directly to individuals. However, Hollinger's second-quarter report, filed May 15, 2001, stated: "Also, as required by CanWest as a condition to the

transaction, Ravelston, Hollinger Inc. and Messrs. Black, Radler, Boultbee and Atkinson, entered into non-competition agreements with CanWest pursuant to which each agreed not to compete directly or indirectly in Canada with the Canadian businesses sold to CanWest for a five-year period, subject to certain limited exceptions, for aggregate consideration received by Ravelston and the executives of Cdn. $80 million ($53 million) paid by CanWest in addition to the purchase price referred to above ..."

5. Ibid., p. 56. The lawsuit relies on company board minutes, interviews with executives, and other corporate documents. The board was originally asked to approve $51.8 million in total non-competes from the CanWest deal, but an additional $1.1 million in interest payments was tacked onto this sum, bringing the total amount collected to nearly $53 million. For purposes of consistency, we are using the latter figure.

6. Ibid., p. 54.

7. Ibid., p. 45.

8. Ibid., p. 46.

9. Ibid., p. 48.

10. Ibid., p. 49.

11. Ibid., p. 121.

12. According to the amended Hollinger lawsuit, p. 14, the special committee says the audit committee "did not retain its own experts or financial advisers to provide independent data and analysis regarding the management fee, and thus it did not put itself in a position where it could negotiate with Black and Radler in a meaningful way." The Cardinal lawsuit, meanwhile, filed on Jan. 4, 2004, accuses the board of being "supine" and "totally quiescent." It refers to board minutes for a variety of transactions in making allegations that the board often accepted Black's requests at face value, without question. Also, in the Report of the Special Committee, published Aug. 30, 2004, the audit committee was described as "inert and ineffective" and allegedly approved management fees in an "unquestioning manner."

13. Report of the Special Committee of Hollinger International, Aug. 30, 2004, p. 496.

14. See *Hollinger International v. Hollinger Inc., Black et al.,* May 7, 2004, p. 69. Also, see the Cardinal suit.

15. *Cardinal Value Equity Partners v. Conrad Black et al.,* Jan. 4, 2004, p. 12.

16. Conrad Black, letter to the editor, *Financial Times,* "No Controversy Over Purchase of FDR Papers," Aug. 20, 2003.

17. *Cardinal Value Equity Partners v. Conrad Black et al.,* Jan. 4, 2004, p. 9.

18. Jeremy Mullman, *Crain's Chicago Business,* June 23, 2003.

19. Testimony of Gordon Paris in Delaware Chancery Court, Feb. 18, 2004, p. 64.

20. See the Report of the Special Committee, Aug. 30, 2004, p. 401.

21. This portion of Burt's deposition was excerpted in Hollinger's pretrial and preliminary injunction statement of facts, filed in Delaware on Feb. 19, 2004.

22. The contents of Black's discussion of Roosevelt and his wife was drawn from Duff McDonald, "The Man Who Wanted More," *Vanity Fair,* April 2004.

Chapter 11 You Want to Fight?

1. Report of the Special Committee of Hollinger International, Aug. 30, 2004, p. 25.

2. Black confirmed in his Delaware testimony, p. 671, that he was the principal author of the letter, which he sent to Finkelstein for minor modifications.

3. Black letter to Thompson, Breeden, and Paris, Nov. 10, 2003, p. 1.

4. Sam Lister, "Enigmatic Success of Double Act," *The Times,* Oct. 5, 2002.

5. Paris testimony in Delaware, Feb. 18, 2004, p. 65.

6. *Hollinger International Inc. v. Conrad M. Black, Hollinger Inc., and 504468 N.B. Inc.* Pretrial and Preliminary Injunction Statement of Facts, filed in the Delaware Chancery Court, Feb. 19, 2004, p. 12.

7. Black testimony in Delaware, p. 698.

8. Zachary testimony, p. 517.

9. Black testimony, pp. 833–834.

10. Ibid., p. 755.

11. Hollinger pretrial statement of facts, filed in Delaware Chancery Court, Feb. 19, 2004, p. 14.

12. *Hollinger International Inc. v. Conrad Black et al.,* Court of Chancery of the State of Delaware, Case no: 183–N, p. 44.

13. Ibid., p. 45.

14. Ibid.

Chapter 12 Gotcha

1. Richard Blackwell, "Black's Darkest Day: Hollinger Scandal Forces Him Out," *The Globe and Mail,* Nov. 18, 2003.

2. Ralph Wragg, "Lord Black's Fall from Grace," *Australian Business News,* Nov. 18, 2003.

3. Tim Arango, "Black Days Ahead for Ousted Conrad," *New York Post,* Nov. 18, 2003.

4. "How a Peer Fell from Grace," *Toronto Star,* Nov. 18, 2003; Richard Blackwell, "Black's Darkest Day: Hollinger Scandal Forces Him Out," *The Globe and Mail,* Nov. 18, 2003; Jacquie McNish and Paul Waldie, "Improper Payments Led to Mogul's Demise," *The Globe and Mail,* Nov. 18, 2003; Jim Kirk, "Hollinger Brass Out in Payout Scandal," *Toronto Sun,* Nov. 18, 2003.

5. Delaware joint exhibit, no. 190.

6. In his Feb. 26 opinion, Vice-chancellor Leo Strine said, "Stated bluntly, Black steered the Barclays toward doing an end run around the strategic process," *Hollinger International v. Conrad Black et al.,* p. 34.

7. Ibid.

8. Delaware joint exhibit no. 200, Black letter to David Barclay, Nov. 20, 2003.

9. Ibid.

10. Ibid., p. 36.

11. Black deposition, *Hollinger International v. Conrad Black et al.,* Delaware Court of Chancery, Feb. 13, 2004, pp. 257–258.

12. Barbara Shecter, "Black Hit by 'Tall Poppy' Syndrome, says Bassett," *National Post,* Nov. 25, 2003.

Chapter 13 **End Run**

1. *Hollinger International v. Conrad Black et al.,* Delaware joint exhibit no. 266.

2. Seitz testimony, Delaware Chancery Court, *Hollinger International v. Conrad Black et al.,* Feb. 19, 2004, p. 283.

3. Ibid.

4. Ibid., p. 264.

5. Delaware joint exhibit, no. 232.

6. Ibid., no. 582.

7. *Hollinger International v. Conrad Black et al.,* Feb. 16, p. 20.

8. Ibid.

9. Ibid.

10. Ibid., p. 36.

11. Ibid., p. 37.

12. Ibid., p. 38.

13. Ibid., p. 36.

14. Strine opinion, p. 40.

15. Ibid.

16. Tina Brown, *Washington Post,* Dec. 4, 2003.

17. Strine opinion, p. 42, and Black dep. 92–97.

Chapter 14 **Et Tu, Brute?**

1. *Cardinal Value Equity Partners, L.P. v. Conrad M. Black et al.,* Jan. 4, 2004, p. 4.

2. Ibid., p. 3.

3. Ibid., p. 18.

4. Ibid., p. 40.

5. Ibid., pp. 44–45.

6. Paris testimony in Delaware, p. 92, in *Hollinger International Inc. v. Conrad M. Black, Hollinger Inc., and 504468 NB Inc.,* Feb. 16, 2004.

7. Paris testimony, p. 95, Feb. 18, 2004. See also the pretrial submissions of Hollinger International, pp. 25–26, in *Hollinger International Inc. v. Conrad M. Black, Hollinger Inc., and 504468 NB Inc.*, Feb. 16, 2004.

8. The threats to fire directors were noted in Paris's testimony in Delaware on Feb. 18, 2004 (p. 96) and also Hollinger's pretrial submissions on Feb. 16, 2004 (p. 26). The brief cites as evidence Black's deposition.

9. Kissinger's contact with Breeden, and the content of his remarks, were summarized in Hollinger International's pretrial submissions on Feb. 16, 2004 (p. 29). Breeden recollected this exchange in his deposition.

10. See p. 29 of Hollinger's pretrial submissions, Feb. 16, 2004.

11. A copy of this email, sent to Breeden by Laurent Wiesel on behalf of Warden, was included as an exhibit in the Delaware proceedings.

12. Paris testimony, p. 98, Feb. 18, 2004. See also Hollinger International's pretrial submissions, p. 27, Feb. 16, 2004.

13. Hollinger's pretrial submissions, p. 30, Feb. 16, 2004. Discussions between counsel for the special committee and the SEC concerning Black's threat to remove the board are cited from Breeden's deposition.

14. This is taken from p. 28 of Strine's opinion in *Hollinger Inc. and 504468 NB Inc. v. Hollinger International*, July 29, 2004.

15. Paris, in his testimony on Feb. 18, 2004, said there was "great concern" about Hicks, Muse. He stated there was evidence "they were very specifically looking at a transaction at Hollinger Inc. to the exclusion of Hollinger International" notwithstanding the firm's commitment to participate directly in the strategic process.

16. Paris testimony, p. 93, Feb. 18, 2004. See also testimony of Breeden, pp. 380–385, on Feb. 19, 2004.

17. This reply is included in Black's Delaware testimony, p. 900, on Feb. 20, 2004.

18. Hollinger International's pretrial submissions, p. 27, Feb. 16, 2004.

19. The events of this meeting are recalled on pp. 358–359 of Breeden's testimony, Feb. 19, 2004. See also Paris's testimony, p. 99, Feb. 18, 2004.

20. This portion of the meeting is taken from Paris testimony, pp. 98–99, on Feb. 18, 2004.

21. Hollinger Inc. press release, Jan. 13, 2004.

22. Paris testimony, p. 105, Feb. 18, 2004.

23. Breeden testimony, pp. 412–414, Feb. 19, 2004.

24. *Securities and Exchange Commission v. Hollinger International Inc.*, Jan. 16, 2004.

25. Mr. Cutler's remarks are taken from a public statement made on Jan. 16, 2004, announcing the SEC's action.

26. *Hollinger International Inc. v. Hollinger Inc., The Ravelston Corporation Limited, Ravelston Management Inc., Conrad M. Black, and F. David Radler,* Jan. 16, 2004.

27. Ibid., p. 4.

28. Ibid.

29. Hollinger International's pretrial submissions, pp. 40–41, Feb. 16, 2004.

30. Black's testimony, p. 906, Feb. 20, 2004.

31. Ibid. The text of Black's testimony actually reads, "Lazard is *always* sending out books next week" [emphasis added]. It appears that the word "always" was read in error, and should have said "only," as is suggested by other evidentiary records.

32. Ibid., p. 907.

33. Paris testimony, p. 112, Feb. 18, 2004.

34. Strine's opinion, p. 48, in *Hollinger International Inc. v. Conrad M. Black, Hollinger Inc., and 504468 NB Inc.,* Feb. 26, 2004.

35. These remarks are taken from a letter sent by Black to the Hollinger International board of directors on Jan. 18, 2004. The letter was publicly released.

36. Seitz testimony, p. 256, Feb. 19, 2004. A note is in order here. The following day, Feb. 20, Black took issue with Seitz's analogy. In his testimony, on p. 790, he said: "If I may expatiate one phrase, Chancellor, I found it very disappointing to read testimony in deposition by directors comparing my offer to the antics of the Nazi government of Germany prior to the occupation of Bohemia in 1938."

37. The pricing details, along with Black's stake, is from p. 1 of an offering circular, dated Jan. 27, 2004, in which the Barclays' company Press Holdings International Ltd. details its bid for Hollinger Inc.

38. The letter to Hollinger International's board was publicly disseminated by the Barclays on Jan. 18, 2004.

39. Taken from a public statement issued by Black on Jan. 18, 2004.

40. Letter from Black to David Barclay, Jan. 18, 2004.

41. Hollinger International's pretrial submissions, p. 34, Feb. 19, 2004. The exact quote referenced here is drawn from Seitz's deposition.

42. Letter from Black to David and Frederick Barclay, Jan. 20, 2004.

43. Letter from Black to David and Frederick Barclay, Jan. 23, 2004.

44. Letter from Black to David and Frederick Barclay, Jan. 24, 2004.

45. *Hollinger International Inc. v. Conrad M. Black, Hollinger Inc., and 504468 NB Inc.,* p. 1, Jan. 26, 2004.

46. Letter from Black to David and Frederick Barclay, Jan. 28, 2004.

Chapter 15 **Delaware**

1. These figures are taken from the State of Delaware's Division of Corporations.

2. Strine made these comments to Rita Farrell, a Reuters reporter, which appeared in a story on Oct. 14, 1998.

3. These excerpts are contained in *Conrad Black v. Richard C. Breeden, Richard C. Breeden & Co., Gordon A. Paris, James R. Thompson, Richard D. Burt,*

Graham L. Savage and Raymond G.H. Seitz, Ontario Superior Court of Justice, Feb. 13, 2004, Case no. 041V-263720cml.

4. *Hollinger International v. Conrad M. Black, Hollinger Inc., and 504468 NB Inc.* Filed in the Court of Chancery of the State of Delaware. See Paris's Delaware testimony, p. 122. Feb. 18, 2004.

5. Ibid., pp. 141–142.

6. Ibid., see Seitz testimony, pp. 203–204, Feb. 18, 2004.

7. Ibid., Seitz, p. 206.

8. Ibid., Seitz, p. 298, Feb. 19, 2004.

9. Ibid., Seitz, p. 277.

10. Ibid., see Breeden testimony, pp. 357–358.

11. Ibid., Breeden, p. 357–358.

12. Ibid., Breeden, p. 432.

13. This scene was first reported in an article in *The New York Times* by Jacques Steinberg, Feb. 23, 2004. The account has also been informed by interviews conducted by the authors.

14. Peter White, "Don't Let Lilliputians Win," *The Globe and Mail,* Feb. 12, 2004.

15. Ibid.

16. *Hollinger International v. Conrad M. Black, Hollinger Inc., and 504468 NB Inc.* See White's testimony, p. 642.

17. Ibid., White, p. 641.

18. Ibid., see Black testimony, p. 698, Feb. 20, 2004.

19. Ibid., Black, p. 727.

20. Ibid., Black, p. 717.

21. Ibid., Black, p. 736.

22. This was first reported by Rick Westhead of the *Toronto Star* on Feb. 23, 2004, and subsequently verified by author interviews.

23. *Hollinger International v. Conrad M. Black, Hollinger Inc., and 504468 NB Inc.* See Black testimony, p. 807, Feb. 19, 2004.

24. Ibid., Black, p. 815.

25. Ibid., Black, p. 817.

26. Ibid., Black, p. 821.

27. Ibid., Black, p. 911.

28. Opinion of Judge Strine in *Hollinger International v. Conrad M. Black, Hollinger Inc., and 504468 NB Inc.* Filed in the Court of Chancery of the State of Delaware, Feb. 26, 2004, p. 1.

29. Ibid., p. 81.

30. Ibid., p. 59.

31. Ibid., p. 34.

32. Ibid., p. 2.

33. Ibid., p. 38.

34. Ibid., p. 58.

Chapter 16 RICO Offensive

1. This excerpt is mentioned on p. 52 of Judge Strine's opinion, dated Feb. 26, 2004, in the matter of *Hollinger International v. Conrad M. Black, Hollinger Inc., and 504468 NB Inc.* Filed in the Court of Chancery of the State of Delaware.

2. Hollinger Inc. public statement, March 12, 2004.

3. Strine refers to these tactics in his July 29, 2004, opinion in the matter of *Hollinger Inc. and 504468 NB Inc. v. Hollinger International Inc.* Strine says that Black "scrambled to put [Hollinger] Inc. in a position to litigate against such a sale [of the *Telegraph*] and to develop an alternative transaction. Black's obvious preference was to forestall any major transaction until the expiration of this court's injunction and the federal Consent Order [by the SEC]." Hollinger Inc. also lost a motion to intervene in the SEC lawsuit, which limited its ability to remove directors at Hollinger International. Judge Blanche Manning, of the U.S. District Court for the Northern District of Illinois, wrote in her May 2004 ruling: "Black has used deceit and threats to derail the special committee's investigation into his wrongdoing."

4. The number and size of the bids are detailed on p. 36 of the above-mentioned Strine decision, July 29, 2004.

5. These amounts were revealed in Hollinger International's proxy circulated, dated March 31, 2003.

6. See p. 36 of Judge Strine's opinion, dated Feb. 26, 2004, in the matter of *Hollinger International v. Conrad M. Black, Hollinger Inc., and 504468 NB.*

7. Ibid., p. 37.

8. Desmond's penchant for bananas has been well documented in the British press. See "7 Things You Need to Know About ... Richard Desmond" in the *Sunday Herald,* April 25, 2004.

9. This meeting was the subject of intense media scrutiny in Britain. The authors of this book have reconstructed the sequence of events through interviews.

10. *Hollinger International Inc. v. Hollinger Inc., The Ravelston Corporation Ltd., Ravelston Management Inc., Conrad M. Black, F. David Radler, John A. Boultbee, Daniel W. Colson, Barbara Amiel-Black, Horizon Publications Inc., Horizon Illinois Publications Inc, Horizon Hawaii Publications Inc., Horizon Publications U.S.A. Inc., Horizon California Publishing Inc., and Bradford Publishing Company.* Filed in the U.S. District Court for the Northern District of Illinois, May 7, 2004, p. 8.

11. Ibid., p. 37.

12. Ibid., p. 8.

13. Ibid., p. 12.

14. Black's response is contained on p. 24 of a transcript of Hollinger International's annual meeting, May 22, 2003.

15. *Hollinger International v. Hollinger Inc. et al.* May 7, 2004, p. 121.

16. Ibid., p. 15.

17. Ibid., p. 22.

18. Ibid., p. 100.

19. Ibid., p. 80.

20. Ibid., p. 19.

21. Ibid.

22. Ibid., p. 75.

23. Ibid., p. 13.

24. Ibid.

Chapter 17 The Hollinger Chronicles

1. The letter was filed with the SEC on June 18, 2004.

2. *Hollinger Inc. v. Hollinger International,* Case no. 543-N, answering brief Hollinger International, July 19, 2004, p. 26.

3. Ibid., p. 26.

4. Richard Blackwell, "Daily Mail Pulls Out of Telegraph Race," *The Globe and Mail,* June 18, 2004.

5. *Hollinger Inc. v. Hollinger International,* Vice-Chancellor Leo Strine opinion July 29, 2004, pp. 49–50; *Hollinger Inc. v. Hollinger International,* answering brief, July 19, 2004, pp. 28–29.

6. *Hollinger International v. Black et al.,* Delaware, joint exhibit no. 212.

7. Strine opinion, July 29, 2004, p. 51.

8. *Conrad Black v. Richard C. Breeden, Richard C. Breeden & Co., Gordon A. Paris, James R. Thompson, Richard D. Burt, Graham L. Savage, and Raymond G. H. Seitz.* Filed in Ontario Superior Court of Justice, Feb. 13, 2004, p. 44.

9. Report of Investigation by the Special Committee of the Board of Hollinger International Inc., August 30, 2004, pp. 24–25.

10. Ibid., p. 2.

11. Ibid., p. 23.

12. Ibid., p. 1.

13. Ibid., p. 46.

14. Ibid., p. 28.

15. Ibid., p. 505.

16. Ibid., p. 496.

17. Ibid., p. 495.

18. Ibid., p. 494.

19. Ibid., pp. 483–484.

20. Ibid., p. 368.

Epilogue

1. John Rigas and his son Timothy were convicted in July 2004 of fraud and conspiracy for looting Adelphia of more than $100 million. Charges against

Tyco's former CEO Kozlowski ended in a mistrial and new trial is set for January 2005. Ebbers pleaded not guilty in March 2004 to charges of fraud and conspiracy relating to an $11-billion accounting scandal at WorldCom, now known as MCI. His trial is set for November. Enron's former chief financial officer Andrew Fastow struck a plea agreement with U.S. prosecutors in early 2004 under which he has agreed to co-operate with investigators and serve a ten-year sentence. His bosses, Ken Lay and Jeffrey Skilling, have been indicted for being part of a wide-ranging scheme to defraud investors. Both men have said they did nothing illegal.

2. Report of the Special Committee, Aug. 30, 2004, p. 22.

3. Ibid., p. 31.

4. Conrad Black, *A Life in Progress,* Key Porter Books, 1993, p. 68.

Index